Social Justice and the Language Classroom

Edinburgh Textbooks in Applied Linguistics series

General Series Editors

Kenneth Fordyce, University of Edinburgh Angela Gayton, University of Glasgow Mairin Hennebry-Leung, University of Tasmania

Consulting Series Editor

Gibson Ferguson, University of Sheffield

The Editorial Board

Paul Baker, Lancaster University, UK
Andy Gao, University of New South Wales, Australia
Maggie Kubanyiova, University of Leeds, UK
Angel Lin, Simon Fraser University, Canada
Diane Pecorari, City University of Hong Kong, China
Jesus Romero-Trillo, Autonomous University of Madrid, Spain

Naoko Taguchi, Northern Arizona University, US
Piotr Wegorowski, University of Glasgow, UK
Clare Wright, University of Leeds, UK

Titles in the series include:

An Introduction to Applied Linguistics
From Practice to Theory
by Alan Davies

Teaching Literature in a Second Language
by Brian Parkinson and Helen Reid Thomas

Materials Evaluation and Design for Language Teaching
by Ian McGrath

The Social Turn in Second Language Acquisition
by David Block

Language Assessment and Programme Evaluation
by Brian Lynch

Linguistics and the Language of Translation
by Kirsten Malmkjaer

Pragmatic Stylistics
by Elizabeth Black

Language Planning and Education
by Gibson Ferguson

Language and Politics
by John E. Joseph

Classroom Discourse and Teacher Development
by Steve Walsh

Materials Evaluation and Design for Language Teaching (2nd edition)
by Ian McGrath

Teaching Language and Promoting Citizenship
by Mairin Hennebry and Angela Gayton

Social Justice and the Language Classroom
Reflection, Action, and Transformation
by Deniz Ortaçtepe Hart

Visit the Edinburgh Textbooks in Applied Linguistics website at
www.edinburghuniversitypress.com/series-edinburgh-textbooks-in-applied-linguistics.html

Social Justice and the Language Classroom

Reflection, Action, and Transformation

Deniz Ortaçtepe Hart

EDINBURGH
University Press

Edinburgh University Press is one of the leading university presses in the UK. We publish academic books and journals in our selected subject areas across the humanities and social sciences, combining cutting-edge scholarship with high editorial and production values to produce academic works of lasting importance. For more information visit our website: edinburghuniversitypress.com

Edinburgh University Press Ltd
The Tun – Holyrood Road
12(2f) Jackson's Entry
Edinburgh EH8 8PJ

Typeset in 10/12pt Baskerville MT Pro
by Cheshire Typesetting Ltd, Cuddington, Cheshire, and
printed and bound in Great Britain

A CIP record for this book is available from the British Library

ISBN 978-1-4744-9175-4 (hardback)
ISBN 978-1-4744-9176-1 (paperback)
ISBN 978-1-4744-9177-8 (webready PDF)
ISBN 978-1-4744-9178-5 (epub)

Contents

Appendices

Series Editors' Preface

This series of volumes published by Edinburgh University Press takes a contemporary view of Applied Linguistics. As such, it is useful to academics, students and all those working in fields relating to Intercultural Communication, Language Education and TESOL who wish to develop a richer theory-informed understanding of the field, particularly given the possibilities opened up by increasing interdisciplinarity.

A specific focus of the series is to make ongoing provision for the wide range of interests in contemporary Applied Linguistics which are provided for at master's level.

Master's postgraduate courses evolve in line with developments and shifts that bring diverse aspects of language teaching and learning and language in use into sharp relief. This has two simultaneous effects:

1. The emergence of similarities across educational programmes in Applied Linguistics facilitates the identification of certain core content.
2. The growth in the range of specialisms, as is the case for any developing discipline. Educational programmes (and professional needs) vary in the extent to which these specialisms are included and taught.

Some volumes in the series address the first development noted above, while others explore the second. As a whole, the series aims to provide students beginning postgraduate courses in Applied Linguistics, as well as language teachers and other professionals wishing to become acquainted with the subject, with a robust introduction for them to develop their own thinking in Applied Linguistics and to further enrich their understanding of specialist areas of their own choosing.

The Edinburgh Textbooks in Applied Linguistics series seeks to theorise approaches to practical experience in the language professions. It is concerned with the problems, the processes, the mechanisms and the purposes of language in use and it draws on theories to explore and explain these. These theories are in turn themselves illuminated by practical experience. This two-way relationship between theory and practice continues to strengthen the theoretical foundations of the field, and this series of textbooks aims to bring these developments to readers.

The volumes in the series are all premised on a view of Applied Linguistics as a discipline with its own distinct theoretical grounding. At the same time, volumes in the series may and do draw on interdisciplinary approaches, recognising their potential for enriching the discipline.

Each volume presents the author's/authors' own view of the state of the art in their area of focus. Volumes are similar in length and in format, and, as is usual in a textbook series, each contains exercise material for use in class or in private study.

Kenneth Fordyce
Angela Gayton
Mairin Hennebry-Leung

26 Eylül 1945

Bizi esir ettiler,
bizi hapse attılar:
     beni duvarların içinde,
          seni duvarların dışında.
Ufak iş bizimkisi.
Asıl en kötüsü:
bilerek, bilmeyerek
hapisaneyi insanın kendi içinde taşıması ...

26 September 1945

They've taken us prisoner,
They've locked us up:
     me inside the walls,
          you outside.
But that's nothing.
The worst
is when people – knowingly or not –
carry prison inside themselves ...

Author's translation

Preface

> Dark days. Recently I was back in the South more than a quarter of a century after the [US] Supreme Court decision that outlawed segregation [of black and white children] in the Republic's schools, a decision to be implemented with "all deliberate speed." My friends with whom I had worked and walked in those dark days are no longer in their teens, or even their thirties. Their children are now as old as their parents were then, and, obviously, some of my comrades are now roughly as old as I, and I am facing sixty. Dark days, for we know *how much there is to be done* and how unlikely it is that we will have another sixty years. (Baldwin, 2021, p. 1024, emphasis added)

First published in the October 1980 issue of *Esquire* magazine, James Baldwin's *Dark Days* cautions its readers that despite the progress made in fighting racism, sexism, genderism, and classism, the world has a long way to go and not as much time to do so. Confirming Baldwin, the Organisation for Economic Co-operation and Development's (OECD) 2018 Teaching and Learning International Survey administered to 260,000 teachers in 15,000 schools across 48 countries reveals alarming findings: More than 10 percent of students have special needs; more than 10 percent come from an L1 background that is not the medium of instruction; 30 percent have socio-economically disadvantaged backgrounds; and more than 10 percent are immigrants or have a migrant background.

Not a day goes by without witnessing the ramifications of the anti-immigrant sentiment that began to ratchet up with Trump's administration in the US, Brexit in the UK, the Syrian war that resulted in more than 6 million Syrian refugees mainly in Turkey but also in other countries; as well as the climate refugees mostly in Bangladesh, South Sudan, and Oceania due to pressing climate change. The Russian invasion of Ukraine in late February 2022 once again displayed race and ethnicity-based inequalities and injustices. Many journalists outwardly distinguished between 'civilized,' 'blue eyed,' 'White,' and 'Christian' immigrants and those from the 'Middle East' who have been suffering years of oppression, war, and poverty in the hands of the so called-Western world.[1] The world has witnessed how White, Slavic Ukrainian people were being treated at the borders with Poland and Romania in comparison to the international students and migrant workers from Africa and South Asia. Various other economic, political, environmental, and societal events and phenomena indicate the need for language educators to be prepared to teach in more linguistically and culturally diverse classrooms and adopt trauma-informed, culturally sustaining pedagogies.

The COVID-19 pandemic exacerbated the economic, social, environmental, political, and cultural inequities in the world. Contrary to what some wealthy celebrities claimed regarding COVID-19 being a great equalizer, the pandemic has disproportionately affected farm workers, people of color, the elderly, and homeless populations, underlining how different forms of deprivation and oppression interacted during the pandemic. A great extent of schoolchildren suffered from patchy and slow internet connections, limited data plans, and not having a quiet place for their online classes and remote studies. Many educational institutions around the world adhered to strict surveillance plans for their online assessments ostensibly making sure students did not cheat and were alone in the rooms while taking their exams, a practice that ignored how having one's own study space is an equity issue disproportionately affecting those families living in small apartments with many children. Just like Baldwin (2021) said, "We are living through a very dangerous time" (p. 501). Nonetheless, there is hope for the future. Language teacher educators and language teachers – whom I will refer to as language educators hereafter – can unlearn, challenge, and dismantle the hegemonic ideologies of capitalism, racism, ableism, sexism, and classism that afflict the society at large. This book is for those who are committed to providing anti-oppressive, transformative, equitable, and inclusive educational opportunities and experiences to students who come from diverse linguistic, cultural, economic, and racial/ethnic backgrounds.

The social justice turn in language education

As interdisciplinary fields that deal with diverse populations, their languages, and cultures, both language education and applied linguistics have long been interested in questions of ideology, hegemony, power, diversity, equity, and inclusion. Many interdisciplinary frameworks have been proposed to investigate these issues, some of which include (critical) multicultural education, inclusive education, critical pedagogy, antiracist pedagogy, feminist pedagogy, anti-oppressive education, culturally responsive/sustaining pedagogies, critical language awareness, and critical applied linguistics.

While issues of gender, race, and sexuality – and teacher and learner identities in general – have long been a concern of language education scholars, the past decade has witnessed a marked intensification of interest in social justice language education (Hawkins, 2011; Ortaçtepe Hart and Martel, 2020). This growing interest in social justice has been closely linked to frameworks and standards proposed by international organizations such as TESOL International Association, American Association for Applied Linguistics (AAAL), the American Council on the Teaching of Foreign Languages (ACTFL), and the Council of Europe's Common European Framework of References for Languages (CEFR). TESOL's Social Responsibility Interest Section (SRIS), for instance, aims to support its members in terms of "social responsibility, world citizenship, and awareness of global issues such as peace, human rights, and the environment" (TESOL, 2022). The Applied Linguistics & Social Justice listserv is an online forum open to all AAAL members who would like to exchange "ideas, resources, publications, and initiatives focused on applied linguistics and social justice" (AAAL, 2022). Similarly, ACTFL's Critical and Social Justice Approaches (CSJA) Special Interest Group aims "to promote and support critical and social justice approaches in language instruction" (ACTFL, 2022). Publications have also appeared which draw parallels between ACTFL's world-readiness standards for learning languages[2] and social justice (Glynn et al., 2014; Osborn, 2006; Randolph and Johnson, 2017). The Council of Europe's 2018 Companion to CEFR was also considered a milestone for underlining the role of languages in human rights and social justice (Council of Europe, 2018).

Two special issues have recently been published in renowned journals – first in *TESOL Journal* by Ortaçtepe Hart and Martel (2020), and then in *Applied Linguistics* by Avineri and Martinez (2021). The theme of the 2022 Conference of the British Association for Applied Linguistics, meanwhile, was *Innovation and Social Justice in Applied Linguistics*.[3] Many other small-scale conferences have been held across the world, such as University of Jyväskylä's *Language Education for Social Justice*[4] in 2021 and Sinop University's *Symposium on Social Justice in ELT*[5] that was held in 2019 and 2022. Amidst these political and socio-economic conjunction in the world and the epistemological and pedagogical developments within language education I started working on the present book in 2019 as a cisgender, heterosexual woman of ethnic minority/color in the United States. In the next section, I will introduce myself and my positionality by describing real events – which might include upsetting and triggering content for some readers – that have brought me to where I am today.

The author's journey as a social justice educator

I was born in October 1980, the very same year James Baldwin published *Dark Days*, and only a month after the 1980 Turkish coup d'état that imposed strict curfews, banned workers' strikes and labor unions, and led to the arrest and exile of hundreds of thousands, including my father. He was the chair of the teachers' union in my hometown of Mudanya. Rallying and protesting was a common family activity for us. Our bookcases were filled with the works of Marx, Lenin, Che Guevera, and Nazım Hikmet. I was given the name Deniz as a homage to the 1960s student leader and activist Deniz Gezmiş, who was hanged with his two companions by the Turkish state in 1972. From the time that I was little through my adolescence, I grew up with the fundamental principle that I should never remain silent in the face of injustice. But that was my personal life. My professional life as a language teacher educator and a scholar – although interested in identity, language socialization, immigration, and assessment – did not really cross paths with my personal commitment to have a more just world. Until the day a school shooting happened in Parkland, Florida in 2018.[6]

It was a normal teaching day in Monterey, California where I was living and working at the time. I woke up, had my Turkish breakfast – like I always do – and went to teach my practicum/placement course. As I walked in, I immediately noticed a dismayed student sitting quietly in a corner. When I asked her whether there was anything bothering her, she mentioned the Parkland school shooting that had happened the day before. Her placement was in a high school, where she had noticed a police car parked in front the day before. She was feeling scared and anxious about her decision to pursue a career in teaching. I listened to these concerns as someone coming from a conflict zone, with bombings happening almost every month at that time.[7] Only a year before I moved to the United States, a failed coup-attempt[8] had taken place, with jets flying literally over our roof in the capital of Ankara where I was teaching between 2011–2017. The jets were shaking the whole apartment building, as we watched from our windows the military helicopters bombing the government buildings and shooting the protestors who were called to the streets by President Erdoğan. So I was right there listening to my student and remembering all the trauma my Turkish students and I experienced during those years. Yet, caught off guard with her concerns regarding the school shootings in the US, I did my best to 'comfort' the student as much as I could. The next day, I had a different student in my office concerned about the previous student's comment and my – obviously failed – attempt to provide a quick fix. This student had been held up at gunpoint in a foreign country where she taught English. She very convincingly argued that discussing school shootings should be within the scope of our practicum course, and that all teacher candidates should be prepared for such scenarios and the realities of the schools. The following week's class focused on school shootings. We discussed what to do when an active shooter is in a school building, and the larger issues around school shootings such as the gun ownership and gun violence in the US. It was not a 'comforting,' 'feel-good' kind of class, but was much appreciated by all students for bringing a real-world issue into their teaching practice course.

And that's how my personal and professional lives finally crossed paths. This was the beginning of a long journey. Since then, I have been a strong advocate for social justice language education, through the projects I have run both in Turkey and in California, and through the course Social Justice Language Education (SJLE) that I designed and taught for the very first time at the Middlebury

xiv   Social Justice and the Language Classroom

Institute of International Studies at Monterey in Fall 2019. This book is both a product of, and a reflection upon, these efforts.

There is no doubt that the past decade has witnessed an increased interest in social justice teacher education, especially in the US, the UK, and Canada. During my years in the States, I have observed how a diversity statement – along with a resume and a cover letter – has become one of the usual documents required for many job applications in higher education. I have seen institutions and programs embellishing their mission statements with words such as diversity, justice, and equity; and phrases such as 'changing the world.' While twenty years ago Nieto (2000) raised concerns regarding "the sluggish pace with which teacher education programs are addressing social justice and equity" (p. 181), already by 2006 Zeichner could remark that it is "difficult to find a teacher education program in the United States that does not claim to have a program that prepares teachers for social justice" (p. 328).

Despite this increased commitment of teacher education programs in social justice, I have also observed their minimal impact on the inequalities in educational systems as well as the society at large. Part of the reason seems to be what Cochran-Smith et al. (2009a) refer to as *the ambiguity critique*, that is, the lack of clarity in the way teacher education programs conceptualize social justice and social justice education (McDonald and Zeichner, 2009). As Hytten and Bettez (2011) discuss:

> [d]espite all the talk about social justice of late, it is often unclear in any practical terms what we mean when we invoke a vision of social justice or how this influences such issues as program development, curricula, practicum opportunities, educational philosophy, social vision, and activist work. (p. 8)

My other observation concerned the literature's heavy reliance on US history, as if the only target audience for social justice teacher education were pre-service teachers in the US. I agree that preparing student teachers for their future teaching context requires a deep understanding and examination of the historical, economic, and political processes that influence the society in which they will be teaching. As Hawkins (2011) states, "learning and teaching … occur in specific situated contexts and are contingent on the time, place and participants in specific interactions that constitute the learning events, all of which, in part, [are] shaped by larger societal and institutional discourses" (p. 3). Nevertheless, I was struggling to find resources for the Turkish pre-service teachers who were part of my Social Justice in ELT project and my international students in the Social Justice Language Teaching course I was teaching in Monterey. Finding ways to make social justice language education relevant to their cultures, lives, and experiences was extremely challenging with the existing US-centric resources. In order to contextualize the issues in ways that are culturally relevant to my learners' experiences and identities, I had to replace the socio-historical exigencies of the US with the ones from the Middle East, Europe, and Asia. During this process, I did come across scholars who have contributed to the body of literature on social justice language education by drawing from their experiences in different parts of the world (e.g., Sierra Piedrahita, 2016 for Colombia; Da Cruz, 2017 for Iceland), but these were quite limited in number. The dearth of publications on social justice education that would appeal to educators from a wide range of backgrounds led me to pose the following questions:

- *How could we, as teacher educators, talk about social justice if our pedagogy only involved one particular group of teacher candidates without providing any guidance on what social justice language education can look like in different parts of the world?*
- *How could we decolonize the knowledge on social justice language education by expanding the scope of our work in ways that would be not only relevant but also transformative in different social, cultural, and political contexts?*
- *How could we talk about epistemological social justice if we are only citing our White colleagues or colleagues from Western cultures, while ignoring the work of scholars of color, ethnic minority, and women, as well as queer scholars?*
- *In what ways could a more global perspective to social justice language education also benefit a US audience, often criticized in other parts of the globe for a certain myopia when it comes to global issues of social justice?*

It is with these concerns and questions in mind that I embarked on this journey to extend social justice language education beyond the borders of a particular country through a book that would include both global and local perspectives. In doing so, my goal was to present the diversity of social justice issues as well as the common ground in order to meet the needs of a diverse range of language educators – not just of English but of all languages – operating in different contexts all over the world.

Overview of the book

This book aims to provide language educators with the knowledge, skills, and dispositions to adopt social justice language education for transformation and social change. Yet it avoids providing a list of 'effective' practices or tips for social justice language education. As Giroux (2011) argues:

… pedagogy can never be treated as a fixed set of principles and practices that can be applied indiscriminately across a variety of pedagogical sites. Pedagogy must always be contextually defined, allowing it to respond specifically to the conditions, formations, and problems that arise in various sites in which education takes place. (p. 75)

Avoiding a prescriptive, one-size-fits-all approach to social justice language education, the book aims to develop language educators' critical consciousness and critical reflection to recognize systems of oppression and inequality and adopt social justice pedagogies for transformation and social change. Overall, this book aims to enable language educators to:

- Acquire and employ the core concepts and the vocabulary to identify, discuss, and address various social justice issues in their classes.
- Examine the myriad ways in which many forms of oppressions intersect and interact with each other within individual, societal, political, economic, and cultural domains.[9]
- Identify, examine, and reflect upon their individual beliefs and dispositions in relation to various social justice issues and to unlearn any misconceptions, misunderstandings, and preconceived notions.
- Value the diversity their students bring to the classroom and make curriculum relevant, meaningful, engaging, and culturally affirming and sustaining by building on learners' talents, strengths, cultural and linguistic resources.
- Establish a caring, inclusive, equitable, and egalitarian classroom environment by demonstrating trust, solidarity, agency, allyship, and advocacy both at the school and societal levels.
- Become curriculum leaders who can participate in difficult conversations and take action to fight against various forms of oppression, marginalization, and discrimination for transformation and social change.

In order to achieve these goals, the book is broken down into three main parts and eight chapters. Part I begins with *Chapter 1: Social justice and social justice education*, which introduces key concepts such as social justice, oppression, ideology, and hegemony. This chapter presents social justice as a continuum of the politics of recognition and the politics of redistribution, with intersectionality at its core. Building teachers' capacity for social justice education as an individual, institutional, and collective journey is also discussed in this chapter. Providing a broad picture of social justice education, this chapter would be of interest to educators not only in language education but also in other disciplines. *Chapter 2: Social justice-oriented critical pedagogy* presents critical pedagogy in relation to language educators' role to realize transformative liberatory education. Considering both the contributions of critical pedagogy to the field of education and the criticisms it has received, this chapter proposes a social justice-oriented critical pedagogy that aims to cultivate learners' critical consciousness, agency, and advocacy for social action. *Chapter 3: Language, education, and social justice* focuses on the nexus of language, power, and ideology and explains social justice language education in relation to the premises and criticisms of multicultural education. The pedagogical implications of the concepts and issues discussed in Chapter 3 will be presented in *Chapter 4: Social justice language curriculum*, which takes a practical approach to discuss four main strategies that situate social justice at the center of the language education curriculum.

Part II delves into three main critical themes and frameworks related to social class, race and ethnicity, and gender and sexuality. *Chapter 5: Neoliberalism,* *social class, and anti-classism* introduces the role of political economy in language education/applied linguistics research and the implications of neoliberalism for classroom teaching. *Chapter 6: Race, ethnicity, and antiracist language pedagogy* unpacks race and ethnicity as social constructs and, by drawing on critical race theory, presents strategies for antiracist language pedagogies. *Chapter 7: Social justice pedagogies for all gender and sexual identities* conveys an integrated and intersectional approach to fighting against sexism, heteropatriarchy, transphobia, and other forms of oppression that impact the lives of lesbians, gays, bisexuals, cisgender women, and trans* and queer individuals, as well as those who are non-binary, genderfluid, and non-conforming. Finally, in Part III, *Chapter 8: The rough and yet traversable road ahead* addresses possible concerns and questions in relation to social justice language education and provides suggestions for further work.

There are several strategies I followed in the organization of this book to make it more reader/user-friendly. The first of these strategies regards the concepts presented in the book throughout all chapters. There is no doubt that defining social justice is not an easy task, neither is explaining race, class, gender, and sexuality. However, as Grant and Agosto (2008) caution, not defining social justice – and any other related concepts in this sense – may lead to "actions in the name of social justice [that] are often superficial, ineffective, and uniformed" (p. 195). Therefore, each chapter in Parts I and II is designed in such a way that first unpacks several critical concepts and then continues to address pedagogical issues related to the chapter's theme.

The second strategy concerns the tasks designed for language educators to engage in. Each chapter in the book starts with a 'Lead-in' that will gauge what readers already know or think about that chapter's topic. Chapters also include problem-posing and reflective tasks that will enable readers to apply the principles and strategies discussed to their contexts and to critically reflect on their practice. The readers can engage with these problem-posing and reflective tasks either as they appear in the text or revisit them after they complete each chapter. There are also multimedia resources and children's books provided at the end of each chapter. I have decided to include children's books as a resource for social justice language education since they can appeal to all learner groups regardless of age and proficiency levels. Multimedia resources are also selected purposefully for language educators who would like to gain additional insights on the topics and find classroom resources (e.g., lesson plans, materials, and activities) that can be used in their classrooms.

Another commonality especially across Chapters 5, 6, and 7 concerns intersectionality. While each of these chapters delves into a particular issue, these critical themes do not constitute compartmentalized systems of oppression but overlap with each other because of the complex and intersectional nature of human experience. Hence, intersectionality is not only discussed in Chapter 1, which familiarizes readers with the concept, but it runs through the whole book, building a bridge between critical pedagogy, political economy, critical race theory, feminist theory, and queer theory. By taking this approach, I aim to depict a more unified social justice pedagogy that enables language educators to fight different forms of -isms (racism, sexism, classism, etc.) while also challenging the neoliberal ideology that circulates in today's schools, institutions, and media. In that sense, this book is in line with Pennycook's (2022) call for critical applied linguistics research and activism through an intersectional approach that embodies a raciolinguistic perspective, a decolonial imperative, an ecofeminist approach that treats feminism and ecology in tandem, a queer focus, and a perspective that deals with the material world through political economy. This book, thus, presents a genuine dialogue across various frameworks and positions in order to help language educators make better connections and develop stronger alliances "to more effectively center a social justice agenda in schools and society" (Hytten and Bettez, 2011, p. 21).

Addressing social justice issues in one's classroom is difficult for everyone, but probably more so for those who work in undemocratic societies that silence all oppositional and marginalized voices, like where I am from. Probably even more difficult is to create social change and transformation. Yet, as Harvey (2020) states, "revolution is a long process not an event" (p. 13). This book is for those who refuse to sit silent, remain 'neutral,' and be a bystander. It is for everyone who chooses to be an advocate, an ally, and an activist for all the injustices in educational settings and across society. Education *is* our hope for brighter days.

Deniz Ortaçtepe Hart
Monterey, Ankara, Glasgow

Notes

1. Bayoumi, M. (March 2022). They are 'civilised' and 'look like us': the racist coverage of Ukraine. *The Guardian.* https://www.theguardian.com/comment isfree/2022/mar/02/civilised-european-look-like-us-racist-coverage-ukraine
2. World-Readiness standards for learning languages: http://www.actfl.org/pu blications/all/world-readi-ness-standards-learning-languages
3. 2022 Conference of British Association for Applied Linguistics: https://www.baalconference2022.com/
4. University of Jyväskylä's conference on *Language Education for Social Justice*: https://sites.google.com/jyu.fi/lang-education-social-justice/home
5. Sinop University's *Symposium on Social Justice in ELT*: www.socialjusticeinelt.com
6. Segarra, L., Reilly, K. and Calfas, J. (2018, February). The latest on the Florida school shooting. *Time.* https://time.com/5158678/what-to-know-ab out-the-active-shooter-situation-at-florida-high-school/
7. Timeline of attacks in Turkey. *Aljazeera* (2017, February). https://www.aljaze era.com/indepth/interactive/2016/06/timeline-attacks-turkey-1606282238 00183.html

8. Turkey's coup attempt: What you need to know. *BBC* (2016 July). https://www.bbc.co.uk/news/world-europe-36816045

9. In this book, the terms political, economic, and cultural will be used to a great extent. In doing so, I follow Steger's (2017) definitions of them: The term economic is associated with "the production, exchange and consumption of commodities." The term political refers to "the practices related to the generation and distribution of power in societies." The term cultural embodies "the symbolic construction, articulation, and dissemination of meaning" (p. 80).

Acknowledgements

This book has been written over several years, spanning the COVID epidemic, over three continents, and with the support of several institutions. I owe thanks to more people than I can acknowledge in person here.

I would like to thank my colleagues at the Middlebury Institute of International Studies at Monterey, especially Laura Burian, Jason Martel, and Anne Campbell for their support and collegiality. The MIIS library staff provided invaluable support, and I would like to extend my thanks to them all, and especially to Lydia Denice Gentry for all her help and for keeping up with my constant demands for interlibrary loans. I would like to also thank Shawna Shapiro at Middlebury College for generously giving her time and expertise and reading and offering feedback on Chapter 4.

My graduate students at the Middlebury Institute of International Studies at Monterey played an important role in shaping this book, and I'd like to thank them for their critical conversations, difficult questions, and insightful comments in the Social Justice Language Teaching course I offered there between 2019 and 2022. I would especially like to thank my former students Kalina Swanson, Sydney Zamudio, and Kathryn DePietro for allowing me to share their lesson plans, materials evaluations, and adaptation projects in various parts of this book. Two other former students deserve a thank you as well: Burcu Chatham for her help with the references and Melanie Kincl for her feedback on Chapter 3. I owe a special debt of gratitude to Greg Ford, my amazing former student/graduate assistant, friend, and colleague, who not only provided constructive comments and suggestions on all the chapters of this book but also offered continuous support and encouragement.

This book was also inspired by the Social Justice in ELT project Adnan Yilmaz and I carried out together in Turkey between 2018 and 2022. I would like to thank Adnan for his dedication and hard work in this project, and Büşra Polat, one of our project participants, for kindly allowing me to share her work (Pavo's story) in this book. Also, a big thank you to Elif Burhan-Horasanlı, who gave me the support and encouragement I needed in times of near despair!

I'd also like to thank my colleagues at the University of Leeds and the University of Glasgow for supporting this work in various ways. I'm also grateful to my Chinese students in the UK for further broadening my appreciation of the complexities involved in moving beyond a Western, Anglocentric understanding of social justice.

I would like to thank my husband, Patrick Hart: his own book with Edinburgh University Press was going through its final edits when he encouraged me to pitch the idea for this one to Laura Quinn (Commissioning Editor) at AAAL 2019, where she and I met for the first time. Thank you for helping me not only to initiate this project, but also to complete it! I'd also like to thank Laura for believing in this project, and Laura, Sam Johnson, the anonymous reviewers from Canada, the UK, and the US, and the entire publication team at Edinburgh University Press for their guidance, support, and insightful suggestions.

Finally, I would like to thank my parents, who paid a high price for their own commitment to social justice in the Turkey of the 1980s. My brother Yaşarcan and my sister-in-law Özge: thanks for always being there for me. Special thanks go to my five-year-old nephew Demir, who always finds a way to cheer me up. *Ailem, iyi ki varsınız.*

Dedicated to my parents, Şule and Doğan, who taught me the fight.

Bana kavgayı öğreten aileme adanmıştır.

Part I

Language teaching for social justice

Chapter 1

Social justice and social justice education

Box 1.1 Lead-in

"If you have come here to help me you are wasting your time, but if you have come because your liberation is bound up with mine, then let us work together."

Often attributed to Lilla Watson, an Aboriginal visual artist, activist, and academic from Queensland, Australia, this quote comes from the work of an Aboriginal Rights group in Queensland, which Lilla was also a part of.

What are your thoughts and reflections on this statement? In what way might your liberation be bound up with Indigenous people's or anyone else's?'

Introduction

Social justice is an elusive and politically charged term, open to multiple and diverse interpretations. Its complexity and fluidity result from the social, economic, political, and cultural contexts that shape its definitions and interpretations (Fook, 2014). As Hytten and Bettez (2011) state, "the more we see people invoking the idea of social justice, the less clear it becomes what people mean, and if it is meaningful at all" (p. 8). Social justice has become a widely appropriated buzzword, making the term vulnerable to negative connotations, backlash, anger, and defensiveness. *Social justice warrior*, for instance, has become a pejorative term to refer to those who support equality and diversity only for the sake of personal validation, rather than to achieve social, political, and economic goals through advocacy and activism.

Social justice education has also been defined, described, and actualized in myriad, often ambiguous ways, to the extent that the term has become "diluted, trivialized or co-opted" (Cochran-Smith, 2010, p. 445). It is not within the scope of this book to provide a comprehensive account of the political and philosophical roots and history of the terms 'social justice' and 'social justice education.'

I do, however, want to describe my own understanding of these two terms and how I am using them in this book. The following issues will, therefore, be explored in this chapter:

- Ideology, hegemony, and oppression as key concepts
- Social justice as politics of recognition and redistribution with intersectionality at its core
- Social justice education: An individual, institutional, and collective journey
- The social justice educator

Box 1.2 Problem-posing task
Talk to at least five people in your school, workplace, classroom, family, etc. Ask them:

- What is your understanding of social justice?
- What do you do to achieve social justice in your life/workplace/ classrooms/community?

Reflect on the responses you receive: Are they in line with each other? What are the commonalities? If the answers diverge, what do you think the reason is?

Ideology, hegemony, and oppression

Social justice has often been framed as a dynamic matter of doing, acting, and becoming, as much as a 'thing' or 'state' that can be defined once and for all. Metaphorically speaking, social justice is a *verb* as much as a *noun*. As a noun, it refers to a set of individual, social, and cultural values that include but are not limited to agency, advocacy, caring, democracy, fairness, equity, diversity, ethics, respect, dignity, recognition, inclusion, and worth. As a verb, social justice is the transformation of these values into political, social, economic, cultural, and environmental strategies and tactics that will challenge, chip away at, and perhaps even eventually demolish existing heteropatriarchal, racist, and capitalist ideologies and hegemonic power relations (Bell, 2016). Three concepts, ideology, hegemony, and oppression are worth explaining here before unpacking the term social justice.

Ideology and hegemony

Ideology and hegemony are both complex but essential concepts that help under-stand and overcome inequalities and injustices. While both concepts have their origins in the work of Karl Marx, the understanding of each has been developed significantly by a broad range of twentieth-and twenty-first-century political thinkers, perhaps most notably by Antonio Gramsci in the case of hegemony, and Louis Althusser in the case of ideology.

Ideology is used today in two distinct senses. The first of these – what might be called the common or everyday understanding of the word – describes a consciously held and more or less coherent set of political convictions. Althusser (2001), however, uses ideology quite differently. For Althusser, ideology refers to the set of unconsciously held beliefs and assumptions by which individuals ration-alize and are reconciled to the socio-economic, political, and cultural status quo. These beliefs are not consciously arrived at but are continually being embedded in individuals from a very early age. These beliefs and assumptions may even contradict or undermine the political positions human beings claim to uphold or support. One of the great strengths of Althusser's account is that it explains why individuals and groups in society may support an ideology – in the first, everyday sense – that is against their own self-interest. It can also account for why those explicitly trying in good faith to challenge a society's dominant socio-political order may nevertheless find their own thinking caught up in its logic.

A key concept for understanding how ideology functions is interpellation. Interpellation refers to how individuals are addressed repeatedly – by authority figures such as parents, teachers, priests, and politicians, and by media and advertising – in ways that establish a particular place for them in the world (or *subject-position*), and invite, compel, or seduce them into occupying that position. At first, individuals may resist being 'made subject' in this way, and fight against occupying the position of the one who should be grateful, who should obey, who should love their nation, who should desire and work and marry and buy. But the remorseless and unavoidable nature of interpellation means that everyone inevitably becomes subjects of the dominant (or hegemonic) ideologies within which they are raised. In most cases, subjects are not even aware that they are being interpellated in this way. Interpellation is most effective precisely when it is invisible, when cultural values are treated as though they were simply natural, given facts (Althusser, 2001).

Althusser's model is especially important for educators for three reasons. First, it places identity formation and how individuals are made into 'subjects' at its core. Second, it sees the education system as one of its key 'ideological state apparatuses' by which individual subjectivity is shaped and molded, alongside entities like the family, mass media, and organized religion. Third, it explains why the work of social justice education is not only so important but also so difficult and why it means – above all – working hard on ourselves as teachers, students, and subjects.

Most associated with the Italian Marxist theorist and activist Antonio Gramsci (1971), *hegemony* refers to the process through which the ruling class (i.e., the dominant groups) who have privilege, power, and access to resources socially and psychologically impose and install a widely accepted worldview, controlling knowledge in order to legitimize, normalize, and naturalize their domination, power, leadership, and control. The ruling class, as Gramsci noted, does not always or not only resort to top-down measures, coercion, or physical force. It also assembles and utilizes a *hegemonic bloc* (e.g., media, schools, family, and religious institutions) that embodies different social forces and relationships to gain population's voluntary consent (Kincheloe, 2007; Apple, 2019). According to Fraser (2019), "hegemony has to do with the political, moral, cultural, and intellectual authority of a given worldview" (p. 35) as well as its capacity to align itself with social forces and classes. Through various hegemonic blocs, populations are informed about "what is just and right and what is not" (Fraser, 2019, p. 10) and socialized into dominant economic, institutional, cultural, and linguistic domains of a society. It is through hegemony that "the roles and rules, institutional norms, historical accounts, and social practices of dominant groups come to be accepted as the natural order" (Bell, 2016, p. 11). For instance, in many countries around the world – regardless of whether same-sex relationships are illegal or protected by law – heteronormativity (e.g., the assumption that erotic love is between a female and a male person) is the hegemonic ideology that is deemed 'normal,' 'legitimate,' and 'natural' by cultural and political institutions. Heteronormativity constantly asserts itself in institutions, organizations, and across society, as recently seen in the 2021 Don't Say Gay Bill in Florida which banned the discussions of gender and sexual identities in the classrooms.

Hegemony and ideology are highly interconnected in socio-cultural domains, including education. According to Apple (2019), various hegemonic ideologies provide individuals with frames of reference that not only "assist them in organizing their world [but also] enable them to believe they are neutral participants in the neutral instrumentation of schooling ... while at the same time, these frameworks serve particular economic and ideological interests which are hidden from them" (p. 21). As will be discussed in more detail in Chapter 2, schools, through selective tradition (e.g., selecting, preserving, and producing certain kinds of knowledge) and a hidden curriculum (i.e., deep structure of schooling), enhance the ideological dominance of certain social classes and groups in a society while ignoring the needs and interests of 'others.' In addition to educational institutions, mass media, social media, corporations, and popular culture are used to create citizens who embrace ideologies that limit access to wealth and cultural power only to the dominant and privileged groups in order to maintain their hegemonic status, power, and authority (Foster, 2012; Hickman and Porfilio, 2012). One telling example for how hegemonic ideologies through digital technologies are conveyed, circulated, and perpetuated in the society comes from the way corporatized outlets such as newscasts, films, television shows, advertisements, and videogames vilified and positioned racialized groups as the sole source of society's problems (Hickman and Porfilio, 2012). Jennifer Eberhardt's book *Biased* (2020) extensively discusses the harmful effects of these messages, rooted in slavery and White supremacy (soon to be unpacked in Chapter 6), on Black people:

> Blacks remain strapped to the ape association by a history of slavery, present-day disparities in almost every significant domain of life, and a collection of overlapping racial stereotypes that reinforce those inequities. In addition to being dark, blacks are seen as cognitively challenged, big, dangerous, aggressive, violent, unrestrained brutes – the very features that, unfortunately, many associate with apes. (p. 145)

Circulated through schooling, media, and other institutions and multimodal technologies, hegemonic ideologies are, therefore, generally held unconsciously and internalized as 'natural.' Difficult to identify within educational institutions and curricula, they lead to oppressive and discriminatory policies and practices that harm Black students, immigrant and minoritized students, and students of color, to name a few.

Oppression

Oppression often derives from hierarchical power relations between individuals based on their group membership. In simple terms, oppression refers to "a harm through which groups of persons are systematically and unfairly and unjustly constrained, burdened, or reduced by any of several forces" (Cudd, 2006, p. 23). Embedded within various cultural, economic, social, and political power relations, oppression is manifested through different -*isms*, such as racism, sexism, ableism, classism, heterosexism, etc.

The terms oppression and marginalization are highly interrelated. According to Kumashiro (2000), "oppression is a situation or dynamic in which certain ways of being ... are privileged in society while others are marginalized" (p. 25). As certain groups gain privileged positions based on their class, gender, race, ethnicity, native language, and so on – which enable these dominant groups to control access to power, authority, privilege, and resources – certain groups are pushed towards the 'margins' of a society. In other words, they are marginalized and represented as inferior and/or deviant in a way that 'justifies' their material and socio-cultural deprivation (Bell, 2016; Glynn et al., 2014; Young, 2011). In classroom settings as elsewhere, hegemonic ideologies operate in such a way as to marginalize certain students (e.g., in the Anglophone Global North, Black, Indigenous, and people of color, and students with limited or no English proficiency in English as a first language settings such as the US and the UK) who are seen as members of these 'inferior' social groups, rather than individuals with unique identities, histories, talents, and abilities (Bell, 2016).

There are different forms of oppression discussed in the literature. For instance, Cudd (2006) discusses *psychological* and *material oppression*, "which mutually cause[s] and exacerbate[s] the effects of each other" (p. 24). Psychological oppression takes the form of causing mental stress, gaslighting, and reducing one's self-image, while material oppression ranges from limiting access to resources (e.g., health care, education, living wage) to harming one's physical well-being (e.g., physical violence, bullying, and rape). The other forms that again interact with each other are interpersonal, institutional, and internalized oppression.

Interpersonal, institutional, and internalized oppression

While oppression is often used in a way that encompasses discrimination, bias, prejudice, hate, and bigotry, these forms of oppression are more associated with individual consciousness and actions. Microaggressions, for instance, are a form of interpersonal oppression that minoritized and marginalized populations face in their lives on a daily basis. Microaggressions in general refer to "the everyday verbal, nonverbal, and environmental slights, snubs, or insults, whether intentional or unintentional, that communicate hostile, derogatory, or negative messages to target persons based solely upon their marginalized group membership" (Sue, 2010, p. 3). Although often associated with racial oppression, any marginalized group based on their gender, sexuality, class, and religion may be the target of microaggressions. Examples range from whistles or catcalls from men towards women, to gay men holding hands on the street being told not to 'flaunt' their sexuality, or White people checking their purses as a Black person walks by (Sue, 2010).

Institutional or institutionalized oppression circulates through cultural, economic, and political institutions. Institutions, in this case, might refer to actual, tangible institutions such as organizations and governments and their practices (e.g., criminal justice,[1] healthcare, and education systems) or more abstract forms such as cultural beliefs and traditions. It is through their policies and practices that customs, norms, beliefs, assumptions, behaviors, and relationships are deemed 'normal,' 'expected,' or 'essential' in societies. In educational systems, institutional oppression may take the form of curricular decisions in terms of whose history and reality are included and whose is omitted. James Loewen's (2007) book, *Lies my teacher told me*, presents an insightful discussion of how knowledge production and curriculum are not neutral and objective processes, but historically embedded, socially constructed, and derived from a complex set of power relations and struggles among different groups.

Lastly, internalized oppression takes place through (un)intentional, (un)conscious and (c)overt stereotypical and biased discourses that are conveyed and circulated through socialization in daily life and through digital media. Internalized oppression refers to marginalized groups' accepting and, in some cases, even replicating their 'inferior' group status and the harmful generalizations ascribed to them by those in power (Bell, 2016; David and Derthick, 2018). For instance, due to the colonizers' teachings of conformity and obedience to authority, internalized racism ended up as one of the reasons colonization was so successful in many parts of the world. Within educational contexts in the US, internalized oppression often takes the form of immigrant English language learners internalizing the explicit and implicit messages that lead to their oppression and marginalization, resulting in feelings of embarrassment, shame, inferiority, and imposter syndrome (e.g., feeling inadequate despite evidence of achievement and/or ability in language learning).

These three forms of oppression – interpersonal, institutional, and internalized – are almost always interrelated and overlapping (Adams and Zúñiga, 2016; David and Derthick, 2018). Perhaps the most salient and illustrative example of such imbrication is the May 25, 2020 murder of George Floyd, a 46-year-old Black man, in Minneapolis, Minnesota by a White police officer while White, Asian, and Black officers looked on and failed to intercede as their colleague slowly choked the life out of Mr. Floyd. While some attributed this event to a single act of racism by a rogue officer (interpersonal), many have argued that such racist violence is systemic within police departments (institutional) and that the other officers of color were complicit in Mr. Floyd's murder (internalized). The harassment of trans people on the street, rape and domestic violence towards women, and the killing of Black men by armed police, while all clearly intentional acts by individual people, also have deep-level roots in cultural, economic, and political ideologies.

Social justice: a continuum of politics of recognition and redistribution

According to Fraser (2019), the current economic world order relies on two complementary, intertwined dimensions – namely, the politics of recognition and the politics of redistribution – that determine individuals' perceptions of what is right and just. Concerned with issues related to respect, esteem, identity, and belonging, the *politics of recognition* fights against various forms of oppression, stigmatization, and discrimination based on group membership (Rampton et al., 2007). The politics of recognition, also known as *identity politics*, acknowledges that every individual has certain identity markers such as race, ethnicity, gender, and sexuality according to which they adopt or are assigned positions of penalty and privilege. Systematic refusal of recognition, that is, nonrecognition or lack of recognition, and misrecognition are two forms of identity-based oppression (e.g., homophobia and racism). Misrecognition differs from nonrecognition: it refers to the process in which individuals are not recognized for who they are. For instance, stigmatized recognition is a form of misrecognition, as in the case of Muslim people from the Middle East being considered terrorists especially after the 9/11 attacks in New York City. Nonrecognition and misrecognition occur both at interpersonal and institutional levels (e.g., unequal rights and discrimination in immigration and citizenship, criminal justice system and in education). Eberhardt (2020) provides a powerful analysis of how stigmatized recognition functions in practice: examining common stereotypes about the 'Black male,' she shows how these work in both obvious and more nuanced ways to associate Black men with criminality, feeding into police brutality and killings.

The *politics of redistribution*, on the other hand, addresses the socio-economic injustices and class-based divisions that are deeply rooted in the political-economic structure of a society at large. Fraser (1997) talks about three overlapping forms of socio-economic injustice: exploitation of labor, economic marginalization, and deprivation, defined as being paid less than the living wage and denied access to adequate standards of living. Therefore, the politics of redistribution aim to restructure the political economy in ways that end class divisions and exploitation through the reorganization of the division of labor, equal allocation of divisible goods (e.g., income), and the transformation of other economic structures.

These two dimensions of justice – recognition and redistribution – have been compartmentalized in various socio-political domains in ways that the former has almost undermined the latter (Fraser, 1997). For instance, Dr. Martin Luther King's thought and rhetoric have been reduced in the public imagination to being solely concerned with questions of race, rather than with race and social class, and the broader transformation of society. The March on Washington for Jobs and Freedom in 1963 has been truncated to 'The March on Washington,' and Dr. King's struggles for economic gains for all people regardless of race have largely been obscured (Cone, 2012). The increased interest in recognition politics since the Civil Rights Movements in the US has contributed to "the relative eclipse" of any focus on economic justice and social class (Fraser, 1997, p. 2). Yet, these two dimensions of justice, recognition and redistribution, are highly intertwined and interdependent:

> Cultural norms that are unfairly biased against some are institutionalized in the state and the economy; meanwhile, economic disadvantage impedes equal participation in the making of culture, in public spheres and in everyday life. The result is often a vicious circle of cultural and economic subordination. (Fraser, 1995, pp. 72–73)

Fraser (1995, 2019), therefore, proposes a transformative framework that would help fight various injustices simultaneously as an alternative to affirmative frameworks that serve ameliorative functions. Affirmative frameworks aim to reallocate goods and resources as well as respect and recognition (e.g., multicultural programs). They support group differentiation and can therefore lead to further misrecognition in the form of stereotyping, oppression, and marginalization, since "little or nothing is done to deal with the underlying conditions that lead to the inequalities emerging from misrecognition and maldistribution" (Block, 2018, p. 174). Fraser's (1995, 2019) transformative framework, on the other hand, aims to challenge the deep structures of cultural and economic power relations by blurring and destabilizing group differentiation (e.g., Black versus White, male versus female) while also promoting solidarity.

This book, therefore, conceptualizes social justice as an amalgam of the politics of recognition and the politics of redistribution as two overlapping and interdependent dimensions of social justice. In doing so, it simultaneously challenges the commonly held belief that the many forms of oppression observed in the world result from a single issue such as racism or sexism and that a straightforward and clear pathway is needed to fight against that singular structural force (Lorde, 1984; Osei-Kofi, 2013). Instead, any attempt towards social justice should acknowledge the intersectionality of various identities and the associated forms of oppression individuals may experience depending on where they stand in the recognition to redistribution continuum.

Box 1.3 Reflective task

In *Sister Outsider*, Audre Lorde (1984) states that, "[T]here is no such thing as a single-issue struggle because we do not lead single-issue lives" (p. 138).

What are your thoughts and reflections on this quotation? What multi-issue struggles do you encounter, observe, and experience in your educational contexts and communities?

Intersectionality

Kimberlé Crenshaw (1991), a Black feminist legal scholar, is often acknowledged for coining and popularizing the term *intersectionality*. She herself, however, noted that this was not a new idea and that various concepts conveying similar meanings had been proposed in the past. Intersectionality refers to the ways in which discrete forms of oppression and identity intersect with each other, as a result of which the nature of oppression experienced by an individual or a group of people is altered and expanded (Block, 2014; Crenshaw, 1991; Osei-Kofi, 2013). Discussing the role of intersectionality in terms of (re)structuring the structure of a society, Pugach et al. (2019) argue that:

> [An intersectionality lens] allows for a reconsideration of how multiple marginalized, complex identities can be addressed in discourses around meeting needs of individuals with complex identities, as well as examining how such identities are situated and interacting within the larger societal structure – thus counteracting an essentialized view of identity based on narrowly defined, single-identity markers. (p. 207)

Intersectionality is about the position or the social location individuals occupy within a context of interrelated systems of power. Yet, oppression is not a binary construct of 'oppressed versus oppressor' (Mann and Grimes, 2001; McLaren and Lankshear, 1994; Tien, 2019). Depending on their position at the crossroads of race, gender, class, and so on, individuals fall within a complex matrix of oppressions and are simultaneously positioned as variously privileged and unprivileged, and as oppressor and oppressed (e.g., a factory worker who is oppressed at work by his boss might be oppressing his wife at home).

For decades, bell hooks (2000) has argued that race, gender, class, and sexual orientation are interdependent in shaping the experiences of women of color. Their experiences, she argues, are significantly different from those of both men of color and of White women since the intersections of race and gender bring about different forms of social identity, lived experience, and oppression. The Obama family presents an interesting case to illustrate the importance of an intersectional lens to understand one's privileges or penalties depending on where they stand at the crossroads of various identity markers. Readers, however, should proceed with caution as the presented racial epithets could be upsetting and/or triggering of past trauma.

The 44th President of the United States, Barack Obama is an African American, heterosexual, cisgender man. He also has religion and class privilege as a Christian who studied at Columbia University and Harvard Law School. At the time of his presidency, media attention focused on his leadership as a Black man, often seeing this as challenging or contradicting common racist assumptions and biases. Considerably less attention was paid to the various privileges which helped Obama rise to a position of prominence in the Democrat Party and become the first Black US president (Adams and Zúñiga, 2016). While Obama was also widely attacked with racial epithets, his wife, Michelle Obama, had to endure epithets attacking both her gender (e.g., her weight and eating habits) and her racial identity (e.g., 'gorilla face'), as well as a combination of both (e.g., 'ape in heels').

Another telling example for the importance of intersectionality comes from the rape of the Central Park jogger that took place in New York City. In the spring of 1989, five Black teenagers were arrested in connection with the rape and assault of a White female jogger. Following police-coerced confessions, they spent 6–13 years in prison until a convicted murderer and serial rapist confessed to the crime in 2002 (Harris, 2019). Crenshaw (1991) has criticized the lack of an intersectional perspective within the public discourse regarding this criminal case in the following terms:

> when feminists fail to acknowledge the role that race played in the public response to the rape of the Central Park jogger, feminism contributes to the forces that produce disproportionate punishment for black men who rape white women, and when antiracists represent the case solely in terms of racial domination, they belittle the fact that women particularly, and all people generally, should be outraged by the gender violence the case represented. (p. 1282)

Intersectionality, therefore, requires an examination of the root causes of intersecting and interlocking systems of oppression that shape the particular social, economic, and cultural realities of learners (Osei-Kofi, 2013). Immigrant student populations are a case in point. Just as the oppression of Black women cannot be addressed by feminism and racism separately but only through a combination of both, issues around immigration cannot be addressed by race or ethnicity alone but should take into consideration their intersection with such matters as gender, sexual orientation, disability, and social class. After-school tutoring programs and other remedial classes that address the academic and social development of children coming from less privileged backgrounds may end up providing insufficient support if they do not address the structural and intersecting and interlocking inequalities impacting these students' lives.

Intersectionality also applies to individual lives and communities that traverse geographical and cultural boundaries (Purkayastha, 2012). Due to various reasons (e.g., globalization, climate change, war, and terrorism), many people live within increasingly transnational economic, cultural, and social networks. This has made the intersections of gendering, racialization, class, and other social hierarchies even more complex, blurred, and fragmented. According to Purkayastha (2012, p. 59):

There are variations of who is part of the privileged majority versus the marginalized minority within a country, and these hierarchies do not always fit the white-yellow/brown-Black [sic] hierarchy extant in Western Europe and North America. Thus concepts such as 'women of color' – which act as an effective framework for indicating the social location of these women in Western Europe and North America, and continuing global hierarchies between countries in the Global North and South – do not work as well if we wish to track the array of the axes of power and domination within countries along with existing global-level hierarchies.

Box 1.4 Problem-posing task

Appendix 1.1 presents the real-life story of Pavo (pseudonym), an Iraqi immigrant who escaped from her country to live in Turkey. Discuss the following questions after reading Pavo's story:

- What role does intersectionality play in Pavo's identity and lived experiences?
- How would Pavo's story help language learners understand the key concepts presented in this chapter?
- In what ways can Pavo's story be used in language classrooms? What would be some potential benefits and challenges?

In other words, transnationality explains how individuals can be part of both a racial majority *and* a minority, to give an example, depending on the different hegemonic ideologies, relationships, and institutional structures in various contexts in which they find themselves. Intersectionality can only retain its explanatory power if multiple intersecting and interlocking forms of oppression are considered in terms of hegemonic structures that shape individuals' lived experiences within, between, and across national borders (Purkayastha, 2012).

Social justice education

A variety of terminologies, principles, approaches, and frameworks exist in education emphasizing the importance of advocacy, equity, diversity, and inclusion in schooling. Some of these include multicultural education, anti-bias education, critical human rights education, culturally relevant/responsive/sustaining pedagogy, antiracist teaching, equity pedagogy, and anti-oppressive education. Social justice education has recently gained prominence as an umbrella term with the overarching goal of confronting, challenging, reducing, and demolishing structural inequalities and discrimination in educational institutions and in society at large based on race, ethnicity, social class, gender, disability, and other socially constructed identity indicators (Adams, 2016; Cochran-Smith et al., 2009a; Cochran-Smith et al., 2009b; Darling-Hammond et al., 2002; Kumashiro, 2009; Zembylas and Keet, 2019).

Like the conceptual conflation around social justice, social justice education as a term has brought about its own collection of conceptualizations and definitions. In a comprehensive definition, Kaur (2012) explains teaching for social justice as:

> ... creating rich learning opportunities for all children ... engaging learners in critical thinking, caring about them and fostering relationships with them and their families and communities, getting to know their lives inside and outside the classroom, valuing and building on the experiences they bring with them into the classroom by making learning meaningful to their lives, noticing and challenging inequities and injustices that prevail in education and society, understanding and interrogating teachers' own positioning, beliefs and attitudes and their role in sustaining the status quo, and at individual and/or collective levels working with and for diverse learners to advocate for a more just and more equitable life chances for all students, to imagine and work for a more just society. (p. 486)

Perhaps one of the most analytic descriptions of social justice education comes from Chubbuck (2010), who discusses social justice education at three levels ranging from the least controversial to the most. At the least controversial level, almost all educators agree that the curriculum, pedagogy, and interactional styles employed in the classroom should provide learning opportunities for every learner, including those typically underserved. Social justice education becomes slightly more controversial when it comes to transforming those educational structures, policies, and practices that impede student learning (e.g., funding opportunities, or language policies). The most controversial level, however, is when social justice education requires teachers to go beyond the school context and examine pre-existing inequalities and disparities in the world and strive to educate their students regarding the social, economic, political, and cultural structures that perpetuate them. The most controversial level also happens to be the most difficult level since teachers, even when they support social justice education and work towards equitable pedagogies in their classrooms, may lack the knowledge, skills, and agency to examine, challenge, and transform the hierarchical power relations in their local and global communities.

Chubbuck's (2010) three levels resonate with the conception of social justice education as an individual, institutional, and collective journey (Cummins, 2009; Nieto, 2000; McDonald and Zeichner, 2009). As an individual journey, social justice education requires teachers to reflect on their biases, power, and privilege, and to develop a lifelong commitment to advocacy, allyship, and social action (Bell, 2016; Chubbuck, 2010; Cochran-Smith et al., 2008; Coney, 2016; Cummins, 2009; Darling-Hammond et al., 2002; Nieto, 2000). According to Giroux (1992):

> A social justice stance is, in part, a disposition through which teachers reflect upon their own actions and those presented by others. Rather than passively accepting information or embracing a false consciousness, teachers take a much more active role in leading, learning, and reflecting upon their relationship with their practice and the social context in which the practice is situated. (p. 99)

Social justice education is also an institutional journey whereby teachers work within and outside the school walls to address the inequalities that affect their students' academic, interpersonal, and societal experiences. Teaching for social justice is more complex than integrating a few activities and readings into the curriculum, inviting guest speakers, and asking students to write petitions to the school principal to change school policies and practices. It necessitates pedagogical changes and transformations at the classroom and school levels. At the classroom level, teachers and learners critically examine existing hierarchies of knowledge in relation to what constitutes knowledge; what varieties or forms of knowledge are (and are *not*) valued and socially legitimized; how knowledge is produced; and how it is transformed into particular power relations in society at large. At the school level, social justice educators work towards understanding the myriad ways racism, heteropatriarchy, nationalism, and other forms of oppressions operate not only in schools but also across society, as well as their interdependence. According to Cummins (2009), challenging the power relations that exist within schools is effectively an act of challenging "the more general operation of coercive power relations in the wider society" (p. 27). Social justice education also calls for a collective journey that brings together learners, parents and families, community activists, and different stakeholders who work collaboratively to challenge and transform the power relations that have an impact on wider political, economic, and cultural systems (Cochran-Smith, 2000; Goodwin and Darity, 2019; Hawkins, 2011). As Zeichner et al. (2016) claimed:

> Continuing to parachute well-intentioned teachers from university and non-university education programs into public schools who know little about their students, their families, and communities, and who are not committed to engaging families and communities in schooling will continue to widen the opportunity and learning gaps that have persisted. The mission of teacher education is not to try and "save" students from their communities, but to work with and for communities to help build on their strengths and develop greater community capacity. (p. 288)

Social justice education as an individual, institutional, and collective journey does not mean that some teachers can restrict their efforts to individual work at the classroom and school levels while some others work outside the classroom settings. The complexities of social justice education and its multifaceted nature require social justice educators to embark on all these journeys simultaneously.

Box 1.5 Reflective task

To what extent has your educational background (e.g., degree and certificate program, training, etc.) prepared you to provide equitable learning opportunities to students coming from diverse communities? What were the strengths and weaknesses of these in terms of preparing you for social justice education for teaching? In what ways could they be improved?

The social justice educator

Teacher capacity for social justice can be explained in terms of an amalgam of teacher dispositions (e.g., values, beliefs, and judgments), knowledge, skills, and practices that encompass equity, ethical values, care and respect, democratic citizenship, civic engagement, and critical inquiry for recognizing inequities and injustices. It also encompasses an appreciation towards all learner identities, diversity, multilingualism and multiculturalism, and a sense of advocacy and activism as agents of social change (Cochran-Smith, 2000, 2004; Chubbuck, 2010; Grant and Agosto, 2008; Howard and Aleman, 2008; Kaur, 2012; Nieto, 2000; Smyth, 2011). But because social justice education is both an individual and collective journey, the first step for all social justice educators is to reflect on their many identities and positionings and understand how the power and privilege they hold might contribute to the many inequities and oppressions in the world (Banegas and Gerlach, 2021; Darling-Hammond et al., 2002). Therefore, teacher identity is an important topic to discuss in relation to teacher capacity to teach for social justice. While there are myriad definitions of teacher identity proposed in the literature, Block's (2007) conceptualization below seems to be the most relevant from the perspective of social justice education. According to Block (2007):

> Identities are socially constructed, self-conscious, ongoing narratives that individuals perform, interpret, and project in dress, bodily movements, actions, and language … Identities are negotiating new subject positions at the crossroads of the past, present, and future … Individuals are shaped by their sociohistories but they also shape their sociohistories as life goes on. The entire process is conflictive as opposed to harmonious and individuals often feel ambivalent. There are unequal power relations to deal with, around the different capitals- economic, cultural, and social – that both facilitate and constrain interactions with others in the different communities of practice with which individuals engage in their lifetimes. Finally, identities are related to different traditionally demographic categories such as ethnicity, race, nationality, migration, gender, social class, and language. (p. 27)

Block (2014), however, cautions that this definition, along with most of the research conducted on language learner and teacher identities in applied linguistics, is based on a culture-based view of identity and is highly associated with identity politics. Therefore, it is important to keep in mind both the politics of recognition and of redistribution when discussing teacher and learner identities, and to underline the intersectional character of different forms of oppression.

Although research on teacher identities presents a vast array of descriptions and experiences through mostly narrative accounts and case studies, explorations of teacher identity from a social justice perspective are more recent and limited (Banegas and Gerlach, 2021; Farnsworth, 2010; Tien, 2019). For instance, Boylan and Woolsey (2015) call for typologies and frameworks of *social justice identity* that go beyond providing fixed reference points in order to allow investigations of the dynamic aspects of identity constructions within "the ambiguous landscapes of teaching for social justice" (p. 15). On the other hand, Appleby (2016) states that language teacher identity research has largely focused on socially and professionally disadvantaged and marginalized groups, while lacking any emphasis on researching the privilege "inherent in the TESOL profession, including the privileges attached to whiteness, native-English-speaker (NES) status, and Inner Circle[2] (Kachru, 1997) origin" (p. 756). Appleby (2016) explains this imbalance in the literature in terms of an uneasiness about empowering participants "who apparently already enjoy favored positioning and treatment in our profession but for whom privilege remains invisible" (p. 758). In that sense, social justice identity or teacher identity for social justice seems to be an area that needs to be further developed in order to help teachers understand the socially constructed nature of teacher and learner identities (i.e., identities not as static and fixed but contradictory, fragmented, and in flux) and explore how their own identities and positionality in different socio-historical contexts embody privilege and oppression.

Conclusion

This chapter first introduced ideology, hegemony, and oppression as key concepts related to social justice which has been described as a continuum of politics of recognition and politics of redistribution with intersectionality at its core. Second, social justice education has been described not just as a set of teacher beliefs and dispositions about diversity, inclusion, and equity but also as an analysis of institutional power relations as well as various social, economic, cultural, and environmental strategies and practices that aim to challenge and dismantle them. This book, therefore, aims to enable language teachers to create equitable, transformative, and inclusive education by examining issues of race, ethnicity, gender, sex, and class from a critical perspective while also cultivating a sense of advocacy and activism for transformative social change. The next chapter will present concepts and practices related to critical pedagogy, a conceptual framework that examines the hegemonic ideologies and power relations in educational systems through transformative, problem-posing education.

Box 1.6 Reflective task: Your identity mindmap

It is now widely accepted that identities are multiple, fragmented, shifting, in conflict, and context bound. For instance, the author of this book is Turkish, a woman, a teacher educator and a researcher. She is cisgender and heterosexual, her pronouns being she/her/hers. She is married and has two cats. When this book was written, she was teaching in a language teacher education program in the US. The US Census Bureau categorizes her as White because she comes from the Middle East. While for many of her students in the US she was a woman of color, she is currently considered an ethnic minority as an academic in the UK.

How would you describe the many identities you have? Create a mindmap of your identities reflecting on the following questions:

- In what ways do your multiple identities interact with each other?
- Do you think these identities are imposed upon you or self-fashioned?

- Are there are any stereotypes associated with any of these identities?
- Were there any times you were held to higher/lower standards or unrealistic expectations because of your identities?
- Can you think of an experience where any aspect of your identity has been negatively interpreted or invalidated?
- Which one of your identities provides a privileged or dominant position in your life and which may be a source of oppression or subordinate position?
- How do your identities and positionalities influence your teaching?

Notes

1. Some prefer the term 'criminal legal system' instead of 'criminal justice system' since they believe that justice can never be achieved through the system as it exists and operates presently. I used the term criminal justice in this book since the term is more widely accessible to a larger audience.
2. Inner circle countries, in Kachru's (1997) description, include the USA, the UK, Canada, Australia, and Aotearoa New Zealand where English is spoken as the native language by most people.

Multimedia resources

The urgency of intersectionality
   https://www.ted.com/talks/kimberle_crenshaw_the_urgency_of_intersec
      tionality
      In this TED Talk, Kimberlé Crenshaw draws attention to the role of intersectionality in order to fight against race and gender in tandem.
The danger of a single story
   https://www.ted.com/talks/chimamanda_ngozi_adichie_the_danger_of_a_
      single_story
      Novelist Chimamanda Ngozi Adichie's TED Talk is about the importance of listening to overlapping stories in order to avoid misunderstandings.
How many is that?
   https://www.howmanyisthat.org/
      How many is that? is a project that displays remarkable statistics to put some of the world's biggest issues into context. The website presents numbers and statistics that can be used in language classes to discuss domestic violence, poverty, bullying, educational access, and so on.
A class divided
   https://www.pbs.org/video/frontline-class-divided/

This episode of the Public Broadcasting Services (PBS) series Frontline tells the story of an Iowan schoolteacher, Jane Elliott, and her class of third graders, who took part in a class exercise about discrimination and prejudice in 1970.

Children's books

Byers, G. and Bobo, K. A. (2018). *I am enough*. Balzer + Bray.
>A beautiful book about acceptance and diversity that teaches children to celebrate themselves and their talents, as well as the talents of others.

Schatz, K. (2016). *Rad women worldwide: Artists and athletes, pirates and punks, and other revolutionaries who shaped history* (illustrated by M. Klein Stahl). Ten Speed Press.
>This book presents Klein Stahl's gorgeous cut-paper portraits and Schatz's empowering descriptions of forty women from all around the world whose names and stories we should all know and be taught in schools.

Williams, N. and Glushkó, S. (2021). *I affirm me*. Running Press Kids.
>A social justice and Black-centric A-to-Z book written for African American children, but which should be read by children of any race, ethnicity, or cultural background.

Chapter 2

Social justice-oriented critical pedagogy

Box 2.1 Lead-in
Joe Kincheloe (2008a), one of the leading scholars in critical pedagogy, has
stated that "[E]very dimension of schooling and every form of educational
practice are *politically contested* spaces" (p. 2, emphasis added).
    To what extent do you agree that education is a political act?

Introduction

Considered the most prominent theorist of critical pedagogy, Brazilian educator
and philosopher Paulo Freire was influenced by his teaching of impoverished
peasants and slum dwellers in Brazil in the 1950s. Critical pedagogy, articulated
in his seminal book, *Pedagogy of the oppressed*, was influenced by Marxist criticism
of capitalism as the driving source of domination and oppression in the world.
While his vision of transformative education shaped language, literacy, peace,
and health education, his influence extended beyond the field of education to
literary theory, cultural studies, philosophy, sociology, and political science.

Critical pedagogy calls for educational institutions, curriculum, and processes
that go beyond serving the needs of those with power and privilege, and, instead,
are grounded in social justice (Crookes, 2013; Giroux, 2011; Kincheloe, 2008a,
2008b; Malott, 2011; Wink, 2011). The role of critical pedagogy to fight against
the many forms of oppressions embedded in educational systems and the society
at large has been underlined by many educational scholars (hooks, 1994; Giroux,
2011; Grant and Agosto, 2008; Kincheloe, 2008a; Nieto, 2000; McLaren and
Fischman, 1998; McLaren, 2020; Shor, 1996). Language education scholars
have also highlighted the importance of critical pedagogy for curriculum design,
teaching methodologies, and assessment (Bartolomé, 2010; Crookes, 2009, 2013;
Daniel, 2016; Pennycook, 2001, 2017; Reagan, 2016; Reagan and Osborn,
2002, 2020; Sung and Pederson, 2012). Critical language pedagogy has connected critical pedagogy to applied linguistics and language education to address

issues such as race, gender, sexuality, and their intersections in language policy, language use, and language teaching practices (Crookes, 2021b; Godley and Reaser, 2018; Pennycook, 2017). The main consensus within this vast amount of literature has been the need to examine schools at the intersection of historical, cultural, economic, social, and political power relations in the world.

The broad aim of this chapter is to lay the conceptual framework this book draws on for social justice language education. In order to do so, this chapter will discuss the following issues:

- The foundational underpinnings of critical pedagogy
- Transformative liberatory education
- Teachers' role in critical pedagogy
- Criticisms of critical pedagogy
- Social justice-oriented critical pedagogy

The foundational underpinnings of critical pedagogy

According to Giroux (2011), one of the founders of critical pedagogy in the United States, critical pedagogy is all about "how knowledge, values, desire, and social relations are always implicated in relations of power, and how such an understanding can be used pedagogically and politically by students to further expand and deepen the imperatives of economic and political democracy" (p. 72). This conceptualization of critical pedagogy can be clarified and elaborated on by discussing three foundational underpinnings of critical pedagogy: education as a political act, hidden/implicit curriculum, and the concept of banking education.

Education as a political act

Those who oppose discussing social justice issues in educational contexts often argue that they prefer to be 'neutral,' 'keep politics out of the classroom,' 'treat everyone equally,' and 'not take a side.' This tendency towards alleged neutrality is what Kincheloe (2008a) calls the "Great Denial of the political dimension of education" (p. 10). There is no neutrality and objectivity when it comes to schooling since *all* education is political (Cochran-Smith et al., 2008; Kincheloe, 2008a; Shor, 1996; Shor and Pari, 1999; Apple, 1990, 2019; Nieto, 2010; Coney, 2016; Wink, 2011).

As Giroux (2011) states, education is an "inherently productive and directive practice" (p. 6). For many, creating informed citizens may seem to be the over-arching goal of education. Yet the deep structure goal of educational systems is to maintain the ideological hegemony in the society by perpetuating the existing socio-cultural and economic hierarchies, normative practices, and consciousness through curriculum, pedagogy, policy, access to resources, day-to-day social interactions between different stakeholders, and everything else that is within the purview of educational systems (Apple, 2019; Anyon, 1981; Howard and Aleman, 2008). Schools are regulatory and reproductive agencies of different cultural, economic, and social power relations and inequalities in a stratified society (Apple, 2019; Anyon, 1981; Shor, 1987; Luke, 2015). According to Kincheloe (2008a), regulation refers to "reducing student and citizen resistance to the interests of dominant groups" and making sure that they "accept their places in the workplaces of global capitalism" (p. 31). Reproduction, on the other hand, refers to "the legitimation and perpetuation of ideologies, practices, and privileges constitutive of present economic and political structures" (Anyon, 1981, p. 31). As discussed in Chapter 1, it is through schooling as well as other institutions and media technologies that the public is convinced that the dominant societal, cultural, and economic order is 'natural' and for everyone's own benefit.

In many countries all over the world, school systems are structured in a way to maintain the existing status quo by determining who has access to which educational resources and opportunities. In the Western world, reproduction through schooling takes the form of reproducing White, middle-class, materialistic, meritocratic, and individualistic values. For instance, although racial segregation (i.e., White and Black students attending different schools) has been declared unconstitutional in US schools with the landmark 1954 ruling of *Brown* v. *Board of Education*, racial and socio-economic segregation still prevails in today's schools. According to a 2019 report by the Civil Rights Project at the University of California Los Angeles, 40 percent of all Black students in the States were enrolled in schools with 90 percent or more students of color (Frakenberg et al., 2019). The divide between state and private schools and school-district policies (i.e., a child needs to attend school based on where they live) both reflect and perpetuate societal, economic, and cultural divisions based on race and class. This form of segregation promotes hegemonic thinking that is used as a justification for the academic failure of students of color and of the working class (Howard and Aleman, 2008). This deficit, 'blame the victim' thinking not only serves to regulate culturally and linguistically diverse learner groups by positioning them as 'less diligent' and 'less hardworking' than their dominant group counterparts, but also reproduces the asymmetric power relations in a society (Bartolomé, 1994).

In different parts of the world, schools reproduce societal homogenization and harmony through dress codes, uniforms, and hairstyles. In Japanese schools, for instance, schoolgirls have been prohibited to dye, perm, or bleach their hair. Those with naturally light brown hair have been asked to dye their hair to standard Japanese black unless they prove with their childhood photos or parents' accounts that it is their natural color[1] (Kidder, 1992; Shiraishi, 1996).[2] In Tamura's (2007) study, Japanese teachers were even found to perceive violations to dress code and hairstyle rules as "an early sign of juvenile delinquency"

(p. 470) – a behavior that needs to be strictly treated to avoid leading up to more serious violations. These findings resonate with the bans around the 1990s Japanese trend *chapatsu* – literally meaning brown color but used for dying/bleaching one's hair – which was a form of self-expression associated with criminality, rebellion, and juvenile delinquency. The policies of Japanese schools' policies for female students' hair color under the pretext of protecting the traditional values for 'natural' physical features, while allowing male students to shave or fix their hair, illustrate how different ideological processes – in this case, homogenization and gender socialization – can intertwine with each other within schools' hidden curriculum.

Hidden/implicit curriculum

Hidden curriculum can be described as (un)intentional yet implicit messages conveyed through the explicit curriculum, classroom contexts, and materials as well as other day-to-day educational processes that "build a replica of the very power structures" (Jean-Marie et al., 2009, p. 14) that exist in society. Some typical examples are calling on boys more often than girls, encouraging boys to pursue STEM education, and teaching only Eurocentric or even ethnocentric histories. Referring to hidden curriculum as the deep structure of schooling, Apple (2019) poses the following questions:

> What underlying meanings are negotiated and transmitted in schools behind the actual formal "stuff" of curriculum content? What happens when knowledge is filtered through teachers? Through what categories of normality and deviance is it filtered? What is the basic and organizing framework of the normative and conceptual knowledge that students actually get? In short, what is the curriculum in use? (p. 52)

Any educational context with its curriculum, classrooms, hallways, playgrounds, and gender-specific restrooms and locker rooms is a contested site where children learn about competition, self-worth, power, aggression, and bullying; and are socialized into the already existing economic, cultural, and social hierarchies (Jean-Marie et al., 2009). For instance, daily routines such as student pledges implicitly teach children messages about life, social order, and status. Let's have a look at the following Turkish student pledge that was recited every morning by all primary school students in Turkey between 1932 and 2013:

Türkçe (Turkish, original)
Türk'üm, doğruyum, çalışkanım,
İlkem: küçüklerimi korumak, büyüklerimi saymak, yurdumu, milletimi özümden çok sevmektir.
Ülküm: yükselmek, ileri gitmektir.

Ey Büyük Atatürk!
Açtığın yolda, gösterdiğin hedefe durmadan yürüyeceğime ant içerim.
Varlığım Türk varlığına armağan olsun.
Ne mutlu Türk'üm diyene!

English (author's translation)
I am a Turk, honest, and hardworking. My principle is to protect the younger, to respect the elder, to love my homeland and my nation more than myself. My goal is to rise, to progress. Oh, Great Atatürk! On the path that you have paved, I swear to walk incessantly toward the aims that you have set. My existence shall be dedicated to the Turkish existence. How happy is the one who says, "I am a Turk!"

The pledge has been criticized for its strong nationalist messages underscoring that if someone is a Turk, they are honest and hardworking, excluding and marginalizing all other ethnicities who live in Turkey. The pledge also conveys that the youth should defend their nation at all costs, leaving no room for critical thinking, agency, criticism, or self-realization. The Turkish student pledge was reinstated in 2017 after being removed from the school curriculum as part of Turkey's 2013 democratization process. Continuing to be part of Turkey's educational curriculum for primary school, the student pledge serves as an ideological tool for social legitimation, regulation, and reproduction.

Hidden curriculum is only one of the reasons that education is a political act. Teachers who believe in the neutrality of their curriculum follow the already made decisions in terms of what curriculum to cover, what messages to convey, whose voices to listen to and silence, and whose reality to reflect within that curriculum. While doing so, they legitimize discriminatory and hegemonic practices that exist in schools; conserve and reproduce the status quo; contribute to sociocultural segregation; and work against any fundamental transformation in society at large. Neutrality, therefore, means being complicit in the further silencing of marginalized voices, epistemologies, and experiences.

Banking education

Narrative education, transmission-model, apprenticeship model, top-down approach, and traditional banking education are some of the terms used to refer to the educational process where the teacher 'fills' their students with content or knowledge that they deem valuable (Freire, 2005b; hooks, 1994; Malott, 2011; Wink, 2011). Students, who are considered to have no previous knowledge, skills, and abilities, are thus positioned as 'receptacles,' or 'containers,' who are expected to memorize and repeat the 'objective' knowledge bestowed upon them with no chance to really understand what this knowledge means for their lives and existence. Banking education is nothing but "an act of depositing, in which the students are the depositories, and the teacher is the depositor" (Freire, 2005b, p. 72).

Shor (1987) lists some of the authoritarian features of banking education as "memorization, mechanical testing, teacher-talk and student silence, abstract subjects remote from student interest, standardized syllabi, balkanized faculties, [and] byzantine administrations" (p. 16). Banking education, in that sense, can easily be identified by taking a closer look at the nature of teacher-student relationships in terms of who decides on the curriculum, who chooses/develops/designs textbooks and materials, who talks more and who listens, how the teacher and students are located within the classroom, and so on. Box 2.2 presents a list of guiding questions for language educators to examine banking education in their classrooms.

Critical pedagogy rejects banking education that reduces teaching and learning processes to a mechanical act of "stuffing volumes of unproblematized data in mental filing cabinets" (Kincheloe, 2008a, p. 109). Instead, it aims to validate and enrich the funds of knowledge – that is, "bodies of knowledge and information that households use to survive, to get ahead, or to thrive" (Moll, 1992, p. 21) – brought to the educational contexts by learners who belong to different religions, social classes, and racial/ethnic backgrounds (Malott, 2011). Fighting against the role of schools in social, cultural, and economic regulation of the society and reproduction of the already existing inequalities, critical pedagogy aims to enable marginalized and oppressed learner groups to think critically about their problems and to share their experiences and knowledge with others (Freire, 2005b).

Box 2.2 Reflective task

Reflect on the following questions to examine banking education in your language classroom or in a context you are familiar with. Based on your responses, consider what changes you might make in this context to reduce the impact of or dismantle banking education.

- Where are the teacher and students located in the physical setting of the classroom?
- How is the seating arrangement?
- Is there a teaching assistant or a second teacher? If yes, what is their physical and social distance to the students?
- What are the teacher-student and student-student relationships like?
- Is the classroom teacher in a position of power and authority or a co-learner/co-explorer? How are these two roles balanced?
- What role do the students play in the decisions made about teaching/learning processes?
- To what extent do the lessons employ or challenge banking education?
- Is knowledge transmitted or co-constructed between the teacher and students?

- What is the method of arranging students into peers and groups?
- Do the lessons include any discussion of explicit and implicit curriculum?
- Do the lessons perpetuate or challenge the already existing status quo and the dominant ideology in the society?
- Are there any stereotypes, biases, and inequalities depicted or challenged in the lessons?
- To what extent do the lessons include real-world examples, critical dialogues, and problem-solving activities?
- In what ways do the lessons draw on students' lived experiences and their communities' funds of knowledge?

Transformative liberatory education

In order to combat against banking education and its hidden curriculum, critical pedagogues propose transformative liberatory education that enables teachers and learners to unveil "how classroom learning embodies selective values, is entangled with relations of power, entails judgements about what knowledge counts, legitimizes specific social relations, defines agency in particular ways and always presupposes a particular notion of the future" (Giroux, 2011, p. 6). Transformative liberatory education breaks down the hierarchies and ideologies embedded in banking education that "stifles inquiry, eliminates creativity, promotes passivity, and reinforces alienation and oppression" (Enns and Forrest, 2005, p. 7). To give an example from the four Anglophone settler colonial societies (i.e., the US, Canada, Australia, and Aotearoa New Zealand), language educators in these contexts can decentralize the experiences of heterosexual, able-bodied, middle- to upper-class, White, Euro-American settlers – especially those that are male – and begin to centralize the stories and histories of traditionally marginalized, maligned, and devalued communities. The overarching goal, thus, should be to promote learners' *critical consciousness* and agency about their current life conditions and possibilities through a *problem-posing approach* and facilitate their participation in social struggles for individual and collective rights and social justice at large (Ball, 2000; Freire, 2005b; Giroux, 2011).

Schools, as part of their regulatory and reproductive functions to maintain the dominant ideologies in societies, serve to reproduce "alienated consciousness" (Shor, 1987, p. 14), a Marxist concept relating to the ways in which capitalism strips individuals' agency and sense of humanity. Therefore, one of the goals of critical pedagogy is to help learners develop their critical consciousness, *conscientização* (Freire, 2005b), through which, crucially, the learners not only get to know themselves better but also articulate and situate their personal experiences of oppression within the larger socio-cultural, political, and economic contexts (Enns and Forrest, 2005).

The process of developing *conscientização* varies according to one's position(s) of privilege in a society. From a privileged position, this process requires an understanding of one's privileges; critically examining the social situations these privileges are embedded in; questioning taken-for-granted beliefs and assumptions and articulating their role in various systems of oppression; and developing skills for social change. For oppressed or less privileged populations (e.g., migrant farm workers, queer students, and racially marginalized children), developing critical consciousness entails the process of refusing any internalized oppression and dismantling the ways their oppressors defined them to be.

Critical pedagogy not only addresses the needs and interests of those who are on the margins of their societies, but also brings their voices, experiences, and perspectives into the classroom context which otherwise relies on Eurocentric, patriarchal, and elitist perspectives (Kincheloe, 2008a). However, the goal of an educator can never be to 'rescue' or 'save' their learners. Freire (2005a) himself cautioned that critical educators should avoid assistencialism,[3] that is offering learners "no responsibility, no opportunity to make decisions, but only gestures and attitudes which encourage passivity" (p. 12). Such attempts of assistencialism would be coming from a paternalistic White-savior complex rooted in colonization and imperialism. Instead, a teacher's role is to provide affordances for their learners to position themselves as "the agents of their own recuperation" (Freire, 2005a, p. 12); as individuals who can critically confront societal, communal, and individual struggles, challenges, and problems. A critical teacher respects all learners and their funds of knowledge and "learn[s] with them about personal empowerment, the cultivation of intellect, and the larger pursuit of social justice" (Kincheloe, 2008a, p. 25).

In order to develop learners' critical consciousness, critical pedagogy employs a problem-posing approach that positions learners as problem solvers and critical thinkers. In order to do so, a problem-posing approach engages learners in critical dialogue, inquiry, reflection, knowledge construction, and exchange as a means of forming the basis of their activism (Enns and Forrest, 2005; Howard and Aleman, 2008; Reagan and Osborn, 2002; Wesely et al., 2016). In transformative liberatory education, teachers and learners are co-learners, co-explorers, and co-teachers who create a collaborative learning community that co-constructs knowledge and skills to understand the barriers oppressed and marginalized groups face and to explore strategies and solutions for social change (Enns and Forrest, 2005; Giroux, 2011; Wallerstein, 1987).

Problem-posing education, therefore, aims to develop learners' critical literacy which refers to the process of decoding the power relations embedded in texts by problematizing all subjects of study. Problematization involves going beyond a surface level understanding and memorization of content knowledge and instead framing any existing knowledge "as an historical product deeply invested with the values of those who *developed* such knowledge" (Shor, 1987, p. 24, emphasis added). Problem posing includes "a mode of analysis that interrogates texts, institutions, social relations, and ideologies as part of the script of official power" (Giroux, 2011, p. 4). By inviting learners to collaboratively identify and problematize aspects of social reality, problem posing helps them draw on their personal experiences to improve their lives through social connectedness and mutual responsibility (Wallerstein, 1987; Wallerstein and Auerbach, 2004). Appendix 2.1 provides language educators with a critical framework to use with their learners in order to develop their critical literacy through problem-posing education.

Teachers' role in critical pedagogy

Critical pedagogy is more than a few pedagogical techniques a teacher can easily adopt. It embodies a deeper-level understanding of the role of education in terms of perpetuating different cultural, social, and economic power relations as well as its capacity to fight against them in ways that bring about social change. Taking on the roles of "public intellectuals, of social activists, of political protagonists," critical pedagogues understand that "what happens inside the classroom cannot be disconnected from what is happening in the local community, the school district, and the wider precincts of democracy" (McLaren, 2020, p. 1246). While radical love, solidarity, critical hope, courage, and humility are virtues critical pedagogues need to develop (Freire, 2005a; Kincheloe, 2008a; Wink, 2011), teachers' critical self-reflection and teachers as collaborative learners are worth mentioning here in detail.

Box 2.3 Reflective task
Reflect on the following questions by considering your current or ideal teaching context.

- What are your pedagogical goals for your language learners?
- What do you hope that your learners would take away from your class besides developing their language skills?
- How do/would you work towards ensuring that your students achieve these goals?
- Which of these goals are in line with critical pedagogy and transformative education? Alternatively, how often do/would you allow your students to set pedagogical goals for themselves?
- What would be the benefits and challenges of such an approach in this context?

Teachers' critical self-reflection

Teachers' critical self-reflection refers to the process of understanding one's own ideological, socio-political, and economic realities and their impact on their positionality and classroom pedagogy. A teacher's interpretive framework (i.e., frame of reference) is shaped by the multiple, shifting, and intersecting social groups they belong to, and, as a result, shapes the way they perceive their learners, educational context, and the world at large. This form of reflection allows educators to "see how [their] ideas, views, and opinions are not objective and independent, but rather the result of myriad social messages and conditioning forces" (Sensoy and DiAngelo, 2017, pp. 66–67). Therefore, critical self-reflection is one of the very first but recurring steps for a teacher to enact critical pedagogy and social justice education (Coney, 2016; Enns and Forrest, 2015; Grant and Agosto, 2008; Goodwin and Darity, 2019; Malott, 2011, Smyth, 2011).

Alsup and Miller (2014) perceive social justice "on a continuum of learning, unlearning and relearning" (p. 205). As teachers inquire into the many ways the process of schooling is embedded within larger social, historical, cultural, economic, and political contexts, they also reflect on their position and role in reproducing the existing power structures in a society. Critical educators, thus, question "the consequences of the subject positions they have been assigned, the knowledge they produce, the social relations they legitimate, and the ideologies they disseminate to students" (Giroux, 2011, p. 79). Unlearning – the process of unpacking and re-examining one's beliefs and assumptions in relation to the roles and privilege they hold in a given society – thus plays an important role in teachers' critical reflection (Britzman, 1998; Cochran-Smith, 2000; Kumashiro, 2000). Understanding and addressing the needs of one's learners and their contexts requires a reflection of "our own roles in the equation" (Hall, 2016, p. 7). Therefore, unlearning what is 'normal' or not in a society is essential for any anti-oppressive education for allowing both teachers and students the opportunity to "examine not only how some groups and identities are Othered … but also how some groups are favored, normalized, privileged, as well as how this dual process is legitimized and maintained by social structures and competing ideologies" (Kumashiro, 2000, pp. 35–36).

Teachers' critical self-reflection also involves self-disclosure. Any educational program that aims to address inequality, oppression, and discrimination should begin with educators' self-disclosure, that is, being open about their power and privileges (Enns and Sinacore, 2005). Self-disclosure is important for "humanizing the classroom, establishing one's authenticity, facilitating the integration of personal and political perspectives, validating diversity and difference, and empowering students" (Enns and Sinacore, 2005, p. 12). Nevertheless, educators' self-disclosure is a vulnerable act: For a White, male, heterosexual teacher, disclosing their identity and showing support for the LGBTQ+ community might be relatively safe, and can be even seen to be 'heroic.' On the other hand, for a lesbian teacher of color, the same act can be criticized for 'having an agenda' (Enns and Sinacore, 2005). The reflective task in Box 2.4 is designed for educators' self-reflection and self-disclosure. This task aims to enable language educators to examine their power and privileges and the underlying hegemonic ideologies behind them in order to help them understand how their learners' lives are shaped by capitalism, racism, and other forms of oppressive and hegemonic ideologies. In doing so, language educators will not only understand their complicity in terms of the inequalities and disparities around them but also learn to transform their power and privileges into the knowledge and skills needed to enact socially just pedagogies. Through their self-disclosure which shows vulnerability, this task will also allow them to develop strong and meaningful relationships with their students coming from underserved, marginalized, and oppressed backgrounds.

> ### Box 2.4 Reflective task: Understanding your privilege (adapted from Chubbuck, 2010)
>
> Reflect upon how, as a language educator, you managed to get where you are in life today in terms of your academic degree, teaching position, etc.
>
> - What kind of support did you receive (financial, collegial, friendship, family, social networks, pastoral, etc.)?
> - How equitably do you think these support systems are distributed in the society you are a part of?
> - How do you think these support systems have shaped – and continue to shape – who you are as a language educator?
> - How do you think these support systems can help you fight injustices in educational contexts and/or in the society more widely?

Teachers as collaborative learners and researchers

Teachers' critical reflection regarding their power and authority also allows them to question and relinquish their role as the 'depositor' and 'the source of knowledge.' Instead, teachers take on the roles of a *facilitator* who allows affordances in the classroom for critical dialogue and inquiry and a *collaborative learner* who no longer "provides students with 'right' answers but pushes them to collect information to support their beliefs" (Howard and Aleman, 2008, p. 167). According to Freire (2005b), "Education must begin with the solution of the teacher-student contradiction, by reconciling the poles of the contradiction so that both are simultaneously teachers *and* students" (p. 72, original emphasis). Removing the teacher-student dichotomy helps reconfigure the traditional teacher/student relationship and enables a context "where everybody teaches and everybody learns" (Jean-Marie et al., 2009, p. 12). Teachers are no longer perceived as the authority or "the dictators" (hooks, 1994, p. 18) in the classroom but as teacher-students who simultaneously teach and learn through critical dialogue with student-teachers (Enns and Forrest, 2005; Freire, 2005b; Shor, 1987).

Kincheloe and Steinberg (1998), however, caution that "[t]o deny the role of authority the teacher occupies is insincere at best, dishonest at worst" (p. 17). In other words, teachers, to some extent, will continue to have power and authority in the classroom as long as they are positioned as 'experts' who determine what learners need to know and who evaluate student learning; and as long as those grades and decisions about student progress are used in ways that impact their current and prospective educational and professional opportunities. In that sense, relinquishing one's authority and power first requires being "self-reflective about the value-laden nature of [teachers'] authority while taking on the fundamental task of educating students to take responsibility for the direction of society" (Giroux, 2007, p. 2). As Shor (1996) argues, the goal is not to deny one's authority in the classroom or expertise in a field but to own and "deploy their power and knowledge as *democratic authorities* who question the status quo and negotiate the curriculum" (p. 56, original emphasis).

Box 2.5 Problem-posing task

For this task you can either observe a class or find a recording of a class that is already available. Here are some resources available for video libraries for both English and World Language Education:

✓ Annenberg Learner: https://www.learner.org/subject/world-langua ges/
✓ Literacy Minnesota: www.literacymn.org/classroom-videos

After the observation, please address the following questions:

- In what ways does this lesson reflect problem-posing education (e.g., teacher's role, student's role, classroom interaction)?
- How would you improve this lesson in order to achieve the goals of critical pedagogy that have been discussed so far in this chapter?

Alternatively, you can also record your own class and reflect on these questions.

Being a facilitator and a collaborative learner requires language educators to regain their agency as many teachers all around the world have been deskilled (i.e., gradually losing control, agency, and ownership of their teaching) by standards-based curriculum, high-stakes testing, accountability measures, and performance management. By engaging in praxis (i.e., an action-critical reflection-action cycle), teachers of critical pedagogy can reconstruct their *agency*, that is "[their] ability to shape and control their own lives, freeing self from the oppression of power" (Kincheloe, 2008a, p. 2). One of the ways teachers can re-establish their agency is through educational action research which enables them to question the power implications of knowledge "that is produced far away from the school by experts in an exalted domain" (Kincheloe, 2008a, p. 17). Understanding the importance of action research within critical pedagogy requires a discussion of the epistemological aspects of knowledge, that is, what is knowledge, who produces it, and who benefits from such knowledge. Rather than following 'top-down' knowledge that is bestowed upon them by 'experts' in the field, teachers become both researchers and learners who seek answers to the problems they face in their own classrooms as well as in the society at large. *Teacher researchers* integrate inquiry with pedagogy in ways that enable them to identify and change the conditions of their teaching in fights against global, national, and institutional policies (Agnello, 2016; Kincheloe, 2011).

Criticisms of critical pedagogy

Despite its immense influence in education, critical pedagogy has received some harsh criticism that mostly revolves around its patriarchal and sexist language as well as its abstract and inaccessible nature that seems to distance itself from the day-to-day experiences of teachers to whom it offered help. Especially the early versions of critical pedagogy have been criticized by feminist critiques for its lack of attention to patriarchy and White male privilege, as well as Freire's frequent use of the male referent in his texts (e.g., man, and his) (Enns and Forrest, 2005; Weiler, 1991, 1994). hooks (1994), a critical feminist whose *engaged pedagogy*[4] has been influenced by critical pedagogy, has underscored the challenges she faced "[to] find a language that offers a way to frame [the sexism in Freire's work] and yet maintain the recognition of all that is valued and respected in the work" (p. 49). Other scholars drew attention to the fact that oppression is a non-binary construct – as discussed in Chapter 1 – that an individual can be oppressor and oppressed at the same time. Weiler (1994), for instance, emphasized how critical pedagogy has failed to "analyze the contradictions between conflicting oppressed groups or the ways in which a single individual can experience oppression in one sphere while being privileged or oppressive in another" (p. 13).

The criticisms over critical pedagogy extended to the White male dominance among critical pedagogy scholars and concerns over whether critical pedagogy is yet another representation of White savior complex. Kincheloe (2007), for instance, has argued that "critical pedagogy has become too much of a North

American (and often European) 'thing,' as White North American scholars appropriate a South American discourse" (p. 11). And although there are many scholars of color working on critical pedagogy, they have not yet received the same level of recognition and status as their White male colleagues (Malott, 2011). The past decade, however, has witnessed an increased attention to the different contexts in which critical pedagogy has been brought to life. Darder, Mayo, and Paraskeva's (2016) edited volume, *International critical pedagogy reader*, for instance, presents a wide range of practices in countries such as Saudi Arabia, Brazil, India, Poland, Japan, Mexico, China, Iran, Spain, Greece, Portugal, Turkey, and many more. López-Gopar's (2019) *International perspectives on critical pedagogies in ELT* and Sung and Pederson's (2012) *Critical ELT practices in Asia* also provide an array of localized critical pedagogies that relate ELT practices to globalization, neoliberalism, post-colonial education, gender studies, sexual diversity, etc. Despite this increased attention to more global contexts and diverse perspectives, critical pedagogy scholars are yet to engage more with African, Asian, African American and Indigenous peoples to learn from their subjugated knowledge and experiences (Kincheloe, 2007; Malott, 2011).

A second set of criticisms has focused on critical pedagogy's language being 'inaccessible,' 'elitist,' and 'academic.' The abstract and theoretical nature of critical pedagogy has posed challenges for educators to enact such pedagogy in their classrooms, thus creating another form of oppression and exclusion (Ball, 2000; Crookes, 2009, 2013; Edelsky and Johnson, 2004; Ellsworth, 1989; Gore, 1993; Hytten and Bettez, 2011; Malott, 2011; Wink, 2011). Apple (2006) has argued that "[critical pedagogy] has become too theoretical, abstract, esoteric, and out of touch with the conflicts and struggles that teachers, students, and activists act on" (p. 83). Some, on the other hand, defended its abstract nature as deriving from an attempt to differ from prescriptive teaching methods that provide 'one-size-fits-all' strategies since "all educational spaces are unique and politically contested" (Kincheloe, 2007, p. 16). Rejecting the 'methods fetish' (Bartolomé, 1994; Macedo and Bartolomé, 2014), critical pedagogy scholars have argued that there is not one single critical pedagogy but situated critical pedagogies that depend on the life experiences of learners and their communities (Freire and Shor, 1987; Giroux, 2011; Malott, 2011; McLaren and Lankshear, 1994; Wink, 2011). Yet, responding to calls to make critical pedagogy more accessible for educators, a growing body of literature has emerged over the last two decades proposing more concrete examples of critical pedagogy for teachers (e.g., Ball, 2000; Crookes, 2013, 2022; Edelsky and Johnson, 2004; Houser, 2007; Walker, 2018; Wallerstein and Auerbach, 2004; Wink, 2011).

Despite all the above-mentioned criticisms, these recent developments indicate that critical pedagogy continues to shape teaching and learning processes all around the world. Commenting on the future of critical pedagogy, McLaren (2020) has stated:

If Freire's work has been decaffeinated over the years such that it no longer proves a threat to the ruling class any more than the work of Freire's educational precursors, then why, moments before his inauguration in early 2019, did Brazilian President Jair Bolsonaro tweet, "One of the goals to get Brazil out of the worst positions in international education rankings is to combat the Marxist rubbish that has spread in educational institutions." And why, on the campaign trail, did Bolsonaro say that he wanted to "enter the Education Ministry with a flame- thrower to remove Paulo Freire" (Bolsonaro to Erase Freire and Feminism from Textbooks, 2019)? Clearly Freire is a figure whose work needs to be reckoned with. If anything, his work is more relevant today than at any other time in its history. (p. 1243)

Considering the criticisms around critical pedagogy as well as the progress made to address them, in this book I have adopted a social justice-oriented critical pedagogy that re-conceptualizes the reciprocal relationship between the schools, the community, and the larger society. A social justice-oriented critical pedagogy, therefore, aims to analyze the role of social, economic, political, and cultural factors in shaping learners' identity and life experiences, and to alter the power relations that operate within and beyond schooling (Adams, 2016; Kincheloe, 2008a, 2008b; Rodas and Osborn, 2016).

Conclusion: a social justice-oriented critical pedagogy

Although schools are structured in a way to maintain and reproduce the already existing inequalities in the society, they also embody nonreproductive possibilities of dismantling and transforming hegemonic structures and ideologies that function and circulate through products, services, and ideas (Anyon, 1981). That's why, as its foundational pedagogical framework, this book relies on critical pedagogy in order to create "critical transformation and a more humane, less Eurocentric, less paternalistic, less homophobic, less patriarchal, less exploitative, and less violent world" (Malott, 2011, p. xxiii). As discussed in Chapter 1, the social justice language education proposed in this book conceptualizes social justice as a continuum of recognition and redistribution; underlines the intersectionality of various forms of oppression; and aims to cultivate critical consciousness, agency, and advocacy for social action. In that sense, this form of social justice language education is in line with Crookes' (2013) definition of critical pedagogy as:

> [T]eaching for social justice, in ways that support the development of active, engaged citizens who will as circumstances permit, critically inquire into why the lives of so many human beings, including their own, are so materially, psychologically, socially, and spiritually inadequate – citizens who will be

prepared to seek out solutions to the problems they define and encounter, and take action accordingly. (p. 77)

Calling into question many forms of oppressions (Keesing-Styles, 2003), a social justice-oriented critical pedagogy fits well with post-colonial education (Abu-Shomar, 2016), critical race theory and antiracist pedagogy (Blake, 2016; Denzin, 2007), liberatory pedagogies (Weiler, 1991), peace education (Brantmeier, 2011; Rivage-Seul and Rivage-Seul, 1994), and feminist (Bender-Slack, 2015; hooks, 1994; Sánchez Bello, 2016; Weiler, 1994) and queer pedagogy (Hickman, 2011; Vavrus, 2009; Vicars, 2016). A social justice-oriented critical pedagogy also draws on critical applied linguistics (Pennycook, 2022), critical language awareness (Alim, 2005; Fairclough, 1992; Shapiro, 2022), critical literacy (Janks, 2010; Kubota, 2010), critical language testing (Shohamy, 2007), and several other frameworks that will be unpacked in the following chapters. This book, therefore, is an attempt to build a bridge across various overlapping yet diverse strands in the social justice literature by highlighting the shared goals as well as their idiosyncratic features to convey the complexity of social justice work and to provide language teachers with a principled approach to implement transformative social action in education and in societies at large (hooks, 1994; Hytten and Bettez, 2011; Smyth, 2011). The next chapter connects the conceptual and pedagogical issues discussed in Chapters 1 and 2 to the fields of applied linguistics and language education, demonstrating in more practical terms their relevance to language educators.

Notes

1. In the early months of 2021, a Japanese student won a lawsuit against her school that imposed strict rules against hair color. The court agreed with the school's policy but decided to compensate the student for the 'psychological toll'. BBC News, April 2021. https://www.bbc.com/news/world-asia-56099237
2. The Tokyo metropolitan government has been reported to have abolished this regulation from its public high schools during the 2022 academic year. *The Guardian*, March 2022. https://www.theguardian.com/world/2022/mar/14/tokyo-schools-cut-controversial-rules-governing-hairstyles-and-underwear?CMP=oth_b-aplnews_d-1
3. According to Freire (2005a), assistencialism is "a term used in Latin America to describe policies of financial or social assistance which attack symptoms, but not causes, of social ills" (p. 17).
4. Building on the principles of critical pedagogy and the philosophy of Buddhism, hooks (1994) proposed a more holistic approach called "engaged pedagogy" that emphasizes teachers' well-being and self-actualization as a catalyst for empowering their learners.

Multimedia resources

EdChange
> http://www.edchange.org/
>> EdChange, an initiative of experienced educators dedicated to educational equity and justice, provides educators with lots of resources to promote equity, social justice, and multiculturalism.

Equity Literacy Institute
> https://www.equityliteracy.org/educational-equity-resources
>> As one of the projects of EdChange, Equity Literacy Institute provides free and downloadable resources and handouts related to equity literacy. The website also includes various links to other multimedia resources that can be of help to language educators.

Teachers for Social Justice (TSJ)
> http://www.teachersforjustice.org/
>> As an organization of a group of in-service and pre-service teachers, administrators, and other educators based in Chicago, Teachers for Social Justice presents resources for multicultural, multilingual, and antiracist classrooms.

Children's books

De La Pena, M. (2015). *Last stop on Market Street*. Penguin Books.
> Written by Matt De La Pena and illustrated by Christian Robinson, this book addresses issues around community, differences, inequity, and happiness.

Hoffman, M. (1991). *Amazing Grace* (illustrated by Caroline Binch). Frances Lincoln Children's Books.
> Selected as the Children's Book of the Year in 1992, this book tells the story of Grace, a Black girl, who longs to play Peter Pan in her school play.

Chapter 3

Language, education, and social justice

Box 3.1 Lead-in
In his 1979 article entitled, 'If Black English isn't a language, then tell me, what is?', James Baldwin states:

> People evolve a language in order to describe and thus control their circumstances, or in order not to be submerged by a reality that they cannot articulate. (And, if they cannot articulate it, they *are* submerged.) A Frenchman living in Paris speaks a subtly and crucially different language from that of the man living in Marseilles; neither sounds very much like a man living in Quebec; and they would all have great difficulty in apprehending what the man from Guadeloupe, or Martinique, is saying, to say nothing of the man from Senegal – although the "common" language of all these areas is French. But each has paid, and is paying, a different price for this "common" language, in which, as it turns out, they are not saying, and cannot be saying, the same things: They each have very different realities to articulate, or control.
>
> It goes without saying, then, that language is a political instrument, means, and proof of power.

What are your thoughts and reflections on this quotation? What does James Baldwin mean by it? What is the role of language in defining and denying 'the other'?

Introduction

It is now widely accepted that there is an internal, bi-directional relationship between language and society, and that linguistic and social phenomena co-constitute each other (Fairclough, 2015; Holborow, 1999). According to

Gramsci (1971), "even in the slightest manifestation of any intellectual activity whatever, in 'language,' there is contained a specific conception of the world" (p. 323). Language takes meaning in historical, cultural, and political contexts, and "as we speak, in all the different contexts of social life, we are saying something about social life" (Holborow, 1999, p. 31). Standing at the nexus of language, power, and ideology, language education thus contributes to the existing economic, cultural, social, and political power relations across societies (Bourdieu and Passeron, 1991; Cummins, 2000; Fairclough, 2015; Holborow, 1999; Norton and Pavlenko, 2004; Reagan, 2019; Ricento, 2000; Wodak and Forchtner, 2018). This chapter will discuss the historical role of language as an ideological tool by drawing on various language ideologies, policies, and practices within English language education, foreign language education, and bi/multilingual education programs. The following issues will be explored in this chapter:

- Language, power, and ideology as interrelated concepts
- The premises and criticisms of multicultural education
- Moving beyond multiculturalism: Social justice language education

The nexus of language, power, and ideology

The term discourse is essential to understanding the role of language in constructing knowledge as social power, common sense, and truth. *Discourse* refers to the ways language, through verbal and multimodal (e.g., gestures, body language, audio, and video) meaning-making forms, is used for social impact through structuring knowledge and social practice (Canagarajah, 1999; Fairclough, 1993; Kress and Leeuwen, 2001). Being influenced by – and influencing – the symbolic power of different speech communities and languages, language education policies and practices, as well as language use itself, perpetuate the existing hegemonic ideologies (Bourdieu and Passeron, 1991; Canagarajah, 1999; Giroux, 2009; Holborow, 1999, 2015; Norton and Toohey, 2004; McKinney, 2017). Here is an example for how hegemonic discourses impact real-life contexts as well as language policy and practice:

We may not be able to say that we don't really want immigrants in our workplaces; we can say, however, that we will only hire people whose linguistic 'skills' meet a certain set of criteria, determined, as it happens, by us. The bourgeoisie of Revolutionary France may not have been able to say that they were not willing to share property with peasants, but they were able to say that only those who mastered standard French merited full participation in the spaces where the resources of the State were distributed (Higonnet 1980). Educated white males of post-Revolutionary Europe may not have been able to say that they didn't want to give women the vote, but they could say that women's discourse is emotional and not rational, and therefore not suited to democratic deliberations (Outram 1987; Bauman and Briggs 2003). (Heller, 2010a, p. 277)

In other words, forms of dominance and oppression are maintained and reinforced through discourses embedded within networks of socio-political control, or 'regimes of truth' (Foucault, 1980). Discourse, then, enables individuals, institutions, and societies to project their practices as universal and common sense, by attributing to them ideological power (Fairclough, 2015). According to Fairclough (1993), "Discourses do not just reflect or represent social entities and relations, they construct or 'constitute' them" (p. 4). It is through different discourses that individuals comprehend different constructs (e.g., literacy, language, culture) and position others as social subjects (e.g., women).

Analysis of discourse requires historical and contextual considerations since different discourses might be combined under particular social conditions to create a new form. For instance, the Black Lives Matter (BLM) movement that began after the acquittal of George Zimmerman in the shooting death of Trayvon Martin in 2012 illustrates how different discourses might shape and overlap with each other. While BLM aims to draw attention to the unequal treatment and police brutality and killings of Black people especially in the US, people all around the world have supported the movement to show solidarity and condemn racism in their own countries as well as abroad. Two main opposing and undermining discourses – All Lives Matter (ALM) and Blue Lives Matter – emerged as a response to BLM. While Blue Lives Matter supports the US law enforcement officers in the US, criticizing the BLM movement for its 'divisive' emphasis on Black lives, ALM has proposed a more 'inclusive' understanding of all human lives. In the United States, ALM has created a discourse that undermines the BLM movement by misinterpreting it to say that *only* Black lives matter. Nevertheless, in several countries around the world (e.g., Turkey), many people have started supporting the supposedly uniting ALM movement to show their solidarity to Black lives. These three different but related discourses show the ways in which language is situated within micro-level interpersonal exchanges (e.g., daily interactions) and macro-level institutional policies and practices (e.g., the criminal justice system); as well as the ways in which hegemonic ideologies (e.g., White supremacy) are constructed in historical, social, cultural, and political discourses. The role of discourse at the intersection of language, ideology, and power can be discussed in relation to English language teaching, foreign/world language education, and multicultural education.

English language teaching and its colonial legacy

English language teaching (ELT) has been widely criticized for its colonial, assimilationist tradition and instructional practices that promote the hegemonic ideologies of the dominant class. The globalization of 'Standard' English, and its effects on ELT policies and practices has been at the center of discussions around linguistic, educational, and cultural imperialism, colonialism, and neoliberalism (Canagarajah, 1999; Fairclough, 2015; Holborow, 1999; Kachru, 1986a; Kubota, 2011; McKinney, 2017; Motha, 2014; Pennycook, 1998; Phillipson, 1992; Schneider, 2011).) Here is a brief historical account of the growth and global spread of 'Standard' English driven by colonialism and capitalism:[1]

> The social dialect which developed into standard English was the East Midland dialect associated with the merchant class in London at the end of the medieval period. This underlines the link to capitalism, for these feudal merchants became the first capitalists, and the rise of standard English is linked to the growing power of the merchants …
>
> 'Standard' English was regarded as *correct* English, and other social dialects were stigmatized not only in terms of correctness but also in terms which indirectly reflected on the lifestyles, morality and so forth of their speakers, the emergent working class of capitalist society: they were *vulgar, slovenly, low, barbarous*, and so forth. The establishment of the dominance of 'standard' English and the subordination of other social dialects was part and parcel of the establishment of the dominance of the capitalist class and the subordination of the working class. (Fairclough, 2015, pp. 84–85)

'Standard' English, which took over major social institutions such as education, government, and religion, while at the same time pushing out Latin and French, not only expanded the number of its domains and users but also gradually gained political, economic, and cultural power. In fact, a critical analysis of the different varieties of English reveals the political nature of language and language education. This analysis can include questions such as which English(es) or whose English(es) to teach; in what ways different varieties are promoted to maintain the existing systems of privileges and socio-economic hierarchies; how unequal communicative rights have emerged especially in regard to 'standard' and 'non-standard varieties' of English; and which varieties are marginalized, stigmatized, and excluded from the language education curriculum (Holborow, 1999; McKinney, 2017). The issue of stigmatized varieties is only one of the examples of how language education often benefits those with more power and privilege since it is often their language varieties that are prioritized and reinforced in the curriculum. As Tollefson (2007) states:

> Stigmatized varieties include social dialects marked as poor or working class, or as ethnic or "racial," such as African American Vernacular English;

regional varieties associated with economically impoverished areas, such as Appalachian varieties in the United States; and pidgins and Creoles, such as Hawaiian Creole English. Medium of instruction policy in most ELT settings requires the use of standard varieties, which are in fact the varieties of the upper middle class that have come to be considered more precise, more scientific, and more expressive than other varieties. (p. 28)

In that sense, discussions around which languages and varieties are privileged and which are stigmatized relate to issues such race, ethnicity, and class.

The hegemonic spread of 'standard' or 'standardized' English has been widely addressed by the literature on English as a lingua franca (Davis, 2010; Jenkins, 2007; Jenkins et al., 2018; Watson, 2018), English as an international language (Holliday, 2005; McKay, 2002; Pennycook, 2017; Sharifian, 2009), and World Englishes (Rose et al., 2021; Kachru, 1986a, 1996; Kirkpatrick, 2007, 2010; Melchers and Shaw, 2011).[2] These scholars have taken six different strands to explore what the global spread of English means at the local and global levels:

> *colonial-celebration*, a traditional view that sees the spread of English as inherently good for the world; *laissez-faire liberalism*, which views the spread of English as natural, neutral and beneficial, as long as it can coexist in a complementary relationship with other languages; *language ecology*, which focuses on the potential harms and dangers of the introduction of English to multilingual contexts; *linguistic imperialism*, which points to the interrelationships between English and global capitalism, "McDonaldization" and other international homogenising trends; *language rights*, which attempts to introduce a moral imperative to support other languages in face of the threat imposed by English; and *postcolonial performativity*, which seeks to understand through contextualised sociologies of local language acts how English is constantly implicated in moments of hegemony, resistance and appropriation. (Pennycook, 2000, p. 108)

Within these six strands of research, the dominant line within ELT seems to be a "liberal laissez-faire attitude … [b]ased on a mixture of general political liberalism and more specific academic apoliticism – a view that academic work should somehow remain neutral" (Pennycook, 2000, p. 109). This liberal approach entails a 'neutral' position towards ideological and political implications of language and language education by relying on "seductive freedom-of-choice arguments" (p. 111). Under the disguise of rendering everyone to be 'free' to do whatever they like with English, this approach, in reality, serves to maintain the existing social, cultural, and economic power relations that shape language education, and its ideologies, policies, and practice as well as language use (Pennycook, 2000).

Among these six strands, linguistic imperialism (Phillipson, 1992) is known to be the best attempt to map out the political and ideological power relations that derive from globalization and capitalism (Pennycook, 2000). Linguistic imperialism – and more specifically English linguistic imperialism – refers to the dominance of English as being "asserted and maintained by the establishment and continuous reconstitution of structural and cultural inequalities between English and other languages" (Phillipson, 1992, p. 47). As Holborow (1999) explains:

> English has a heavy historical load for many peoples across the world and to ignore this fact by claiming that it is simply an 'additional language', a linguistic *tabula rasa,* is to deny the fact that for many English has been an *alien word,* brought at the point of a sword and synonymous with oppression. That is why the question of linguistic rights of all minority (and majority) languages is at the centre of the politics of English. The dichotomy in many African states where the home language seldom reaches the school is the result, not of linguistic functionalism, but of social inequality bolstered by the legacy of imperial oppression. (p. 87)

The research on linguistic imperialism, thus, focuses on the dominance of English in former multilingual and multi-ethnic colonial countries, its role in North-South power relations, and the way ELT contributes to the hierarchy and eradication of languages worldwide. Linguistic imperialism also explains the reasons why English has become the predominant language internationally and whose interests its spread and dominance serve (Phillipson, 2000, 2006).

Questioning how and why some languages are privileged or marginalized, Phillipson (2006) discusses the implications of linguistic imperialism on foreign language education:

> Is it fair that some should be able to communicate, negotiate, trade, and be culturally productive in their mother tongue, whereas others have to use a second or foreign language? Is it fair that the United States and United Kingdom can avoid investing substantially in foreign-language education, whereas virtually all other education systems are obliged to in order to access the global economy and cultural industries? Such inequity is largely unrecorded and unquantified, since the structural and ideological underpinning of global linguistic hegemony tends to be regarded as legitimate, despite the massive economic and cultural advantages this gives the English-speaking world. (p. 350)

English in multilingual and multi-ethnic countries – in terms of language ideologies, policies, and practices – is also worth discussing in terms of linguistic imperialism. For instance, post-apartheid South Africa is an interesting case as "a highly unequal and diverse society that is explicitly grappling with the deeply ingrained effects of institutionalized racism, and struggling to decolonize" (McKinney, 2017, p. 10). South Africa's 1994 Constitution embraced an extensive multilingual status with eleven official languages, which ironically paved the way for English to emerge in public spheres including education (Newfield, 2011). Seeing English as a tool for upward mobility and for access into the local and international marketplace, most educational institutions have started to provide English medium instruction (EMI), although English is not the mother tongue of a majority of children in South Africa. The language ideologies and policies in South Africa have legitimized the prestige varieties of English at the expense of "non-English languages and non-mainstream varieties that they [students] bring to school and continue to use on a daily basis" (McKinney, 2017, p. 10). Similar cases were observed in other multilingual, multi-ethnic countries in West Africa. For instance, in Ghana, Hamile respondents reported mixing Dagara and English, since an indicator of superiority in social status and upward social mobility was "the image of a well-bred Dagara-English bilingual" (Beyogle, 2014, p. 88). In Nigeria, English, being considered an ethnically neutral and economically advantaged language, has been adopted as the official language (Schneider, 2011).

Given the global spread of English, scholars have coined terms such as linguicism which refers to "ideologies, structures and practices which are used to legitimate, effectuate, regulate and reproduce an unequal division of power and resources between groups which are defined on the basis of language" (Skutnabb-Kangas, 1988, p. 13). Scholars have also discussed the linguistic genocide especially of Indigenous languages (Phillipson, 1992) and have even argued whether English is a 'killer language' (Kachru, 1986b, 2005). Shank Lauwo (2019), for instance, has discussed how Tanzanian mainstream schooling has muted over 130 different local languages like Maa and marginalized Maa-dominant learners, while speakers of dominant languages such as Swahili and English were given privileged access to school knowledge. According to Schneider (2011), only three post-colonial countries, Tanzania, Malaysia, and the Philippines, deliberately aimed to develop their Indigenous languages to fulfill the role of their national language as a symbol of their national identity, yet English not only remained important but became more widespread. Taking a 'language ecology' approach that related languages to environmental protection, scholars such as Robert Phillipson and Tove Skutnabb-Kangas have perceived the problem with the global spread of English as "a complex disruption to an ecology of languages" (Pennycook, 2000, p. 110). Linguistic rights, linguistic diversity, and multilingualism are recognized as part of human rights while subtractive education through a dominant language is seen as a "crime against humanity" (Skutnabb-Kangas, 2009, p. 341). Acknowledging the significance of linguistic ecology, linguistic human rights, and linguistic imperialism, Pennycook (2000) also has proposed *post-colonial performativity* as a framework that underlines the local context, sense of agency, resistance, and appropriation.

Foreign language education and Otherness

Many of the ideological issues and power relations mentioned in the previous section in relation to teaching English are relevant to and show similar implications within foreign language education programs. To begin with, linguistic legitimacy – that is "which language varieties are deemed by the society (or some subset of the society) to be legitimate, and which are not" (Reagan and Osborn, 2002, p. 34) – is an issue that is pertinent in both English and foreign language education. Just as 'English' in ELT has historically referred to 'Standard' English – a euphemism for American or British English in most cases – foreign language education also endorses normativism that emphasizes 'standard' language(s) (e.g., Castilian Spanish) at the expense of non-native or 'non-standard' varieties. Native speakerism – a topic that will be discussed in more detail in Chapter 6 – has long been a hegemonic ideology that privileges native speaker teachers over local ones, regardless of the language taught (Moussu and Llurda, 2008; Llurda, 2005; Phillipson, 1992).

As a name for a field of practice and research, 'Teaching English to Speakers of Other Languages (or TESOL)' has also been criticized for indirectly perpetuating the dichotomous Self-Other subject positions of Anglo-teacher and learner, and thus contributing to the asymmetrical native versus non-native divide (Lin and Luke, 2006). Similarly, the 'foreign' in 'foreign language education' has been challenged as an ideologically charged concept constructing Otherness and as an invitation to xenophobia (Holly, 1990; Reagan and Osborn, 2002). While foreign language education is the widely used term in different parts of the world to refer to English language education (e.g., English as a foreign language), within the US especially, an attempt to eradicate the subtle bias and 'Othering' of the target languages has been a shift from 'foreign' to the more politically correct label 'world' (i.e., world languages). These attempts, however, might run the risk of removing "what might be termed articulated bias" (Reagan and Osborn, 2002, p. 8) while brushing over the deep-structure discriminatory practices that exist within the field. Overall, the discussions around terminology of the larger fields in language education (e.g., foreign language education, TESOL) illustrate how labels, concepts, and names attribute or remove power from individuals and the wider communities.

Similar to how English language education is more accessible to those with more economic and cultural capital, foreign language education can also be considered an elitist activity for being offered in private schools or in wealthy school districts (Kubota, 2010; Reagan and Osborn, 2002). In fact, its Eurocentrism in terms of languages available for learners to choose from can be listed as one of its elitist features. According to the United States' K-12 Foreign Language Survey Report (2017), Spanish had the highest number of enrollments with 7,363,125 students (69.21 percent) of foreign language education overall, while French had the second highest enrolment with 1,289,004 students (12.12 percent). The lowest enrollments belonged to Russian (14,876), Latin (21,306) and

Arabic (26,045), all three making up less than 1 percent of foreign language education in the States. In the UK, according to the British Council's 2021 Language Trends survey, French is taught on the curriculum across 72 percent of primary schools, while Spanish as the second most commonly taught language is offered across 29 percent of the schools. Less than 3 percent of the surveyed schools offered one of Arabic, British Sign Language, Danish, Hebrew, Italian, and Japanese (Collen, 2021). Phipps (2021) explains this dominance of certain languages over others in relation to hegemonic power dynamics rooted in linguistic and cultural colonization and oppression. Therefore, a decolonization of the foreign language curriculum is called for, so as to "re-orientate the curriculum towards those languages which have suffered marginalisation and attrition, and towards nurturing speakers – be they heritage, native, or simply communities of interest – in languages which have not enjoyed the same levels of resourcing as dominant languages" (Phipps, 2021, p. 6).

As discussed in this chapter so far, language ideologies, which lie at the nexus of language, ideology, and power, are concerned with which languages are counted as legitimate and valued; which languages are marginalized and devalued; how language minority students or students of 'non-standard' varieties are educated; and how these processes are embedded within English language education, bi/multilingual programs in post-colonial countries, and foreign language education. The next section will focus on multicultural education, an interdisciplinary, pedagogical framework drawing on sociology, anthropology, history, economics, political science, social psychology, and communications. Concerned with issues that regard language, power, and culture, multicultural education has aimed to address the educational needs and experiences of students of color, low-income students, and English language learners (May and Sleeter, 2010). Yet, its focus has shifted to a more liberal and depoliticized multiculturalism which has received criticism even from its own supporters (e.g., Banks, 1995). The rest of this chapter will first discuss the premises of multicultural education along with its criticisms. It will then move onto social justice language education, which underlines the ideological nature of language(s), and the role of language education in challenging the existing social, cultural, and economic hierarchies.

Box 3.2 Problem-posing task

What kind of language ideologies, policies, and practices exist in your society and how do they reflect the concepts and issues discussed in this chapter so far? Which language(s) and/or varieties are valued or marginalized? What are some of the beliefs and practices towards non-mainstream languages or varieties? What actions would you take to raise awareness towards these non-mainstream languages or varieties in your classrooms and community?

Multicultural education: premises and criticisms

Since emerging in the 1960s as part of the Black civil rights movements in the United States, a variety of approaches within multicultural education have been offered, ranging from liberal multiculturalism to critical multiculturalism that aims to transform pedagogy and curriculum (Dover, 2013; May and Sleeter, 2010). Despite its intention to move beyond integrating diverse racial, ethnic, and cultural content into the educational curriculum in order to promote social equality among different learner groups (McGee Banks and Banks, 1995), multicultural education has become more associated with the liberal, 'tourist' or 'Heroes and Holidays' approach. This tends to trivialize and reduce multiculturalism to a mere 'celebration of diversity' through ethnic celebrations, multicultural dinners, festivities, and so on. Contemplated as reminiscent of colonialism, liberal multiculturalism has presented a depoliticized, essentialized view of culture as a set of concrete practices, by overlooking the processes of how knowledge is reproduced, maintained, and marginalized in classrooms (Britzman et al., 1993; May and Sleeter, 2010).

Multicultural education embodied the colonial legacy of English language in terms of spreading cultural and religious enlightenment while deculturizing Indigenous and local communities, with the overarching goal to gain political, economic, and cultural power. The tourist approach reflected this legacy through instructional practices and materials such as engaging learners in 'cultural' activities (e.g., celebration of Christian holidays) rather than exposing them to different religious traditions; or celebrating Thanksgiving without conveying the historical and cultural events that took place around that period as well as the genocide of Indigenous people. Nieto (2000) also elaborated on the weaknesses of multicultural education by drawing on her own experiences:

> The field was in its infancy in 1980 when I taught my first course in multicultural education, but it was already clear to me that much of what took place in classrooms and schools in the name of diversity was little more than window dressing. Back then, adding a unit on "Christmas Festivals Around the World," or an assembly program during "Brotherhood Week" was about as far as attention to multicultural perspectives went. A few years later, some schools were commemorating Dr. Martin Luther King Jr.'s birthday and including a few examples of multicultural children's literature in the curriculum. Yet, I was beginning to see that most approaches to multicultural education avoided asking difficult questions related to access, equity, and social justice. (p. 180)

Similarly, hooks (1994) has also criticized the tokenism within multicultural education programs, which often entail no more than a symbolic gesture towards inclusivity:

> What does it mean when a white female English professor is eager to include a work by Toni Morrison on the syllabus of her course but then teaches

that work without ever making reference to race or ethnicity? I have heard individual white women "boast" about how they have shown students that black writers are "as good" as the white male canon when they do not call attention to race. Clearly, such pedagogy is not an interrogation of the biases conventional canons (if not all canons) establish, but yet another form of tokenism. (p. 38)

Multicultural education has also been criticized for its lack of emphasis on political economy; more specifically, for representing different ethnic groups without including their "cultural *and* economic inequities" (North, 2006, p. 511, original emphasis), and for normalizing the middle-class values and practices in a way that legitimizes and reproduces the already existing socio-economic inequalities. Overall, widely criticized for its colonialist, essentializing approach to teaching culture(s) with its superficial celebration of positive cultural features, feel-good additive content, and tokenism, liberal multicultural education failed to address the structural and cultural inequalities that exist within and beyond educational institutions (Nieto and Bode, 2018; Ladson-Billings and Tate, 1995; Lee et al., 1998; Macedo and Bartolomé, 2014; May and Sleeter, 2010; Skutnabb-Kangas, Phillipson, Mohanty, and Panda, 2009).

Not only have multicultural education programs fallen far from achieving their overarching goals of equity and social justice, but they have also become one of the 'master's tools' (Lorde, 1984) utilized to perpetuate the hegemonic ideologies in the world. Social progress or triumph narratives about women's rights, the legal status of same-sex marriages in twenty-nine countries, anti-bias and anti-bullying programs at schools, and diversity, equity, and inclusion (DEI) committees and trainings enabled the schools and other institutions to circulate meritocratic messages in relation to how class-based differences no longer exist, and that if individuals work really hard, they can move up the ladder and achieve their dreams. These narratives often lay at the center of multicultural programs for their potential to reassure individuals that they are different from their ancestors who enslaved people for profit, who fired gay people, and who did not allow women equal status in social and political life (Quinn and Meiners, 2016). In addition to meritocracy, multicultural education programs have also been criticized for perpetuating language ideologies that marginalize and oppress multicultural and multilingual learners. As Macedo and Bartolomé (2014) discuss in their article, 'Multiculturalism permitted in English only,' bilingual and multicultural education programs in the US continued the legacy of colonialism with their preference of 'standard' language use over students' vernaculars, devaluing their cultural capital and linguistic heritage.

Different frameworks have been proposed to address these criticisms around the appropriation of multicultural education to serve dominant discourses and hegemonic ideologies. For instance, Nieto and Bode (2018) have proposed an antiracist multicultural education rooted in critical pedagogy and social justice. Critical pedagogy scholar Kincheloe (2008a) has also argued that multiculturalism needs to move beyond "supposedly depoliticized taco days, falafels, and Martin Luther King's birthday" and focus more on "the subtle workings of racism, sexism, class bias, cultural oppression and homophobia" (pp. 9–10). Among these frameworks was critical multicultural education that draws on critical race theory, antiracist education, critical pedagogy, multiculturalism, and critical language awareness (Fairclough, 1992; Kubota, 2004; May, 1999; May and Sleeter, 2010; Pennycook, 2001; Shapiro, 2022). One common goal of these frameworks is to develop learners' critical consciousness; that is, the critical thinking and inquiry skills learners need to challenge processes of knowledge construction (Byars-Winston et al., 2005, p. 134). For instance, Glynn et al. (2014) have argued that a Spanish language class can encourage its learners to move beyond representing Spain in terms of flamenco dance, song, and guitar to learning about Roma people who have been oppressed for centuries not only in Spain but also in different parts of the world. Overall, these frameworks aimed to address the above-mentioned criticisms of liberal multiculturalism by offering a structural analysis of culture "in the context of how unequal power relations, lived out in daily interactions, contribute toward its production, rather than framing it primarily as an artifact of the past" (May and Sleeter, 2010, p. 10).

Going beyond multiculturalism: social justice language education

It is a common assumption in the fields of language and literacy education that social justice education and multicultural education are almost synonyms (Hytten and Bettez, 2011). Some have even argued that the field of language education, with its emphasis on multilingualism and multiculturalism and its diverse body of language learners coming from different linguistic and cultural backgrounds, is almost "half-way there" (Glynn et al., 2014, p. 3), and, therefore, better equipped for social justice language education (Nieto, 2000). While social justice language education partly grew out of the efforts of multicultural education that focused on the educational experiences of students of color and low-income students as well as English language learners (McDonald and Zeichner, 2009), it underlines the need to go beyond linguistic and cultural diversity and inclusion to uncovering the ideological nature of language and challenging the existing interpersonal and institutionalized social, cultural, and economic hierarchies that are promoted through language education and language use. In other words, shifting the focus from the individual to the societal/institutional, social justice language education examines issues of oppression and marginalization from a systemic and institutionalized perspective rather than as individual acts of prejudice and ignorance or simply a result of cultural differences (Howard and Aleman, 2008). Often considered "an extension of the social action approaches within multicultural education" (McDonald and Zeichner, 2009, p. 598), social justice language education requires a critical analysis as well as transformation of the socio-cultural and institutional structures that perpetuate inequalities and oppression.

Conclusion

Language not only allows human beings to interact with each other and develop a general understanding of themselves and their surrounding world but also serves as a political and ideological instrument in the reproduction of the many inequalities that exist in the society. Yet, as Holborow states (1999), "Language both *arises* from the social demands and needs of the material world and, through human cooperation and activity, *contributes* to the transformation of that world. It is then itself transformed as human society changes" (p. 18, original emphasis). In order to achieve societal change through language and language education, various frameworks have been proposed, including critical pedagogy (Freire, 2005b [1970]) and multicultural education, two frameworks that are widely discussed in Chapter 2 and this chapter, respectively. Various other inclusive and equity-oriented approaches concerned with language and literacy education have been proposed, such as funds of knowledge (Moll et al., 1992; González et al., 2005), multiliteracies (Cope and Kalantzis, 2000; New London Group, 1996), multimodality (Kress and Leeuwen, 2001), translanguaging (Garcia and Wei, 2014; Wei, 2022), culturally responsive and sustaining pedagogies (Gay, 2018; Paris and Alim, 2017), critical multiculturalism (May, 1999; May and Sleeter, 2010), and critical language awareness (Fairclough, 1992; Pennycook, 2001; Shapiro, 2022). The social justice language education I propose in this book brings together these approaches in order to underline the need to acknowledge the linguistic and cultural resources different learner groups bring to the classroom; to develop their critical literacy skills in ways that enable them to question relations of power in the world; and to achieve transformation and social change not only in educational institutions but also in the society at large. The next chapter, therefore, will take a more pedagogical approach by delving into the social justice language curriculum in terms of lesson planning, instructional materials, and social action projects. In doing so, the goal is to help language educators consolidate and put into practice the many conceptual issues around language, power, and ideology discussed in this book so far.

Notes

1. Similar arguments can be made with most languages where there is a central locus of power (e.g., Parisian French, Hanoverian German, Hanoian Vietnamese, Beijinger Mandarin, and Florentine Italian).
2. English as a lingua franca refers to the communication that takes place between those different users of English who do not speak English as their native language. English as an international language highlights the global use of English, while World Englishes refers to the different varieties of English (e.g., British, South African, Nigerian, Jamaican) usually taking into account Kachru's (1986a) three circles of inner, outer, and expanding.

Multimedia resources

Rethinking Schools
  www.rethinkingschools.org
    As a non-profit publisher and advocacy organization, Rethinking Schools provides magazines, books, and other resources that can be used by language educators to promote equity and justice in the classroom.
So Just
  http://www.sojust.net/index.html
    So Just, a sister website of EdChange (http://www.edchange.org) and Equity Literacy Institute (https://www.equityliteracy.org), is a source for historic speeches, songs, poetry, and manifestos on human rights and social justice.
Social Justice Books
  https://socialjusticebooks.org/
    As a project of Teaching for Change (https://www.teachingforchange.org), Social Justice Books provide teachers and parents with a list of multicultural and social justice children's books as well as other resources to help children to read, write, and change the world.

Children's books

Tonatiuh, D. (2013). *Pancho rabbit and the coyote: A migrant's tale.* Abrams Books for Young Learners.
    This allegorical tale is about the external and internal factors that lead people to leave their homelands in order to find work in the US, and pulls no punches about the dangers people face on their journey.
Binford, W. (2021). *Hear my voice/Escucha mi voz.* Workman Publishing Company.
    Drawing on first-hand accounts, this bilingual book is a look at the experiences of immigrants from Latin America to the United States and their dehumanizing experiences with U.S. Customs and Border Protection.
Muhammad, I. (2019). *The proudest blue: A story of hijab and family.* Little, Brown Books for Young Readers.
    A beautiful story about Faizah's first day of school that demystifies and destigmatizes the wearing of the hijab.

Chapter 4

Social justice language curriculum

Box 4.1 Lead-in

Audre Lorde (1984), in her famous essay, 'The Master's tools will never dismantle the master's house', argues as follows:

For the master's tools will never dismantle the master's house. They may allow us to temporarily beat him at his own game, but they will never enable us to bring about genuine change. (p. 183, original emphasis)

What are the 'master's tools' Audre Lorde refers to in this essay? If the 'master's tools' will never dismantle the 'master's house,' what tools do language educators need to gather, acquire, and/or develop to bring about genuine change in their classrooms and the society at large?

Introduction

Language and language education stand at the intersection of social, cultural, and political ideologies that empower certain populations while marginalizing others (Avineri et al., 2019; Glynn et al., 2014; Hastings and Jacob, 2016; Hawkins, 2011; Skutnabb-Kangas, 2009; Osborn, 2006). Language education is a political act since "many decisions about what gets taught, to whom, how, when, and where, are made at high levels of the political hierarchy" (Pennycook, 1989, p. 590). Everything language teachers do in their classrooms – from macro-level processes (e.g., curriculum development and textbook selection) to micro-level activities (e.g., lesson planning and classroom interactions) – has social, political, and economic implications on language learners' lives and the society at large (Auerbach, 1995; Pennycook, 2001). Social justice language education, in that sense, encompasses epistemological beliefs, ideological dispositions, and pedagogical practices that help language learners develop a sense of advocacy and activism that transcends classroom walls (Coney, 2016; Hawkins, 2011;

Ortaçtepe Hart and Martel, 2020). The present chapter will take a pedagogical approach to discuss the following four strategies that situate social justice at the center of a language curriculum:

- Centralizing social justice within lesson planning
- Cultivating activism for social change
- Deconstructing language education materials
- Reconstructing materials to develop learners' critical literacy

Box 4.2 Reflective task

Reflect on your reasons – or the reasons others might have – for pursuing a career in language teaching. Which of these are related to achieving social justice in the world? In what ways can social justice language education enable language educators to enhance teaching and learning practices in educational contexts within which they find themselves, while also affirming their learners' identities and improving their life experiences?

Centralizing social justice within lesson planning

The integration of content and language objectives is one of the key features of language classrooms adopting content-based instruction (CBI) or content and language integrated learning (CLIL) (Baecher et al., 2014; Cammarata, 2016; Martel, 2022; Morton, 2016). In a similar vein, the social justice language curriculum embodies three sets of overlapping learning objectives: content, language, and social justice (Adams and Zúñiga, 2016; Glynn et al., 2014).

Language objectives describe what language learners should be able to do with the language by the end of the lesson in ways that support their language development (Kong and Hoare, 2011; Shrum and Glisan, 2009). *Content objectives* are related to the understanding of new topics and concepts, as well as the development of cultural knowledge and intercultural skills (Kong and Hoare, 2011). Content objectives, however, need to go beyond content knowledge and lead to "new insight and ability in the learner in which content is meaningful and useful going forward" (Wiggins and McTighe, 2011, p. 45). In order to distinguish between simple facts and meaningful takeaways, language teachers can ask themselves "If they [students] really did understand this content, what would they then see and do differently? What's the point of teaching that content?" (Wiggins and McTighe, 2011, p. 45). *Social justice objectives*, on the other hand, include reflections about one's positions, identities, and privileges

TABLE 4.1 Sample language, content, and social justice objectives

Content objectives	Language objectives
The students will be able to: • Explain the term "herstory." • Demonstrate an understanding of the Herstory movement.	The students will be able to: • Review and use the past simple and progressive. • Review and use passive voice in writing. • Write a short biography (~300 words) about a female leader from their own culture who made a positive impact on the world.

Social justice objectives

The students will be able to:
- Compare and contrast "herstory" in the 1970s when it was coined by Robin Morgan and today with the Herstory Movements.
- Develop an informed and respectful story detailing the accomplishments of a female historical figure.
- Think critically about the role of intersectionality in terms of the under-representation of women in history books.
- Take action to bring more female voices into history by posting their biographies onto the Herstory Movement Website.

as well as critical thinking about structural inequities and injustices (Adams, 2016). Social justice objectives can be articulated jointly either with content and language objectives or stated separately. For instance, being able to articulate different LGBTQ+ related vocabulary or using gender neutral pronouns could be stated under either language objectives or social justice objectives. Above are some sample language, content, and social justice objectives taken from a lesson plan on the HerStory movement.[1]

There are several affordances of formulating lesson plan objectives in terms of language, content, and social justice. First, the integration of language-related knowledge and skills with meaningful and relevant content will allow language learners to use the language for real-life purposes in contextualized ways (Glynn et al., 2014). Second, designing lesson plans based on language, content, and social justice objectives will not only enable language educators to address social justice issues in their classes but also to think about the cultural, economic, and political impact of their teaching. Finally, it will help break down the false dichotomy between teaching for social justice and teaching for "academic knowledge," the former being considered "trivial and limited in intellectual substance" (Cochran-Smith et al., 2009a, p. 630).

Knowledge and social justice are in fact complimentary goals that allow language educators to know not only how to teach kids to read but also to "know that the inequalities of schooling and society make it much easier for some groups of kids to learn to read than others" (Cochran-Smith et al., 2009a, p. 646).

Box 4.3 Reflective task

Using the lesson plan template presented in Appendix 4.1, design a lesson for your current or ideal teaching context. Once you complete your lesson plan with language, content, and social justice objectives, use the provided checklist to evaluate and reflect upon your lesson plan. Which features of your lesson plan support a social justice curriculum and which features need to be changed to make it more in line? Alternatively, you can examine an already existing lesson plan and use the checklist to evaluate and modify it.

Cultivating activism for social change

While a social justice language curriculum engages language learners in personal insights, reflection, and deep inquiry with regard to social justice issues, it is also important to translate and apply one's learning and unlearning to generate social change within their classrooms, schools, and the society more widely (Boyd, 2017; Byars-Winston et al., 2005). Thus, social responsibility or social action projects that build bridges between language learners' educational contexts, lived experiences, and communities would not only help learners develop their critical consciousness but also engage them in social transformative action. Service learning and fieldwork projects will also enable learners to contextualize the course content; situate themselves both locally and globally; and connect with different stakeholders within their community (Byars-Winston et al., 2005; Harven and Gordon-Biddle, 2016).

Within a social justice curriculum, *activism* precedes *social action*. The difference between these two terms is similar to what Ladegaard and Phipps (2020) describe as "*talking about* intercultural communication and social injustice, to *doing* intercultural communication and promoting a social justice agenda" (p. 70, original emphasis). This distinction is especially relevant in today's digital world where one common form of activism is what is called social media, cyber, or hashtag activism (Dixon and Janks, 2014). Phipps (2020), while acknowledging the role social media played during the Arab Spring and the Black Lives Matter protests, cautions against this form of 'click-tivism' where "the personal gratification of signing a petition or posting on a hashtag *can be* the primary or only outcome" (p. 88, original emphasis). Language educators, therefore, should not only cultivate advocacy and activism in their learners, but also encourage them to take action in ways that will lead to social change (Edelsky and Johnson, 2004).

Boyd (2017) describes a four-step process to facilitate learners' social action projects: contextualizing, organizing, acting, and reflecting (COAR). First, students working as a whole class or in small groups identify a list of problems they want to address in their communities. While topical clarity is a starting point, the other important consideration at this stage is the topic's viability for real change. Volunteering with a soup kitchen, however, may not lead to social change unless community engagement involves a critical analysis of the community as well as an action plan (Crookes, 2013). Once language learners have a chance to examine the topic through archival research, interviews with local communities, or each other's own experiences, they then design and implement the action plan with clear executable steps. Assessment of social action projects should be formative as well as summative. Teachers' ongoing feedback during the process can be accompanied by reflection questions about the action plan, its impact, and the way ahead. Learners can also engage in self-evaluations discussing their contribution to the group project and reflecting on its perceived impact.

While social action projects have the potential to alleviate some of the injustices across society in a direct or indirect way, they also have pedagogical affordances at the classroom level. These projects help promote language learners' multimodal literacies by allowing them to utilize different modes of communication to accomplish their goals. They also provide opportunities for language educators to demolish their authority in the classroom by giving learners the agency to work on an issue that is of interest and relevance to them, and that falls within their own fields of knowledge and expertise. Lastly, activism through social action/social responsibility projects is essential in order not to leave students in despair, guilt, and negative dispositions (e.g., powerlessness and helplessness) in the face of all the atrocities they read about, discuss, and deconstruct (Boyd, 2017; Edelsky and Johnson, 2004). There is, however, a delicate balance to maintain between cultivating learners' sense of agency for social change and helping them understand that while individual attempts do make a difference, they cannot cure all systemic problems (Boyd, 2017).

Although a social justice curriculum adopts a perspective of advocacy, activism, and action, it would also be unrealistic to demand language teachers to have an action-oriented activity at the end of each lesson. As Crookes (2013) reasonably poses, "If a teacher intends to manifest a critical pedagogy but [their] course doesn't result in action, does it then in a sense 'fail' to be critical pedagogy?" (p. 72). Similarly, would it still be social justice language education if there was no action-oriented activity in the lesson plan? While actionable social justice objectives should be part of the social justice curriculum, language lessons tend to proceed in a developmental order appropriate to the learners' readiness both in terms of content knowledge and language skills. Therefore, while some lessons may focus on awareness raising, others might lead to more action-oriented projects and activities. The key is that discussions of different socio-historical and economic perspectives, policies, and practices should be complemented with explorations of possible solutions and actionable strategies.

Deconstructing language learning materials

The instructional materials language teachers use in their classrooms range from textbooks, realia, flashcards, multimodal, digital, and literary texts to audio-visual materials. While these materials are adopted or adapted to teach a particular linguistic function or a communicative skill, they are by no means neutral curricular and cultural artifacts, but economic commodities and ideological tools that reproduce the already existing power relations in the world (Apple, 1992; Bori, 2018; Gray and Block, 2014; Hickman, 2011; Pennycook, 2001). As Apple and Christian-Smith (1991) have mentioned:

> All texts are at once the results of political, economic, and cultural activities, battles, and compromises. They are conceived, designed, and authored by real people with real interests. They are published within the political and economic constraints of markets, resources, and power. And what texts mean and how they are used are fought over by communities with distinctly different commitments and by teachers and students as well. (pp. 1–2)

The following sections will discuss language textbooks as economic commodities, ideological tools, and cultural artifacts. Yet many of the arguments presented here are applicable to any authentic or inauthentic materials and texts used in language classrooms, ranging from digital, multimodal texts to more traditional readers.

Textbooks as economic commodities

Textbooks are economic commodities that need to be sold by publishing companies in global markets. English language textbooks, for instance, have historically focused on American or British culture and Kachru's (1992) inner circle countries since the goal is to produce cost-effective, lucrative textbooks that are marketable across different cultures and countries. To achieve their sales target, textbook companies have chosen to produce anodyne textbooks with watered and dumbed down, bland, and 'neutral' content (Apple, 2019; Hickman, 2011; Tomlinson, 2012). This content represents today's teenagers as *only* caring about traveling and tomorrow's party in a sanitized world (Cook, 2003). 'Inappropriate,' 'controversial,' and 'taboo' subjects are mostly avoided, following an implicit practice called 'No PARSNIP,' which stands for no politics, alcohol, religion, sex, narcotics, -isms (e.g., feminism), and pork within language textbooks (Gray, 2002; Risager, 2018).

Cook (2003) argues that "[T]he blandness of these coursebooks is partly dictated by fears of giving offence on religious or political grounds and of going out of date" (p. 279). In a current study examining English, German, French, Spanish, Danish, and Esperanto textbooks used in Denmark, Risager (2021) found two textbooks that included references to religion. The English textbook, *A piece of cake*, included many branches of Christianity, Judaism, Hinduism, and Aboriginal religions, while no references were made to Buddhism and Islam. Similarly, Ndura's (2004) study with ESL books used in the United States also revealed minimal reference to Christmas and Hannukah, while religious diversity was not mentioned at all. That's why, in addition to being economic commodities driven by market needs, textbooks embody hegemonic ideologies through their explicit and/or hidden curricula, that is, what is included and what is (un)intentionally omitted (Apple, 2019; Phillipson, 1992). The role of textbooks as ideological, hegemonic tools requires an examination of what constitutes legitimate knowledge in language textbooks, whose social worlds are represented, which identities are included and excluded, and what social behavior, values, and attitudes are imposed (Canagarajah, 1993; Canale, 2016).

Textbooks as ideological, hegemonic tools

In many language education contexts, there is "an unfortunate tendency to confuse and conflate the curriculum with the textbook" (Reagan, 2016, p. 176). Often constituting the flesh and blood of the curricular knowledge that students are expected to learn, textbooks serve to reproduce the economic, cultural, and political hierarchies in the world (Hickman, 2011). Discussing English language education as 'the White man's burden' dating back to "the colonial mission of spreading Enlightenment values for civilizing purposes" (p. 12), Canagarajah (1999) states:

> Contemporary education as a whole (not only ELT) is considerably influenced by the knowledge produced, disseminated, and defined by the materially-developed center communities … Western centers of education, research, and publishing – whether funded by state or non-governmental agencies – provide financial backing, donate textbooks, share expertise, train teachers and scholars, and sometimes even run ELT enterprises in the periphery. (p. 12)

In other words, this form of mandated, legitimized knowledge embodied in textbooks is a cultivated effort of international and local textbook companies which are driven primarily by the needs of the market, and then the governments, school principals, teachers, and, rarely, students.

Often recognized as the source of 'legitimate knowledge,' language textbooks – for all languages – have been found to perpetuate White supremacy, nativism, sexism, heteronormativity, ableism, consumerism, and classism. In Turkey, Ulum and Köksal's (2019) study examined the ideologies, value orientations, and hegemonic practices in international textbooks produced by publishers such as Cambridge University Press, Pearson Education, National Geographic Learning, as well as local textbooks produced by the Ministry of Turkish National Education, and Ministry of Education in Iran. Their study revealed that the three US- and UK-produced textbooks emphasized the cultural and economic values of Kachru's (1986b) inner and expanding circles, while the Iranian and Turkish textbooks reinforced religious values and nationality. In Iran, sexism, consumerism, and cultural stereotypes were also present in the commonly used EFL textbooks (Abdollahzadeh, and Baniasad, 2010; Taki, 2008). The ESL textbooks used in the United States were found to promote a hegemonic worldview rooted in imperialism and colonialism that values "profit over human agency" (Montaño and Quintanar-Sarellana, 2012, p. 28). Similarly, examinations of the EFL textbooks published by Korean companies provided evidence for how the existing ideologies of globalization in Korea (e.g., an admiration for the West, West referring to dominance rather than geographical location, and White meaning power and privilege) were woven into the fabric of the language textbooks while omitting any discussion on multiculturalism, poverty, slavery, racism, or gender-related issues (Lee, 2009, 2011).

In addition to examining the non-verbal content in textbooks, studies have also focused on their verbal content; more specifically, the language variety presented in textbooks. Despite evidence that language variety is a marker of social, cultural, economic, and other forms of identity, language variation rarely occurs in today's language textbooks, reflecting their role as "instruments of standard language ideology" (Tollefson, 2007, p. 30). There is no doubt that language teaching materials should raise learners' awareness of the different varieties of the language they are learning that differ from the prescribed norms and standard language ideologies presented in most textbooks (Galloway, 2018; Matsuda and Friedrich, 2011; McKay, 2012, 2018). The work of Nicola Galloway and her colleagues on Global Englishes for Language Teaching (GELT) is, therefore, significant in order to bring different language varieties into the English language classroom (Galloway, 2017; Galloway and Rose, 2014; Rose et al., 2021). Although GELT offers an analytical framework for English language teachers to examine norms, recruitment practices, and models of English(es) presented in language education materials and ways to "critically evaluate ELT materials to ensure that they equip students with the skills necessary to participate in global contexts" (Galloway and Rose, 2018, p. 5), its principles can be expanded to other languages and language varieties.

The representation of different identities in textbooks is also a matter of who has more power and privilege, since those who are included and excluded in textbooks are often "proxies for wider questions of power relations" (Apple, 1990, p. 19). The widespread class, gender, and racial bias in textbooks reflects the already existing political, economic, and cultural relations while excluding the life circumstances and cultural expressions of women, people of color, the poor, and other marginalized groups/communities. To illustrate, Speakout Intermediate (first edition), a well-known English textbook published by Longman in 2011, had a unit called 'Millionaires.' This unit presents an image of a middle-aged White man's face with his skull, half-open, spouting materialistic images such as a fancy sports car, a gold watch and a ring, a yacht, diamonds, a bar of gold, and a jet plane. In the second edition of this textbook, published in 2015, Longman kept the reading text as was but replaced the visual content with an image of a young, wealthy, handsome man in a suit, with a diamond ring and an expensive watch in the foreground and a tropical island in the background. The imagery used in both editions exemplifies the role of textbooks in constructing a social reality that enfranchises capitalism, paternalism, and White supremacy (Song, 2013; Shardakova and Pavlenko, 2004).

Textbooks and other curricular materials "are a rather salient source of vetted identity options for language learning students" (Paiz, 2017, p. 4). In other words, as Auerbach and Burgess (1987) have argued, "[b]eyond *describing* an oversimplified reality, texts often *prescribe* particular roles for students" (p. 158, original emphasis). For instance, in Risager's (2021) study, only one of the analyzed textbooks, *A piece of cake*, had a short comment on homosexuality in a non-fiction text based on Oscar Wilde's life. The same book, however, failed to engage with sexism, genderism, ableism, and racism in the US or the UK. In addition to (mis) representing different countries, aspects of world history, and cultural and social identities, textbooks also have the potential to (re)construct and mediate imagined identities and imagined interlocutors in the target language and culture. In their analysis of Russian beginner-level textbooks, Shardakova and Pavlenko (2004) found the imaginary Russian learner to be a "heterosexual White middle-class male who goes to Russia to experience titillating adventures and perhaps even to 'educate the natives'" and their possible interlocutors to be mostly "White middle-class men, as well as women who constitute romantic interests and supportive characters" (p. 43). The authors further argue that:

> Misrepresentation, stereotyping, and oversimplification of these imaginary worlds could lead to cross-cultural miscommunication, frustration, offence, and conflict, as well as to resistance from students in cases where their own linguistic and cultural values come into conflict with those imposed on them by the texts. (p. 28)

Several scholars have argued that today's teachers are more informed and critical about material evaluation and textbook selection and can refuse to consume the ideological content they are prescribed by center-based publishing industries (Apple, 1990; Bori, 2018; Canagarajah, 1993; Gray, 2010; Taylor-Mendes, 2009; Tomlinson, 2012). Nevertheless, underlining the nature of textbooks as economic commodities, Kumaravadivelu (2016) has criticized this line of research:

> I do not see how "oppositional readings" or marginal doodles can make any difference to the commercial bonanza or the ideological agenda or the dominating agency of center-based textbook industries. After all, even if they are put to subversive use, textbooks have to be prescribed by teachers and bought by learners in the first place. When they do that, it is "mission accomplished" for the publication industry. (p. 75)

In that sense, there is certainly a need for more localized textbooks that contradict publishing companies' interests; provide culturally responsive materials that will also promote global citizenship and intercultural learning; challenge native speaker norms; and dismantle the existing power relations in the society at large (Alptekin, 2002; Bori, 2021; Risager, 2021; Shin, Eslami, and Chen, 2011; Tajeddin and Teimournezhad, 2015). Identity-focused pedagogies can be helpful to challenge these prescribed forms of identities presented in language textbooks (Fisher et al., 2020; Schachter and Rich, 2011). Language education materials that include a variety of learner identities will not only help learners to develop awareness of their multilingual/multicultural identities but also enable them to reconceptualize their future selves and investments.

Textbooks as cultural artifacts

Language textbooks have been traditionally perceived as a gateway into the target language community by representing 'native speakers'' ways of being and ways of acting through thematic chapters that reduce culture to holidays, cuisine, eating habits, leisurely activities, families, and friends (Canale, 2016; Clarke and Clarke, 1990; Alptekin, 1993; Gray, 2010; Shin et al., 2011; Vinall and Shin, 2019). This essentialized, homogenous, and knowledge-oriented view of culture ignores the many ways in which culture involves complex and intricate "social and political relationships informed by history as well as by race, ethnicity, language, social class, sexual orientation, gender, and other circumstances related to identity and experience" (Nieto, 2010, p. 9).

Language textbooks employ politics of exclusion *and* inclusion to convey a homogenous view of different cultures (Canale, 2016). *Politics of exclusion* avoid any aspects of cultural diversity, for instance, depicting Latin Americans as light-skinned while erasing other racial or ethnic groups who are not part of the White culture. *Politics of inclusion*, on the other hand, reflect diversity *between* cultures rather than *within* a particular culture. That is, cultural diversity and representation is reduced to products (e.g., books, landmarks, music, food, and art), practices (e.g., social interactions), and perspectives (e.g., attitudes, values, and ideas). This framework perceives culture as simplistic, static, predictable, and neutral in terms of objects, artifacts, and behaviors with the help of which cultural comparisons can take place in terms of what learners do/have in their own culture versus what *others* do/have and not (Kubota, 2003; Canale, 2016). As Canale (2016) argues, "comparisons between 'our' homogeneous culture and 'their' homogeneous culture tend to reinforce mono-dimensional and stereotypical comparisons of everyday practices" (p. 240). Cultural meanings are conveyed with pictures, stories, and dialogues that might misalign with or contradict language learners' life conditions and experiences.

In one of the earliest studies on textbook evaluation, Clarke and Clarke (1990) discussed how intentional and unintentional inclusion and exclusion of cultural elements in ESL textbooks used in the United Kingdom reinforced racial, gender, and class-based stereotypes and prejudice. In Brazil, the "made-in

Hollywood version of culture" (p. 77) represented in the EFL textbooks led to impressions of the US as a country of White, wealthy elites and of Black folks as poor and powerless (Taylor-Mendes, 2009). In Korean textbooks, information about students' own and other cultures were based on stereotypes around the Eiffel Tower, Christmas, kebab and baklava, and traditional clothing (Vinall and Shin, 2019). Especially with the influence of globalization and neoliberalism, the tourist approach to multicultural education – as discussed in Chapter 3 – has also become predominant in language textbooks. In Cook's (2003) analysis of English, Italian, and French textbooks, the most common themes were tourism, tourist attractions, and making plans and arrangements for activities such as parties, shopping, and dealing with hotels, illustrating language textbooks' role as the "advertising arm of the tourist industry" (Clarke and Clarke, 1990, p. 42). Vinall and Shin's (2019) study, on the other hand, focused on how the 'tourist gaze' presented in EFL textbooks approved by the South Korean government contributed to the construction of Koreanness and the construction of global citizenship. Their findings revealed the ways in which English textbooks simultaneously positioned language learners as tourists *and* tour guides and presented English as "a passport to travel everywhere" (p. 177). This touristic, consumerist approach was not limited to the images and content of the textbook but extended to the lingua-pragmatic functions language learners were expected to attain. Language learners were often exposed to conversations on 'light' subjects such as 'the weather' accompanied by formulaic expressions they could use to talk to their friends rather than engaging in deeper conversations (e.g., discussing different values and beliefs regarding friendships) (Vinall and Shin, 2019).

Box 4.4 Problem-posing task

Using the critical framework provided in Appendix 4.2 for materials evaluation and adaptation, examine a language textbook you use in your classes, or one that you are familiar with. To what extent does the textbook support a social justice language curriculum and how can it be adapted to make it more in line?

There are several strategies language teachers can adopt in order to avoid binary conceptualizations and comparisons of 'us versus them' and 'similarities versus differences.' Language textbooks can be adapted or supplemented with additional materials that represent cultural diversity not only *between* cultures but also *within* cultures. Appendix 4.2, in fact, provides a critical framework for the evaluation and adaptation of materials that language educators can use by reflecting on one's own pedagogical purposes, contexts, learners, curriculum, and the wider community. Regardless of the material at hand, it is also important that both language educators and learners adopt a dynamic, fluid, constructed, and transformed view of culture influenced by historical, political, and ideological forces (Kubota, 2003;

Canale, 2016). Learners, then, should be encouraged to critically reflect on the "sociocultural and sociopolitical realities of the culture in question" (Canale, 2016, p. 240) in ways that can help develop their critical cultural awareness.

Reconstructing materials as tools to develop learners' critical literacy

Language learners, instead of passively decoding pre-established meanings (Canale, 2016), can actively contest the representations and ideologies textbooks aim to reproduce by bringing their own background to the text and constructing their own meanings. Therefore, language educators should seek ways to avoid a 'textbook-equals-curriculum' approach, acknowledge the ways texts and textbooks operate in social, economic, and political contexts, and move towards an "understanding of how texts and discourses can be constructed, deconstructed and reconstructed to represent, contest and indeed, transform material, social and semiotic relations" (Luke and Dooley, 2011, pp. 856–857). Developing learners' critical literacy, thus, plays a paramount role in providing opportunities to deconstruct the hegemonic ideologies embedded in texts and to develop their critical consciousness, and in language educators' work towards social justice, equity, and social change. Drawing on Althusser and Gramsci, Janks (2010) explains critical literacy as an emancipatory project:

> Part of the work of critical literacy is to make these workings of power visible, to denaturalise 'common sense' assumptions (Gramsci, 1971) and to reveal them as constructed representations of the social order, serving the interests of some at the expense of others. (p. 36)

Critical literacy encompasses all kinds of paper-based, digital, and multimodal texts (e.g., aural, textual, visual, animated, spatial, gestural, and kinesthetic). Hence, the term 'literacy' loses its traditional sense of capabilities related to reading and writing print text since its meaning extends to multiliteracies, a term that underlines "the multiplicity of communications channels and media" (Cope and Kalantzis, 2000, p. 5). In other words, critical literacy not only allows language learners to interrogate all kinds of print, multimodal, and digital texts for assumptions and values that promote hegemonic ideologies but also allows them to develop their critical consciousness, agency, and capacity for social change. As Kubota (2016) further elaborates:

> critical literacy raises learners' awareness of how various linguistic and discursive means in texts (e.g., choices of modality, lexical item, discourse marker, nominalization, passive or active voice, genre) mediate the production of particular knowledge (Freire & Macedo, 2013; Luke, 2000). It encourages the learners to employ critical awareness to actively read and write for social change. (p. 193)

When used critically, textbooks – like almost any text – have the potential to engage learners in an analysis of real-world problems that have an impact on their economic, political, social, and cultural realities (Apple, 1992). A good starting point for all language educators in that sense is to ask themselves how to "design classroom environments in which learners can understand textbook discourse as a genre which operates socially, historically and ideologically, and not as the accumulation of incontestable factual (verbal and visual) evidence about language and culture" (Canale, 2016, p. 240). To give an example, one of the ways language teachers can bring social justice issues into their language classrooms and promote their learners' critical literacy is through commonly taught vocabulary about professions presented in language textbooks. Some of the questions that can be raised in classroom discussions are "What professions are taught? What do the visual representations used in the textbook, on posters, on worksheets, or on visual flash cards say about who typically works in each profession?" (Glynn et al., 2014, p. 7). Critically examining the professions presented both in terms of the verbal and non-verbal content would allow a discussion on which professions are privileged in a society, which ones have more inferior or superior status, and which identities are represented as doing what. As Kubota (2010) suggests, "teachers need to raise students' critical awareness of racial, gender, and class representations in textbooks and other materials and engage them in discussions of the discursive construction and sociopolitical consequences of these images" (p. 108). Thus, reconstructing texts by examining how race, gender, sexuality, disability, and social class interact with (un)employment, salaries, poverty, and wealth will not only help develop learners' critical literacy but also debunk the already existing stereotypes and challenge the status quo in the society at large.

> **Box 4.5   Reflective task**
> Despite all the criticisms they have received, textbooks and other commercially produced materials are likely to remain. How can you as a language educator fight the tyranny of textbooks in your educational context? How can you raise learners' awareness and critical literacy in ways that can contribute to social change?

Conclusion

Language professionals who acknowledge the political nature of language education "use all languages to decolonize minds, so as to facilitate equitable dialogue and to counteract occupation, physical and mental" (Phillipson, 2008, p. 40). A social justice language curriculum, therefore, can not only help

language teachers disrupt the deficit ideologies regarding minority populations, immigrants, and those who are under-represented and marginalized
but also challenge hegemonic ideologies in the world by drawing on language
learners' talents, strengths, funds of knowledge, and cultural capital (Cummins,
2009).

In this chapter, I focused on four main strategies language teachers can adopt
and adapt in order to situate social justice at the center of their language education programs. These were (1) centralizing social justice within lesson planning,
(2) cultivating activism for change and transformation through social action projects, (3) deconstructing materials as commercial, ideological tools, and cultural
artifacts, and (4) reconstructing materials to develop learners' critical literacy.
This is neither a prescriptive list of strategies nor an exhaustive one. These four
were chosen for this book because they addressed the core elements of a language
curriculum: lesson planning, materials, and praxis. The next three chapters in
Part II will delve into the critical themes of this book: social class, race and
ethnicity, and gender and sexual identities. These chapters will not only unpack
the conceptual issues related to these critical themes but also present how the four
strategies mentioned in this chapter can inform the discussion of these issues in
language classrooms.

Note

1. The objectives presented here come from Kalina Swanson's lesson plan that
   was submitted as an assignment in the Social Justice Language Teaching
   course offered at Middlebury Institute of International Studies at Monterey
   in Fall 2020. The lesson plan was designed for an advanced level Reading and
   Writing course offered at an Intensive English Program at the tertiary level.
   Kalina currently works as a manager at an educational organization called
   NewGlobe.

Multimedia resources

Center for Media Literacy
   http://www.medialit.org
      Center for Media Literacy offers publicly available courses (currently in
      English, Spanish, and Lithuanian) on media literacy to raise informed
      citizens in this complex, global media environment.
Films for Action
   https://www.filmsforaction.org/
      Since its founding in 2006, Films For Action has curated more than 1,000
      documentaries and 4,000 short films – all free for everyone who wants to
      change the world.

American Council on the Teaching of Foreign Languages (ACTFL)
> https://www.actfl.org/resources/resources-language-educators-address-issues-race-diversity-and-social-justice
>> ACTFL provides lots of resources for language teachers as well as links to other platforms that address issues of race, diversity, and social justice.

Children's books

Nagaro, I. (2013). *A is for activist*. Triangle Square.
> This lovely board book – also available in Spanish – introduces children to the alphabet of ethical values, social awareness, and activism.

Tonatiuh, D. (2014). *Separate is never equal: Sylvia Mendez and her family's fight for desegregation*. Abrams Books for Young Readers.
> Seven years before the landmark *Brown* v. *Board of Education* decision of 1954, the Chicano Mendez family fought for their children to attend school with White children in Westminster, CA. This is the story of how their efforts led to the desegregation of California's schools in 1947.

Part II

Critical themes and frameworks

Chapter 5

Neoliberalism, social class, and anti-classism

Box 5.1 Lead-in
In her book, *Where we stand: Class matters*, bell hooks (2000) mentions that:

> [My mostly white neighbors in Greenwich Village, New York City] are social liberals and fiscal conservatives. They may believe in recognizing multiculturalism and celebrating diversity (our neighborhood is full of white gay men and straight white people who have at least one black, Asian, or Hispanic friend), but when it comes to money and class they want to protect what they have, to perpetuate and reproduce it – they want more. The fact that they have so much while others have so little does not cause moral anguish, for they see their good fortune as a sign they are chosen, special, deserving. (p. 3)

To what extent do you talk about poverty, universal basic income, and universal health care with your friends, families, colleagues, or students? Do you think social class is an unpopular subject in comparison to race, ethnicity, gender, and sexuality? What factors contribute to the erasure of class while other issues of inequality, oppression, and discrimination have come to the fore?

Introduction

This chapter aims to introduce the role of political economy in language education and applied linguistics. Regardless of Gal's (1989) and Irvine's (1989) initial calls for applied linguistics research to situate itself within political economy in order to underline the interplay of linguistic and economic phenomena, language education scholars and applied linguists have engaged more widely with issues around race, ethnicity, gender, and sexuality than with class, and in ways that often ignore the role of political economy in these issues themselves. It is only very recently that language education scholars have started to discuss neoliberalism, capitalism, and social class with the aim of understanding the distribution of linguistic and economic resources, as well as the material and symbolic value of languages, particularly of English (Badwan, 2021; Block, 2012a, 2014, 2018; Block et al., 2012; Heller, 2010b; Rampton et al., 2007; O'Regan, 2021; Ricento, 2015a). This chapter therefore aims to help language educators – who may have had less exposure to issues around social class, especially as opposed to issues relating to race, ethnicity, gender and sexuality – understand the concept and its relevance to their professional and personal lives, as well as its intersections with other forms of oppression.

In particular, the following issues are discussed in detail in this chapter:

- Political economy and neoliberalism
- Conceptualizing class: Karl Marx and Pierre Bourdieu
- Classism, intersectionality, and immigration
- Neoliberalism, social class, and language education
- An anti-classist, anti-neoliberal framework to dismantle classism

The chapter's final section presents a framework designed to help language educators analyze elements of classism embedded in their own language teaching activities and materials, and to work towards eliminating them. Because social class and economic injustice have been relatively neglected within language education and applied linguistics, this anti-classist, anti-neoliberal framework offers a more focused tool and more immediate takeaways than the more general strategies offered in the two following chapters, relating to race and ethnicity (Chapter 6) and to gender and sexual identities (Chapter 7). Based on Block's (2018) constellation of interrelated class dimensions, it is placed just before these latter chapters to encourage readers to keep in mind how deeply issues of gender, sexual identity, race, and ethnicity are informed and inflected by questions of social class and political economy.

Political economy and neoliberalism

As an interdisciplinary field that draws on philosophy, sociology, anthropology, political and social sciences, education, geography, and communication studies, political economy refers to the political, social, and cultural inquiry into economic phenomena. Political economy, in general, aims to understand how the policies and practices of social institutions (e.g., education, health, and criminal justice systems) interact with neoliberal and global capitalism at individual, societal, national, and global market levels (Block, 2014, 2018).

According to many cultural analysts, many of the inequalities and forms of oppression that exist in the world today are not the result of a multiplicity of separate dysfunctions but are interconnected and ultimately have a common derivation: neoliberalism, which is often considered a more globalized and enhanced form of capitalism. Neoliberalism's precise genealogy is disputed, but it is commonly associated with economic doctrines that became dominant in the 1980s in Britain under Prime Minister Margaret Thatcher and in the USA under President Ronald Reagan (Harvey, 2005). Thatcher's and Reagan's governments promoted private ownership, the 'free market' and individual choice while attacking nationalized public ownership (of, for example, housing and transportation) and other social democratic policies. Extending the 'laissez-faire' economics of a certain brand of nineteenth-century liberalism, neoliberalism transformed itself into an institutionalized social order that, for its critics, exacerbates and perpetuates social and economic inequality across the globe (Chomsky, 1998; Fraser, 2019; Giroux, 2008; Harvey, 2005, 2020).

As an ideology with specific sets of economic and cultural policies and practices, neoliberalism serves to justify and maintain existing power structures and a status quo that elevates a global economic elite of transnational corporations (TNCs), bankers, financiers, bureaucrats, and politicians (Block, 2018; Giroux, 2008; Harvey, 2005, 2020; Steger and Roy, 2010). Neoliberalism not only entails hegemonic and dominant processes of capital circulation and accumulation (e.g., economic policies and practices) but also shapes the cultural and social spheres (e.g., socio-cultural and ethical beliefs, norms, and practices) (Harvey, 2014). This socio-cultural, economic, and political impact of neoliberalism on the societies can be explained in terms of two overlapping processes: roll back and roll out. *Roll back* involves processes of deregulation and the corporatization of economic and business activities (e.g., free markets and free trade); reducing government control and regulation through privatization and cutbacks in infrastructure and public services in areas such as education, transportation, housing, and health; increasing global trade and financial markets in the form of global flows of goods, services, and labor; and reducing labor costs through outsourcing and part-time employment and removing or limiting the power of organized labor (e.g., the right to strike) (Block, 2018; Steger, 2017). However, as Harvey (2020) argues, neoliberalism's roll back measures for 'reduced government control' have only meant a shift from supporting people through health care, education, and social services, to supporting capital.

These roll back policies promote "the cutthroat downsizing of the workforce, the bleeding of social services, the reduction of state governments to police precincts, the ongoing liquidation of job security, the increasing elimination of a decent social wage, the creation of a society of low-skilled workers, and the emergence of a culture of permanent insecurity and fear" (Giroux, 2008, p. 7). *Roll out*, then, refers to the processes and strategies that arise in order to compensate for the gaps in basic public and social services and infrastructure resulting from roll back – that is, from the reduction and even elimination of certain forms of public expenditure (Block, 2018; Steger, 2017). Examples of roll out include the empowerment of charities, community organizations and NGOs; the promotion of skills development programs for the unemployed; and the offering of subsidies to families by private initiatives and NGOs. These are just some of the measures put into place in order to reduce the state's responsibility for the consequences of unemployment or low wages (Giroux, 2008).

In summary, the role of the state in a neoliberal system is to secure private property rights, to liberate and reinforce individual entrepreneurship, and to develop and ensure the smooth functioning of the market in areas such as housing, water, education, health care, and social security (Harvey, 2005). Yet neoliberalism is a "variegated phenomenon" (Block, 2018, p. 51) that can be perceived as an amalgam of both global and local ideologies governing economic policies and practices. Therefore, neoliberalism may not display itself in the same way in every context and local forms do emerge based on various social, historical, cultural, geographical, and political characteristics.

Social class

The field of political economy has been long concerned with class-based inequalities that derive from resource allocation, capital accumulation, and income inequality grounded in neoliberal and global economic activity (Block, 2012a, 2014). As Harvey (2020) states, neoliberalism is "always defined as a class project, a project to accumulate wealth and power within a small elite class" (p. 14). Social class, as "a mode of social differentiation that is rooted in the political-economic structure of society" (Fraser, 1995, p. 75), however, is a complex issue to define and discuss (Block, 2012a, 2014; hooks, 2000; Sayer, 2002). For some, the very notion of class is divisive or no longer relevant, while others have an instinctive understanding of class structures and can talk in nuanced ways about their own positions within those structures.

According to Fraser (1995), "A class only exists as a collectivity by virtue of its position in that structure and of its relation to other classes" (p. 75). In other words, class is about individuals' and groups' relative standing in social relations and one's class position can only be discussed in reference to others (i.e., the position of upper class only makes sense in relation to the middle or working classes). This aspect of class as relative standing, however, has also led to a confusing proliferation of models for understanding and analyzing class. Marx's fundamentally two-part model of class stratification within capitalism, consisting of the bourgeoisie and the proletariat, has largely been replaced or obscured in the popular understanding by more ill-defined, one-dimensional, lay notions such as 'upper, middle, and lower class' or 'upper, middle, and working class' (Block, 2014). This is partly because Marx's own writings on class are challenging, while the academic theorizing about class that emerges out of much twentieth- and twenty-first-century Marxism is frequently even more opaque. Other models for thinking about socio-economic stratification, especially those emerging out of fields such as market research, have also influenced, and further muddied, public discourse about class (in the British context, for example, the National Readership Survey social grades, with their A/B/C1/C2/D/E classification system, based on occupation rather than property ownership or wealth).

Class can, therefore, seem a muddled, unhelpful concept, and is often passed over or marginalized by those eager to promote social justice in favor of a focus on race, gender, and sexuality. Yet as this chapter will argue, class plays an absolutely central role in cementing the injustices of neoliberalism. Failing to give proper consideration to class and to the economic factors that underpin it can fundamentally undermine well-intentioned attempts to promote social justice in the language classroom. Worse still, they can render them complicit in the very injustices they aim to challenge. The following sections, therefore, will discuss Marxist and Bourdieusian understandings of social class in ways to help language educators understand social class in regard to various economic, political, social, and cultural power relations that derive from patterns of production, distribution, exchange, and consumption existing at different layers of society.

Marxist and Bourdieusian understandings of social class

According to Anyon (2011), "Capitalism, in Marx's terms, is an economic system based on private ownership of the means of production" (p. 7). Human labor, the process "by which man, through his own actions, mediates, regulates and controls the metabolism between himself and the nature" (Marx, 1990, p. 283), therefore, lies at the heart of the Marxist understanding of social class. Within capitalist societies, working class refers to those who must sell their labor-power under the tacit agreement that those who control the means of production, that is the capitalist class, will be the ones benefitting from the surplus (Fraser, 1995). As Marx and Engels ([1848] 2008) state in the *The communist manifesto*, "The bourgeoisie cannot exist without constantly revolutionising the instruments of production, and thereby the relations of production, and with them the whole relations of society" (p. 35). The Marxist understanding of class, thus, revolves around the idea that "societies are divided in such a way that individuals live under different economic conditions, which in turn give rise to different ways of behavior and thought, and ultimately lifestyles in different cultures" (Block, 2014, p. 28).

Marx's distinction between base and superstructure is crucial to examine the ways in which the production, regulation, and distribution of the goods and services are managed and controlled in ways that impact not only the economic but also the socio-cultural circumstances of a society (Block, 2018). In Marxist understanding of social class, base refers to the economic base of a society that is "constituted by the organization of production in that society, that is, the activity engaged in to satisfy basic needs (food cultivation, cattle raising, factory-based commodity production, etc.)" (Block, 2014, p. 28). Superstructure, on the other hand, is about the social relations that derive from an individual's relationship to the means of production. Superstructure composes the social, political, and intellectual domains of a society, which ultimately rest upon and derive from the economic base. The role of a state emerges from this distinction since the state, being the legal and political superstructure of a society, "serves as a guarantor of the class-based status quo which emerges from the organization of production" (Block, 2014, p. 29).

While acknowledging the importance of economic states and processes (e.g., income and occupation), Bourdieu's (1984) conceptualization of class diverges from the Marxist model of class in the significance it attaches to various social and cultural practices. Bourdieu's model has been influential across the humanities and social sciences, including language education and applied linguistics research, and has played a significant if also problematic role in thinking about social class. For Bourdieu, economic capital (i.e., material resources in the form of income and wealth) cannot provide a sufficient explanation for the class-based inequalities that exist in societies. He points to the various opaque and often seemingly arbitrary entry requirements to elite society, for example, those around sports such as golf, skiing, and sailing. Merely having the required economic capital to take part in these activities is often not enough to win access, even if it can pay for the necessary club memberships. Instead, as Bourdieu (1984) notes, "there are more hidden entry requirements such as family tradition and early training, or obligatory manner (of dress and behavior), and socializing techniques, which keep these sports closed to the working class" (p. 217). Those who would join the elite have to establish their legitimacy by complying with these hidden (or at least implicit) rules and practices, which function to maintain the status quo.

Bourdieu expanded Marx's concept of *capital* from the solely economic to include broader socio-cultural aspects of human life. In particular, Bourdieu proposed four forms[1] of capital that relate to social class: economic, symbolic, cultural, and social (Apple, 2019; Bourdieu, 1990; Skegg, 1997). *Economic capital* corresponds to the Marxist understanding of capital, including monetary assets and inheritances, income, wealth, and so on. According to Bourdieu (2005), *symbolic capital* "resides in the mastery of symbolic resources based on knowledge and recognition, such as 'goodwill investment', 'brand loyalty', etc.; as a power which functions as a form of credit, it presupposes the trust or belief of those upon whom it bears" (p. 195). *Cultural capital* refers to accumulated and legitimized cultural knowledge, skills, and know-how, and is acquired through education and socialization. Cultural capital can take embodied form (e.g., language knowledge, accent, gestures), objectified form (e.g., books, paintings, music), and institutional form (e.g., academic qualifications such as degrees and certifications). Although all class cultures (i.e., the norms, values, and traditions shared by those within a similar class) have their own forms of cultural capital, they are ranked and valued differently in terms of their attributed worth and status (Adams et al., 2016). Lastly, *social capital* is built upon one's economic and cultural capital and extends to the development of social relations such as institutionalized relationships, group memberships, networks and connections, as well as recognitions from others (Bourdieu, 1986, 2005). Often associated with the social networks of the privileged such as rotary clubs and elite memberships, social capital can also derive from family, friends, and neighborhoods that poor and working-class people rely on for childcare, down payments, housing, and so forth (Adams et al., 2016). There is, therefore, a mutual relationship between one's economic, social, and cultural capital. While it is true that one's economic and cultural capital provide access to various social networks and memberships, the social capital gained through the recognition offered by these networks also develops and sustains one's economic and cultural capital.

Bourdieu's conceptualization of capital has been very helpful in understanding the social, cultural, and economic experiences of immigrant populations. Even though every socio-cultural group has its own cultural capital, not having access to the cultural capital of the dominant and privileged groups can be problematic for immigrant populations in a new society since this type of information allows one to navigate social institutions such as health care, the tax system, education, and the courts. In that sense, education, which Bourdieu (1986) refers to as institutionalized cultural capital, is an important class index and a commodity that can be traded for further education or better employment opportunities. However, Block (2014) cautions that education as academic capital may not always lead to economic advantages (e.g., an academic with a PhD in the UK might be making less than a successful interior decorator) and thus education as cultural capital should be separated from education as economic capital.

Bourdieu's framework has been employed by many scholars in applied linguistics and language education, especially in relation to teacher and learner identities, language socialization, and the integration of cultural elements into language teaching (Darvin and Norton, 2014; Wong and Grant, 2007; Gunderson, 2007; Heller, 2001; Ortaçtepe, 2012). So influential has his work in these disciplines been that language educators are likely to be more familiar with his theories of capital than with those of Marx. But Bourdieu's work has been widely challenged by scholars working in the Marxist tradition for foregrounding the cultural and symbolic at the expense of engagement with the brutal, shaping realities of the economic capital. Bourdieu's critics note that although his use of the term capital is derived from the Marxist theory and his framework itself on market metaphors, it conflates the material aspects of capital with questions of status (Block, 2018; Harvey, 2005). To compound matters, any meaningful economic analysis is missing from Bourdieu's framework (Holborow, 2015). Bourdieu's relative lack of engagement with political economy and global capitalist ideology has been criticized for allowing "symbolic dominance to take the lead in establishing and reproducing the prevailing neoliberal social order" (Holborow, 2015, p. 60). The next sections, therefore, revisit the politics of recognition and redistribution discussed in Chapter 1 in order to underline the importance of an intersectional class struggle, especially in the lives of immigrant populations.

> **Box 5.2 Problem-posing task**
> In the article, *Documenting reproduction and inequality*, Luke (2015) argues that:
>
> > class is not a stand-alone determination, but works in relationship to gender, ethnicity/race, affiliated culture and subcultural context, linguistic disposition, and sexual preference of student *[sic]*. It is always a factor in the formation of background knowledge and capacity via the differential uptake as student habitus for exchange value in the field of the classroom. But, like race and gender, it is never "stand alone." (p. 176)
>
> How does social class intersect with other identity markers in shaping the lived experiences of yourself, your students, families, and friends?

Intersectional class struggle and immigration

Despite the widening economic inequalities in many countries since the 1980s, other axes of inequality and difference such as gender, race, sexuality, and disability have rightfully gained prominence, while their recognition has come at the expense of class (Malott, 2011; Sayer, 2005). Just like race, gender, and sexual identities, class is a source of stigmatization and discrimination. Yet class is not addressed within identity politics (i.e., politics of recognition) since there is little that identity politics can do to reduce income inequalities as long as human beings live in a class-based society governed by neoliberalism.

Fraser (2019) attributes this shift from politics of redistribution to identity politics to the view of progressive neoliberalism, which refers to the combination of a free market system and mainstream liberal-meritocratic social movements that show interest in feminism, environmentalism, multiculturalism, antiracism, and LGBTQ+ rights, to name a few. Supporters of neoliberalism argue for its role in economic growth, technological innovation, scientific advancement, and overall, the realization of a better world. Neoliberalism also promotes a meritocratic ideology; that is, with hard work and effort anyone can achieve these resources and if they do not, it is because they did not work hard enough or they lacked the necessary entrepreneurial skills and self-branding. Therefore, one of the goals of progressive neoliberalism has been to diversify the social hierarchy by "ensuring that 'deserving' individuals from 'under-represented groups' can attain positions and pay on a par with the straight white men of their own class" (Fraser, 2019, p. 13).

Given that the neoliberal economy, by relying on inequalities of resources, income, wealth, and political rights, threatens the living standards of the vast majority, it "couldn't be sold politically at face value," and therefore, "required some window-dressing" (Fraser, 2019, p. 38). Harvey (2020) explains this window-dressing as follows:

> The 1960s had seen a very strong movement of people wanting individual liberty, and freedom, and also social justice. That movement of the '68 generation, if you want to call it that, was antagonistic to what capital was about. The response of capital was to say "We give you the individual liberty, and we value the individual liberty too, and we will structure things around individual liberty, particularly in the market, so that you get lots of freedom of choice in the market. But the bargain is that you forget about the social justice. (p. 18)

In other words, neoliberal policies protect the ruling class by justifying social positions and class (in)equalities that allegedly derive from (the lack of) individual merits (Adams et al., 2016; Block, 2014; Collins, 2006; Giroux, 2008; Mann and Grimes, 2001; Rampton et al., 2007; Sayer, 2005). The progressive politics of recognition that idealize diversity, empowerment, and multiculturalism, while making real and important gains, has also created a hollow version of equality – as already discussed in relation to multicultural education in Chapter 3. Therefore, for Fraser and others, the way to overcome class inequality is not through recognition but through redistribution and the regulation of economic activities through means such as minimum wage legislation, universal health care, employment rights, and progressive taxation.

Despite these tensions between the politics of recognition and the politics of redistribution, various scholars have agreed that social class, just like race and gender, *is* related to identity. Social class is not only "about being in the world – about who we are" (Block, 2018, p. 93), but also "always entangled with other forms of social being and social consciousness" (Rampton et al., 2007, p. 72). Classism, which refers to beliefs, policies, and practices based on which individuals receive differential treatment according to their social class, is often combined with other forms of bias, oppression, and discrimination and "produce[s] situations of double jeopardy" (Smith and Redington, 2010, p. 182) for poor women, poor people of color, poor LGBTQ+ youth, and poor people with disabilities. Therefore, class needs to be analyzed in relation to other identity markers such as race, ethnicity, gender, sexuality, disability. In his introduction to the 2008 edition of the *Communist manifesto*, Harvey has written about the importance of an intersectional class struggle as follows:

> to the degree that capitalists can distract attention from their own perfidious role in the ruthless exploitation of labour power in the workshops of production, by blaming immigrants, foreign competition and the 'uncivilised' habits of despised others for all the problems that local workers face, so the prospective

unity of the working classes is rendered far more difficult. The divide and rule tactics of exploiting not only national but also ethnic, gender and religious differences within the working classes take an inevitable toll and all too often end up fomenting and even entrenching a politics of exclusions rather than of incorporation into a global dynamic of class struggle. (pp. 14–15)

The migrant farm workers of California, one of the groups most severely affected by the COVID-19 pandemic, offer one US-based example of the ways in which intersectionality manifests itself within class struggle. According to a report published by the California Institute of Rural Studies (2020), farm workers, the majority of them Latinx, were three times more likely to contract COVID-19 than other workers. In Monterey County, California, 77 percent of those tested positive for COVID-19 by November 2020 were Hispanic/Latinx, and agriculture was the most affected industry with 21 percent of those working in that sector contracting COVID-19. While the pandemic has illustrated the intersectionality of class, race, and environmental justice, the efforts to contain the pandemic have also exemplified the systemic discrimination against farm workers in California. Perhaps the most emblematic example of this classist racism – or racist classism – came from an emergency flyer designed by Ventura County in California, with two versions in English and Spanish. The English version showed two people (whose facial and bodily features were drawn in detail) separated by a ski, with an accompanying text warning that said: "6 feet is about the length of skis." The Spanish version of this flier was almost the same as the English one, except the two people were not presented in detail but presented as silhouettes, and the image of the ski was replaced by an illustration of three vegetable crates. The message was: "6 pies (2 metros) es la distancia de 3 cajas de verduras," translating as "6 feet (2 meters) is three crates of vegetables." Although the flyer was quickly removed by the county in the face of withering criticism, the issue was approached purely from a racial perspective, rather than being seen as also one of social class. The pandemic and its repercussions have shown once again the need for more intersectional and transformative frameworks in order to fight cultural, societal, and economic inequalities by "combining egalitarian redistribution with nonhierarchical recognition" (Fraser, 2008, p. 24).

Neoliberalism, social class, and language education

There are myriad studies that underline the complicity of educational institutions in class differences (Anyon, 1981, 2011; Apple, 2006; Bourdieu and Passeron, 1991; Carpenter and Mojab, 2011, 2017; Weis, 2016). According to Holborow (2015), "education, now an enabler of human capital development, becomes the crucial driver of the economy, a power-house of economic potentiality from which anything non-functional, not measurable in monetary terms or not immediately economically useful, is expelled" (p. 16). The privatization of education, high-stakes tests that are increasingly run by corporations, the standardization of curricula, and the gradual decrease in teacher autonomy and agency can be seen as the inequitable forces of a neoliberal system. The differences between private versus public schools and urban versus rural schools, and the likelihood that students of similar socio-economic backgrounds attend similar schools, are only some of the factors that reproduce class status by socializing younger generations into inferior or superior positions in the capitalist world.

Box 5.3 Problem-posing task

Torres' (2006) book chapter entitled, 'Schooling, power, and the exile of the soul,' discusses the role of schooling in reproducing hegemonic ideologies as follows:

> Schooling reproduces authoritarian, classist, racist, homophobic, and patriarchal relationships in capitalist societies. This is the result of the authoritarianism of administrators and school bureaucrats and is compounded by the authoritarianism of parents, politicians, and the authoritarianism of knowledge production, distribution, exchange, and consumption once it's defined as 'official knowledge. (p. 51)

Given this quotation, what kind of influence do you think neoliberalism has on language education? How does this influence manifest itself in an educational context you are familiar with?

Just as educational policies and practices are marked by neoliberal policies, applied linguistics and language education are also closely linked to political economy. According to Irvine (1989), one of the first scholars to bridge the gap between sociolinguistics and political economy, "[T]he allocation of resources, the coordination of production, and the distribution of goods and services, seen (as they must be) in political perspective, involve linguistic forms and verbal practices in many ways" (p. 249). In a paper published within the same year as Irvine (1989), Gal (1989) investigated the interplay of language structure, language use, and political economy. Notwithstanding these early attempts in applied linguistics, relatively few scholars stand out for integrating class and political economy into their research (Bale, 2015; Block, 2007, 2012a; Block et al., 2012; Bruthiaux, 2008; Collins, 2006; Ramanathan and Morgan, 2009; Rampton et al., 2007; Ricento, 2015a; Vandrick, 2014). This lack of engagement with political economy has even been described as threatening to undermine applied linguists' credibility as scholars supposedly concerned with real-world language issues and "the social injustices they so rightly deplore" (Bruthiaux, 2008, p. 20). In fact, several researchers have argued that only a political economy approach can help understand the role of neoliberal policies in the trajectories of global and non-global languages and the maintenance of minority languages, cultures, and multilingualism (Ricento, 2015a). More interdisciplinary research which connects language, communication, and political economy has been called for in order to open up new paths of inquiry within applied linguistics research (Block, 2018; Pennycook, 2022).

Within this limited body of research, a particular area of interest has been the commodification of language, an area that relates Marx's conceptualization of commodity to language and language education. The next section, therefore, first introduces the Marxist concept of commodity and then discusses – and problematizes – language-as-commodity in relation to the call center industries and edutourism, widely recognized as the two representative outcomes of the interplay of neoliberalism and the global spread of English.

Commodification of language

From a Marxist perspective, a commodity refers to a product of human labor with an exchange value at the market (Block, 2018; Holborow, 2015). Commodities cover any objectifiable, interchangeable, and measurable goods or products that have market value (i.e., money equivalence) (Ball, 2012). For Holborow (2015), commodities range "from yogurt to jeans, iPads to houses, cars to carbon emissions, kilowatts to kitchens" (p. 18). In language education, language textbooks, published readers, materials, and assessments, and even educational institutions can be considered commodities. Commodities are not limited to tangible and physical objects (including mechanically or digitally reproducible products such as movies, music, video games, software, and apps) but also extend to affective products that sell an experience or feelings of satisfaction and higher status.

Language-as-commodity has emerged as a contested topic of interest among language educators and researchers who are interested in exploring the relationship between neoliberalism and language education (Heller, 2010b; Ives, 2015; Kubota, 2011, Shin, 2014). According to Bourdieu (1977), in class-based societies, linguistic differences acquire an economic conversion rate and, as a result, perpetuate class-based inequalities. Drawing on Bourdieu, Heller (2010b) defines language-as-commodity in terms of linguistic resources that can be "produced, controlled, distributed, valued and constrained" (p. 108). Language commodification brings about questions in relation to *which* languages are considered 'legitimate' and 'commodifiable;' and *who* has the right to make these decisions, and to produce and distribute these linguistic resources (Heller, 2003, 2010a). The commodification of language is also related to the extent to which one's language skills determine the economic and social benefits they can gain at individual and national levels (Irvine, 1989; Heller, 2010b). In other words, one's language, language variety, dialect, and style may determine one's access to higher status, prestigious social networks, clubs and memberships, promotions, and other means or trappings of upward mobility. In short, "language varieties, linguistic utterances, accents, and their embodiments are all like commodities on a market – the linguistic market" (Park and Wee, 2012, p. 27). For instance, in many contexts, the de facto status of native speakerism provides a disproportionate advantage to those who acquire a language as their mother tongue as well as to those who have the means to be educated in it.

On the other hand, language-as-commodity has been approached with skepticism by Marxist applied linguists such as Block (2014) and Holborow (2007). First, as Block (2014) claims, "language is not a machine, a piece of linen, a bed sheet made from linen, or wheat, or anything else material, what Holborow (2007: 56) calls the 'real products' on which capitalist systems are dependent. And this is a problem" (p. 137). Second, language does not fit into "the Marxist sense of a product embodying the congealed labour of workers that, when sold, produces surplus value for capitalists who control the means of production" (Block, 2018, p. 14). The Marxist concept of a product is of something that a worker produces at the end of their labor, after which not only is the person who produced it alienated from it, but it also begins to serve as a tool that exercises power over them. Language commodification involves no congealed labor, and the language learner (i.e., the "buyer") might be "the hardest worker and the maximum beneficiary" (Block, 2018, p. 6). To clarify, an exchange of a commodity requires the human laborer to give up the use rights to that commodity in return for an economic gain. In the case of a t-shirt, the human labor involved in its production is concealed from the consumer, as the t-shirt is reduced to an object with a price tag and a label. A language user does not give up the rights to their language skills every time they engage in a conversation, write a document, or talk to a friend. This lack of alienation in language raises concerns regarding its identification as a commodity in anything approaching the Marxist sense of the word.

Despite these fundamental differences between the Marxist conceptualization of what a commodity is and applied linguists' understandings of language-as-commodity, several researchers have proposed a view of language as a soft communication skill that can be constructed as a measurable commodity with market value (Heller, 2003; Urciuoli, 2008). Coulmas (1992), who has been influential on the theoretical framing of language commodification, acknowledges that "like other intangible goods, the commodity language has the peculiar property that by selling it the sellers do not diminish their own stock, since, obviously, the language teacher does not lose what the student acquires" (p. 79). Instead, what is sold in linguistic markets is a service that yields a product, and that the buyer and seller play different roles than in a more tangible exchange.

Linguistic instrumentalism, which explores the "usefulness of language skills in achieving utilitarian goals" (Kubota, 2011, p. 248), requires an understanding of the concept of human capital in a neoliberal discourse where individuals are held accountable for maintaining their employability through lifelong learning. Thus, human knowledge and skills are commodified to the extent that people sell their potential to work in the labor market by competing against those with similar knowledge and skills through 'performance reports' and 'annual reviews' that ensure that they have fulfilled their economic potential. Holborow (2015) could not have put the neoliberal perspective on human capital in better words: "Neoliberalism presents all human skills as simple commodities with a price tag" (p. 20). With neoliberalism's influence on the workplace, employees have become personally responsible for their professional development, to the extent that they have become commodities themselves (Urciuoli, 2008). This process, also known as *self-commodification*, has resulted in an increased emphasis on soft skills such as communication, teamwork, and leadership. Thus, one particular area of interest in language education has been the global spread of neoliberal policies which have naturalized the use of English as an international, commodified language (Heller, 2010b; Piller and Cho, 2013, 2015). English, as "the language of capitalism" (Holborow, 1999, p. 1), is now seen as a global language that can facilitate and intensify not only social relations (Block, 2007) but also upward socio-economic mobility through economic, social, and cultural capital (Gao, 2014; Holly, 1990; Martin, 2010; Ricento, 2015a, 2015b). According to Phillipson (2000):

> Globalization and Englishization are discreetly penetrating a mass of economic, political, and cultural domains in complex ways (Phillipson & Skutnabb-Kangas 1999). As well as being a means of communication and a marker of identity, English is a big commodity, second in importance to the British economy after North Sea oil. (p. 91)

The historical roots of [English] language commodification can be traced back to colonial contexts in which the White savior colonizer sought to 'rescue and civilize the natives from their sins and ignorance.' The tight control over educational resources, especially at higher levels of education, which determined and limited access to linguistic resources, led to the stratification of the sociolinguistic market where "English equaled elite identity" (Rampton et al., 2007, p. 76). After colonialism, the nationalist leaderships in post-colonial contexts maintained and expanded the very system that reproduced the same class privileges and linguistic hierarchies in colonial times. While colonial languages were retained for the purposes of establishing and/or maintaining national identity in ethnically divided societies with multiple languages, the children of these leaderships acquired the languages of the former colonial countries in order to "become part of a global elite with mobile, well-paid employment" (Rampton et al., 2007, p. 76).[2] The vast majority of the people in these societies, who did not have access to the same material and linguistic resources, either remained in the margins or migrated to the former colonial countries to become part of the local working class in low-wage sectors. While the life experiences of these migrant children underline the intersection of class, immigration, and language education, Rampton et al. (2007) draw attention to the erasure of class in the discussions around these contexts since "the class element is normally misread or reconfigured as an ethnic minority problem, with the main emphasis on transition to European languages as the key to educational achievement" (p. 76).

Applied linguists who endorsed the idea of language-as-commodity focused on two language industries, call centers and edutourism, which Heller and Duchêne (2012) refer to as "hallmarks of late capitalism" (p. 13).

The call center industry

In many parts of the world, but especially in the Philippines, Pakistan, and India, two outcomes of neoliberal policies, outsourcing and the offshorization of the service industry[3] and the commodification of language seem to be acting together as an interlocking system. Influenced by neoliberalism's offshorization, the call center industry has witnessed various TNCs firing their employees in the countries in which they operate and sell their products, and, instead, outsourcing the jobs to those in less economically well-off countries around the globe. The call center industry, in that sense, is one of the examples of how neoliberalism shapes the political economy and language ideology. Within the call center industry, the commodification of English influences language policies and practices among customer services representatives (CSRs) with demands for linguistic and social capital (Antony, 2013; Cowie, 2007; Rahman, 2009; Sonntag, 2009). These linguistic demands are met through accent-neutralizing training that helps CRSs achieve an accent without mother tongue influence (MTI). In Pakistan, for instance, a 'neutral accent' often takes the form of "the substitution of certain phonetic, phonological, and prosodic features of native (American and British) varieties of English for Pakistani ones" (Rahman, 2009, p. 235). On the other hand, demands related to social capital are met through the creation of an alternative identity involving the adoption of Western pseudonyms, location masking, and synchronicity (i.e., pretending to be within the same time zone) (Rahman, 2009). In order to enable CSRs to attain these linguistic and social forms of capital, the soft skills agencies in these countries provide training to their customers not only in achieving a 'neutral accent' through Anglosphere English and phonetics but also in developing their skills and dispositions for customer care through cultural elements (Cowie, 2007).

This type of outsourcing serves another neoliberal agenda as well. Concealing employees' identities through linguistic and cultural means allows TNCs to portray themselves as "nation-less, agency-less, global entities" (Sonntag, 2009, p. 14). This portrayal in turn can be used as an anti-immigration tool, as seen in the case of the 45th President of the USA, Donald Trump, who promoted a xenophobic discourse that conveyed messages around immigrants 'stealing' jobs from American workers and that the United States of America needed a wall to keep such 'job-stealing immigrants' out. In reality, TNCs, through outsourcing and offshoring, are the ones that relocate the jobs from the Global North to the Global South. While this brings certain economic opportunities to the Global

South, it often comes "at the high price of the racialization and feminization used in the service of exploitation" (Heller, 2010b, p. 109).

Studies have also documented how call center industries – and their accent and identity reduction/concealing training – have impacted language education programs in these countries. Documenting the case of the Philippines, Martin (2010) states:

> The textbook [*E-way to better communication 1* (Ala-bastro and Panelo, 2003)] cover presents an attractive call-centre agent in a business suit. As early as the first year of high school, when Filipino students are still in their early teens, the image of call-centre agents earning US dollars is already being ingrained into their minds. In fact, schools have increasingly become targets of call-centre head-hunters ... The Philippine government's formula for economic success may be summarized as follows: improve English in schools to produce more English-proficient graduates in order to supply the ICT sector with skilled human resources so that they may earn US dollars for the Philippine economy. The formula is painfully simplistic: English equals money. Whether these graduates are capable of critical and creative thinking, or have acquired basic life skills other than language, is not a concern. (p. 255)

This view of 'English equals money' has not only shaped the industries of assessment and textbooks, but also the upper- and middle-class parents' demands for private K-12 schools and language schools with English medium instruction (see López-Gopar and Shugrua, 2014 for Mexico; Gao, 2014 for China; Kubota, 2011 for Japan; Cho, 2017 for South Korea). This demand has also contributed to an increase in short-term or long-term language learning related travels in order to build multilingual repertoires and gain access to global and local markets (Heller, 2010b), a phenomenon also known as *language edutourism* (Yarymowich, 2003).

Edutourism: English for upward mobility

In South Korea, English is perceived as a key to upward mobility through better employment opportunities and neoliberal global citizenship. The country, therefore, has been of particular interest to researchers who examine the intersection of neoliberal policies and English language education (Block, 2012b; Park, 2009; Piller and Cho, 2013, 2015; Shin, 2007, 2012, 2014). The *yeongeo yeolpung* – or English fever or frenzy – in South Korea has made proficiency in English the hallmark of academic excellence at the higher education level, to the extent that in many institutions English has become the medium of instruction across all subjects in the curriculum, even in foreign languages such as Chinese or Japanese (Piller and Cho, 2015).

The Early Study Abroad (ESA) program is representative of what language edutourism looks like in South Korea. The ESA program allows middle-class

Korean families to send their children to English-speaking countries to acquire proficiency in English. According to Shin (2014), one category of such families is the *gireogi gajok*, or 'wild goose family,'[4] which splits geographically, with the mother leaving Korea with the children while the father remains in Korea to provide financial support. Shin (2014) discusses this trend of ESAs as a form of "social polarization resulting from differential access to English instruction" (p. 100) and the marketization of education – the twin outcomes of neoliberalization in many non-English speaking countries.

On the other hand, the alleged need for vast swathes of the population – including many low-income language learners – to learn English for upward mobility and participation in the globalized economy is also contested. Summarizing concerns in relation to English as an international language, Pennycook (2007) discusses two interrelated myths: that English is a language of equal opportunity, and that social and economic advantages await those who learn English. In contrast to these myths, Pennycook (2007) outlines the "collusionary, delusionary and exclusionary effect[s] of English" (p. 133) as follows:

> This thing called English colludes with many of the pernicious processes of globalization, deludes many learners through the false promises it holds out for social and material gain, and excludes many people by operating as an exclusionary class dialect, favouring particular people, countries, cultures and forms of knowledge. (pp. 100–101)

Box 5.4 Reflective task

In the book chapter, 'A critical pedagogy of hope in times of despair,' Farahmandpur (2009) asks:

> Why should teachers be concerned with the political economy of schooling under global capitalism and the new imperialism? How can they recognize the decisive role they play in the ensuing battle between labor and capital? Why should teachers be troubled with the growing class polarization and the maquiladorization of the global economy? What lasting impact, if any, will the persistent wave of attacks of neo-liberal social and economic policies have on the working conditions of teachers? Can teachers join workers and resist the corporatization and privatization of schools? (p. 111)

Based on your experiences as a language learner or a language teacher, how can you reflect on Farahmandpur's questions? Taking an educational context you are familiar with, what can you say about language educators' role in the battle between labor and capital?

In Shin's (2014) study, for instance, those ESA students who went to Canada faced downward mobility – also known as *declassing* – and racial and linguistic discrimination from their White classmates as well as the other long-term Korean immigrants. These experiences not only limited their use of English but also prevented them from obtaining the "'global' capital of 'authentic' English" (p. 100).

This chapter so far has introduced the Marxist and Bourdieusian concepts of social class and discussed how political economy and neoliberalism have shaped the limited body of applied linguistics research that focuses on issues such as language-as-commodity and English for upward mobility. Given that there is even less engagement with social class within language education, in the next section I take a more pedagogical approach, first discussing classism in language education and then presenting an anti-classist, anti-neoliberal framework based on Block's (2018) constellation of interrelated class dimensions.

An anti-classist, anti-neoliberal framework to dismantle classism

Within language education, classism, which refers to "the normalization of the dominant class culture and the devaluation or disregard of others" (Adams et al., 2016, p. 216), often establishes a power relation between learners and those represented in the activities and materials used in their classrooms. Classism in language education has been examined in relation to classroom activities and materials to understand how different social classes are represented, valued, and legitimized.

In one of the earliest studies on the hidden curriculum of survival ESL programs, Auerbach and Burgess (1987) provided evidence for classism in texts used with adult ESL students in the US. According to the authors, these survival texts prepared learners for menial positions and taught them to be submissive through language functions such as "asking for approval, clarification, reassurance, permission, and so on, but not praising, criticizing, complaining, refusing, or disagreeing" (p. 159). Three years after Auerbach and Burgess' (1987) study, Ramirez and Hall (1990) revealed that the Spanish books used in the US omitted references to poverty, malnutrition, and political strife and instead depicted Spanish-speaking communities as middle to upper class.

In a series of more recent studies, Gray and Block (2014), Block and Gray (2018), and Gray (2010) have examined how textbooks brand – or in Althusser's (2001) terms *interpellate* – language learners as neoliberal global citizens: that is, as cosmopolitan, individualistic, and entrepreneurial. According to Gray (2010):

> Essentially branding is about the construction of a set of associations and a recognizable identity for products (whether material or symbolic). Ultimately the aim is to create identifications through which consumers can insert themselves into the 'world' of the brand. (p. 729)

By erasing any references to the working class, textbooks represent the ideal speakers of English as supposedly class-less, independent individuals, though in reality what is represented is an upper-middle-class lifestyle filled with digital technologies, international travel, and shopping. Gray's (2012) study also draws attention to the pervasive use of celebrity figures in textbooks, and the ways in which textbooks' 'aspirational content' reinforces neoliberal values through individualistic self-branding. The neoliberal ideology conveyed through this self-branding, commodification, conformism, and consumerism is not only common in English textbooks (Bori, 2021; Gray and Block, 2014; Gray, 2010; Sokolik, 2007), but also in French (Block and Gray, 2018; Coffey, 2013) and Catalan textbooks as well (Bori, 2018). As Bori (2018) states:

> [...] what Catalan textbooks almost always show are the voices of the economically well off. They can be women and men, LGBT (in [*sic*] a lesser extent but steadily gaining ground) or heterosexual; they can be African, Asian and Caucasian, atheist, Christian or Muslim. The only thing that people in the texts cannot be is poor, or at least not in any great numbers. The textbooks for Catalan will do everything they can to get the poor to at least aspire to become wealthy – using all the mechanisms of neoliberal capitalist management, gurus, self-help, self-responsibilization technicians, celebrities, alternative lifestyle, yoga and meditation coaches. To put it bluntly, they will use every tool they can to alienate people, turning away from making humans more human and less zombie.

The Catalan textbooks examined in Bori's (2018) study did not include any "single example of [an] activity or text that stimulates a social awareness of the injustices in the world of which we are part" (p. 164), confirming the findings of Auerbach and Burgess (1987) and Ramirez and Hall (1990). Bori (2018) further states that Catalan textbooks:

> promote the conformism or even the alienation of individuals, in endowing them with a 'happy consciousness' (Marcuse 1964), the pressing need to consume (Debord 1970) and the 'instrumental reason' to achieve only utilitarian purposes (Horkheimer and Adorno 2002 [1944]). (p. 163)

Considering the role of language education in promoting the neoliberal ideology and associated classist perspectives that ignore the cultural and linguistic capital of certain language learner groups, I have developed an anti-classist, anti-neoliberal framework in order to help language educators analyze and dismantle the reproduction of already-extant structural inequalities through language education. This analytical framework is built upon Block's (2018) constellation of interrelated class dimensions, which draws on both Marxist and Bourdieusian perspectives. According to Block (2014), social class is fundamentally a material phenomenon relating to "one's position in relation to the ownership and control over the means of production but it may also be seen as symbolically realized, communicated into existence in complex and sometimes unexpected ways, through linguistic phenomena such as accent, grammar and lexis" (Block, 2018, p. 3). Social class indices, therefore, range from the traditional/tangible ones such as education, food/nutrition, dress/ clothing, income, family background, place of residence, occupation, wealth, property, spatial behaviors (e.g., travel and mobility) to more intangible and symbolic social practices such as social status, language, values, lifestyles, social networks, patterns of consumption, cultural tastes, political associations and aesthetic values (Block, 2012a, 2018; Gao, 2014).

Table 5.1 below describes Block's six dimensions of social class in terms of key words and guiding questions for language educators to engage with in relation to various themes that are commonly present in language education.[5]

TABLE 5.1 Anti-classist, anti-neoliberal framework to examine classism in language education

Interrelated class dimensions	Key words	Guiding questions	Possible themes in textbooks
Material life conditions	Relations of individuals, groups, or societies to the means of production	What do the activities and materials suggest in terms of who owns and controls the means of production and who provides labor power? Whose material life conditions are included and whose are missing?	Professions, Business, Technology
Economic resources	Land and housing property as well as ownership of other material possessions, income, and wealth	What do the activities and materials suggest in terms of the economic resources of individuals, groups, cultures, and societies?	Professions, Family, Housing
Socio-cultural resources	Occupation, education, and cultural and social capital, including technological know-how	What kind of socio-cultural resources are associated with the individuals, groups, cultures, and societies represented in the activities or materials?	Technology, Professions, Art/ Literature

TABLE 5.1 (continued)

Interrelated class dimensions	Key words	Guiding questions	Possible themes in textbooks
Behavior	Consumption patterns, lifestyles, and symbolic capital	What kind of embodied, multimodal, and symbolic behaviors are associated with the individuals, groups, cultures, and societies represented in the activities or materials?	Hobbies, Interests, Entertainment, Food, Friends
Socio-political positions	Political power, physical and psychological well-being, as well as living conditions	What do the activities and materials suggest in terms of living conditions (e.g., type of neighborhood, housing) and physical and psychological well-being of the individuals, groups, and cultures, and their relative position within the hierarchies of power in a society?	Health, Weather, Housing
Spatial conditions	Local and global mobility, proximity to others	What kind of spatial conditions are associated with the individuals, groups, cultures, and societies represented in the activities or materials?	Travel, Tourism, Transportation, Housing

General questions:

- In terms of Block's (2018) class dimensions presented above, what can be said about the class-based positions represented in language teaching activities and materials?
- Whose economic and socio-cultural resources are included? Whose are missing?
- What are the living and work conditions of the people represented in the activities and materials (e.g., property, occupation, wealth, place of residence, education)?
- Are there any conflicts (i.e., class struggles) depicted between different class positions (e.g., material life conditions, socio-political conditions, and economic resources), interests, and practices?

TABLE 5.1 (continued)

- Do the people represented in the activities and materials show awareness of their class positions and interests?
- Do the people represented in the activities and materials engage in any endeavor to advance their class positions?
- Do the people represented in the activities and materials show awareness of their class privilege – that is, the advantages and resources they are granted for their class position?
- How does the representation of different class positions intersect with other forms of oppressions such as genderism, sexism, racism, ableism, and so on?

General questions about social class are presented at the end of the table for further exploration on the representation of class-based positions, class awareness, and class struggle in language teaching activities and materials. Following Block's (2018) recommendation for not putting "class into little compartments" (p. 91), I would recommend that language educators use this analytical framework to examine classism in language education without adopting an essentialist, compartmentalized understanding of class limited to these dimensions. It is hoped that this framework will provide a starting point for language educators to engage with social class in their praxis, as a result of which they will start exploring the ways in which they can begin to dismantle class-based hierarchies both in their schools and societies.

Conclusion

This chapter has aimed to raise language educators' awareness of social class, a topic that is less likely to be explored within language education textbooks and teacher education programs than such matters as race, gender, and sexual identity. Despite the recent attention social class has received within the field of applied linguistics, especially in relation to language ideology, multilingualism, and language commodification, it still remains a highly charged and 'non-grata' concept that often creates ambivalence and unease (Sayer, 2002). Yet, just like race, ethnicity, gender and sexuality, social class influences the identities, experiences, and social relations of different language learner groups. Language educators, therefore, need to find ways to engage with political economy not only to eliminate aspects of classism in their educational institutions, but also to understand the impact of neoliberalism on language education policies, practices, and ideologies. Further explorations are particularly needed within the field of English language teaching given the global spread of English and its colonial legacy that continues to entrench inequalities in various parts of the world. As Ricento (2015b) argues:

the bald claim that English is a means to social mobility, let alone necessary to promote global justice – even in the long run – while not acknowledging and addressing the underlying dynamics of transnational capitalism, the role of high-income states in maintaining and benefiting the current system, and the effects on employment and migration patterns that often work against the sustainable development of local economies, especially in low-income countries, cannot be justified. (p. 38)

And although English has been at the center of these discussions, neoliberalism and classism have a tremendous influence on practically all language learners since "not all languages are equal in their social status, both within and across societies … this inequality extending to individuals as members of language communities" (Ricento, 2015b, p. 34). Therefore, educators of all languages should reflect upon the following questions: *To what extent does language learning serve sustainable economic and social development all around the world? What kind of implications does classism have for language teachers and learners in educational contexts as well as the society more widely? In what ways does classism in language education programs contribute to and benefit from neoliberalism?* The answers to these and similar questions can be provided only through a political-economy perspective that would take into account a range of fields from history, sociology, economics, politics, education, and linguistics (Ricento, 2015a). Only an interdisciplinary and intersectional approach can account for the impact of neoliberal policies on the status and usefulness of [learning] languages for social mobility and socio-economic development and help dismantle the class-based inequalities in the world.

Notes

1. In his 2005 book, *The social structures of the economy*, Bourdieu expands this list to "financial capital (actual or potential), cultural capital (not to be confused with 'human capital'), technological capital, juridical capital and organizational capital (including the capital of information about the field), commercial capital, social capital and symbolic capital" (p. 194).
2. Similar phenomena exist in different parts of the world or with different languages as well. Some examples include Afrikaans (Namibia and South Africa), Dutch (Surinam), Portuguese (São Tomé and Príncipe; Angola, Mozambique, Timor-Leste, Cabo Verde, and Macao), Spanish (Equatorial Guinea), and Russian used in the other former Soviet Republics that are now independent and still use Russian to some extent.
3. Outsourcing occurs when a company contracts with an external third party located abroad or at home, while offshorization involves when the business is sent overseas.

4. Coming from the fact that geese are species that migrate, *gireogi gajok* references the lengths to which Korean families will go for the education of their children.

Multimedia resources

David Harvey
> http://davidharvey.org/
>> In this website, David Harvey, the leading Marxist geographer and theorist of neoliberalism, presents podcasts, courses, and manuscripts that break down Marx's political economy and neoliberalism.

Capernaum (2018) (Netflix)
>> This Lebanese movie tells the story of a 12-year-old boy who sues his parents for the 'crime' of bringing him to life. This documentary-like movie portrays the intersections of poverty, child abuse, negligent parents, and immigration.

Children's books

Sturgis, B. R. (2017). *Still a family: A story about homelessness* (illustrated by Jo-Shin Lee). Albert Whitman & Company.
>> In this book, Brenda Reeves Sturgis addresses the challenges and difficulties faced by a family experiencing homelessness and family separation.

Roberts, J. and Casap, J. (2018). *On our street: Our first talk about poverty* (World Around Us Series) (illustrated by J. Heinrichs). Orca Book Services.
>> Jillian Roberts and Jaime Casap tackle the subject of poverty and homelessness in a question-and-answer format that will help younger readers build a foundation of knowledge on these complex issues.

Nielsen, S. (2018). *No fixed address*. Andersen Press.
>> This novel is about a 12-year-old boy whose mother is not able to maintain employment and their struggle to remain housed.

Chapter 6

Race, ethnicity, and antiracist language pedagogy

Box 6.1 Lead-in: Understanding racism

Excerpt 1: In the Turkish version of the TV show *Survivor*, one of the Turkish contestants used the N-word to refer to a Black contestant, a former football player in Turkey. When the recipient of this racial slur got angry, the producer of the TV show tried to make peace by saying "It was not meant to be offensive, since there is no racism in Turkey."

Excerpt 2: The documentary *Farmingville* presents the story of a hate-based attempted murder of two Mexican day laborers in the town of Farmingville, New York. For the directors, the strength of the documentary lies in how it reflects both sides of the story, that of the town's anti-immigration residents and that of the day laborers, and leaves viewers to construct their own interpretations of the unfolding events. In one scene, one of the residents leading the fight against 'illegal immigrants' states: "I was at first shocked when people started calling me a racist. It felt like a slap in the face." Then she adds, "I got used to being called a racist and it was almost a reassurance that I was doing something good."

Excerpt 3: My Catalan neighbors were called in to school by the teacher of their 4-year old daughter who, with a group of friends, was not accepting another classmate in their games "because of her black curly hair." My neighbor, knowing the work I was doing, asked me, "We are not racist: how is she picking up these forms of behavior?"

Excerpt 4: Reflecting on her experiences as a member of a racial minority in an American higher education institution, Kubota states, "Once, I gave a presentation to my colleagues about my thoughts on the need to include issues of politics and ideologies in second and foreign language teaching and teacher education. I mentioned something to the effect that we should address issues of race and ethnicity more. A couple of years later, in a reappointment review, I was criticized as being racist in my presentation" (Kubota and Lin, 2006, p. 472).

Considering the excepts above, what do you think racism is? How can language educators talk about racism with their students, colleagues, families, and friends when it is such an elusive concept?

Introduction

Race[1] and ethnicity are two concepts that have been prominent within language education, a field that brings together teachers, learners, and teacher educators from different linguistic, cultural, and religious backgrounds (Curtis and Romney, 2006; Jenks, 2017; Kubota and Lin, 2006). Issues around race and ethnicity have been widely discussed in relation to the identities, literacy skills, and multicultural/lingual development of ethnic minorities in ESL contexts (Kubota and Lin, 2006, 2009; Michael-Luna, 2009; Nieto and Bode, 2018; Norton Peirce, 1995; Sleeter and Zavala, 2020; Wong and Grant, 2007). Conceptual and pedagogical frameworks have been proposed to draw attention to the role of race and ethnicity within language education: Anti-Blackness in language education (Anya, 2021), the global spread of English and native speakerism (Q. Charles, 2019; Galloway, 2017; Holliday and Aboshiha, 2009; Motha, 2014; Ruecker, 2011), raciolinguistic ideologies (Alim et al., 2016; Flores and Rosa, 2015, 2019) and culturally responsive, relevant, sustaining, revitalizing pedagogies (Ladson-Billings, 2009; Paris and Alim, 2017; Sleeter, 2001), to name a few.

Yet, just as with social class, discussing race and ethnicity also has been increasingly difficult and unpopular especially in White settler colonial contexts such as the US, Canada, Australia, and New Zealand. The complexity and fluidity of race and ethnicity – as seen in Box 6.1 – not only make these conversations difficult, but also often obscure the understanding of the term racism itself. As a morally and politically loaded term, "racism has become a term of political abuse" (Miles and Brown, 2003, p. 3), and talking about racial equity has proven to be a challenge for scholars of color even in teacher education programs (Kubota and Lin, 2006; Moule, 2005; Williams and Evans-Winters, 2005). Macro-level policies also accelerated the challenges around any antiracist endeavor. Due to the impetus of the Trump administration, since 2020 several school districts across the US have banned the teaching of critical race theory and ethnic studies with threats to cut the already limited budgets provided to schools and other governmental institutions. In the UK, former Prime Minister Boris Johnson set up the Commission on Race and Ethnicity as a response to the Black Lives Matter protests in 2020. The April 2021 report attributed differences in social domains such as health, education, employment, crime and policing to family structures and socio-economic status. The report controversially concluded that the 'divisive' term institutional racism should be avoided since it no longer existed in the UK. Yet, racism, in its many forms, still permeates society. This chapter therefore aims to inform language educators about the many ways language classrooms not only mirror but also reproduce the racial or ethnic hierarchies in the society at large. It also helps them become antiracist educators who can actively fight against race and ethnicity-based inequities and injustices. This chapter addresses the following issues:

- Race and ethnicity as socio-historical constructs
- Racialization, ethnicization, and racism
- Critical race theory and antiracist language pedagogy

Race

One commonly held understanding of race is that it is biological: that different races of people are separated by distinct genetic differences observed through phenotypical variations (e.g., hair texture and color, ear shape, eye and skin color, the shape/size of the skull). This notion of race has a long history but became especially prominent in the West during the early years of the United States, when the US economy depended heavily upon both the Atlantic slave trade and the displacement and genocide of Indigenous peoples. To justify the kidnapping and forced labor of millions of Africans, the brutal subjugation and extirpation of Indigenous peoples and the dispossession of Indigenous lands, and all the other socio-economic processes that disproportionately enriched a very small group of people (predominantly the White bourgeoisie and 'plantocracy'), a whole sophisticated but bogus apparatus of race science, race theory, and racial hierarchies was developed (Bell et al., 2016; Omi and Winant, 2015).

This biological understanding of race is (at best) wholly mistaken. According to the results of the National Human Genome Project (2003), at the base-pair level an individual's genome is 99.9 percent the same as every other human being on the planet. The same report also describes how skin color has evolved over time based on the environment, with multiple genomic variants all originating in Africa. There is no biological basis to race-based differentiation and discrimination: "'races' do not exist" (Miles and Brown, 2003, p. 88). Instead, race – defined as a 'natural difference' between groups of people – is a social construct that has been used repeatedly to legitimize inequitable, exclusionary, and discriminatory socio-economic structures, policies, and actions that benefit particular "races," usually White populations (Darder et al., 2009; Kubota and Lin, 2006; Sensoy and DiAngelo, 2017). As Miles and Brown (2003) have argued:

In Europe, North America, and Australasia, the idea of 'race' is now usually (though not exclusively) used to differentiate collectivities distinguished by skin colour, so that 'races' are either 'black' or 'white' but never 'big-eared' and 'small-eared'. The fact that only certain physical characteristics are signified to define 'races' in specific circumstances indicates that we are investigating not a given, natural division of the world's population, but the application of historically and culturally specific meanings to the totality of human physiological variation. (p. 89)

Given that different races actually do not exist from a biological standpoint and race itself is a socio-historical construct rooted in racism, scholars such as Darder and Torres (2009) have even argued the need to move away from race-based terminology:

> Our intention is to contest the notion that the color of a person's skin and all it has historically come to signify within the sociological, political, or popular imagination, should continue to function as such … We argue that we must disconnect from "race" as it has been constructed in the past, and contend fully with the impact of "race" as ideology on the lives of all people – but most importantly on the lives of those who have been enslaved, colonized, or marked for genocide in the course of world history. (pp. 150–151)

And although the idea of race as a social category is indeed invented, "[races] are *socially real* and reenacted in the everyday life in encounters in all sorts of situations and spaces" (Bonilla-Silva, 2015, p. 1360, original emphasis). Therefore, deconstructing race as a social category runs the risk of contributing to colorblind racism or to the claims that racism no longer exists (Bell, 2016). As Kendi (2019) states:

> … if we stop using racial categories then we will not be able to identify racial inequity. If we cannot identify racial inequity, then we will not be able to identify racist policies. If we cannot identify racist policies, then we cannot challenge racist policies. If we cannot challenge racist policies, then racist power's final solution will be achieved: a world of inequity none of us can see, let alone resist. Terminating racial categories is potentially the last, not the first step, in the antiracist struggle. (p. 125)

Therefore, attention should be drawn to the realities of racialized groups in terms of social outcomes (e.g., poverty and incarceration) in ways that mobilize racially oppressed people and create solidarity and resistance (Bell, 2016; Kubota and Lin, 2009).

Ethnicity

Just as with race, ethnicity as a social construct is used to distinguish groups of people based on group affiliation and socio-cultural differences such as ancestry, religion, language, culture, customs, norms, and values. Being equally problematic as race, ethnicity as a term raises questions around how culture is defined and how cultural boundaries are drawn (Kubota, 2003; Miles and Brown, 2003). To illustrate, one of the most brutal ethnic conflicts in recent memory was the genocide that took place across Rwanda from April to July 1994, in which more than half a million Tutsi were brutally murdered by their Hutu compatriots (Verpoorten, 2020). The 2004 movie *Hotel Rwanda* depicted a dramatized version of the horrific events of the Rwandan genocide after the Belgian colonization. In one scene, the conflict between Hutu and Tutsi was explained by one of the locals to a White journalist as follows:

> According to the Belgian colonists, Tutsis [*sic*] are taller ... more elegant. It was the Belgians that created the division. They picked people. Those with thinner noses, lighter skin. They used to measure the width of people's noses. Belgians used the Tutsis to run the country, and when they left, they left the power to the Hutus [*sic*]. And of course, Hutus took the revenge for years of oppression.

While one of the problems around ethnicity is the blurred cultural boundaries between different ethnic groups, another issue regards the term's being conflated and used interchangeably with race. As Miles and Brown (2003) state:

> [Ethnicity] is often used as a politically correct code word for 'race' – that is, it signifies a group that is identified as an ethnic group according to common-sense phenotypical indicators. On this criterion, African-Americans in the USA or Asians in Britain might constitute an ethnic group (though not necessarily 'white' people, because 'ethnic' often connotes 'Other' or 'minority'). Sometimes, the ethnic group is smaller and more local. For example, 'ethnic cleansing' was added to the lexicon in the early 1990s to denote mass murder and forced migration within the conflicts in Bosnia and Herzegovina, and other parts of the Balkans. There, the ethnic groups were identified as Serbian, Croatian, Bosnian Muslim, Romani ('Gypsy') and Albanian. In this context, phenotypical indicators of ethnicity were less important than cultural, linguistic or religious ones, but the use of mass rape as an instrument of war suggests that 'other' ethnic groups were perceived as biologically distinct and self-perpetuating, and that this distinctiveness and self-perpetuation could be negated by forced insemination. The difference between such a concept of ethnic distinctiveness and a concept of 'racial' distinctiveness is entirely elusive. (pp. 93–94)

The relationship between race and ethnicity becomes clearer when the processes of racialization and ethnicization – both of which result in racist beliefs, dispositions, ideologies, and practices – are considered.

Racialization, ethnicization, and racism

Racialization refers to the process of historically, socially, and politically constructing race and racial categories based on individuals' biological features. Racialization provides the foundation for racial social systems through mechanisms such as creating racial categories, structuring race relations within social domains (e.g., law, education, health), and developing ideologies and justifications for racial rationale and violence (Christian, 2019). Similarly, ethnicization takes place when populations are divided into various ethnic groups according to their skin color, language, religion, or other relevant cultural characteristics. Miles and Brown (2003) explain the interplay of these two concepts as follows:

> [E]thnicisation as a dialectical process by which meaning is attributed to socio-cultural signifiers of human beings, as a result of which individuals may be assigned to a general category of persons which reproduces itself biologically, culturally and economically. Where biological and/or somatic features (real or imagined) are signified, we speak of racialisation as a specific modality of ethnicization. (p. 90)

Racism, in that sense, refers to the discourse where certain racialized and/or ethnicised groups – those who are categorized on the basis of their phenotypical traits or cultural norms and practices – are overtly or covertly deemed inferior or superior in relation to each other within an institutionalized system of social, political, and economic hierarchy. As Darder and Torres (2004) state, "'race,' simply put, is the child of racism. That is to say, racism does not exist because there is such a thing as 'race'" (p. 100); rather, race exists because of and is produced by racism. Discussing racism as a product of colonialism, slavery, and labor migration, Bonilla-Silva (2015) argues in similar terms:

> Racism produced (and continues to produce) "races" out of peoples who were not so before, whether one is thinking of the various nationalities and peoples from Europe who shed (somewhat) their regional, tribal, and local identities and slowly became "White" (Jacobson, 1999; Painter, 2010); the aboriginal peoples of the Americas who became "Indian" (Forbes, 1993); or the multiple ethnic and tribal groups from the African continent who became "Black" (Wright, 2004). (p. 1359)

Racism embodies not only the assumption that different races exist but also a potentially negative evaluation of those races that racist individuals do not regard themselves as belonging to (Miles and Brown, 2003). And while racism is often associated with White supremacy and the oppression of Black people and people of color, its scope has certainly extended to different ethnic and religious groups. The most obvious example comes from the era following the September 11, 2001 attacks on the Twin Towers in New York City, in Washington DC (the

Pentagon), and Shanksville, Pennsylvania, which constructed Middle Eastern identities and positioned Islam as a global threat (May and Sleeter, 2010). Essentializing the diversity of Muslim nation-states, languages, religious sectarian affiliations, ethnicities, and cultures, Islamophobia has racialized religion to circulate religious and racist fears, hostility, and violence against peoples of North Africa, Asia, and the Middle East (Adams and Joshi, 2016). Rooted in the colonialist and Orientalist assumptions of the West and Christianity (Said, 1978), Islamophobia argues for – or presupposes – the superiority of the West over the East and leads to the devaluation of and discrimination against Muslim people.

Although racism is an ideology that permeates organizations, institutions, cultures, and societies, the dominant tendency is to define or identify racism with only individual acts and expressions of overt or extreme prejudice and discrimination. Individual racism takes place at personal and interpersonal levels through verbal and non-verbal behaviors as well as beliefs, values, and attitudes. Reducing racism to individual acts also leads to the fallacious *good versus bad* binary. This common misconception sees good, nice, progressive, multicultural, well-intentioned, non-racist people on the one hand, and mean, willfully ignorant racists on the other (Sensoy and DiAngelo, 2017; Sullivan, 2014). Apart from its obvious childishness, the binary of good versus bad people is problematic for two main reasons. First, individuals who believe in this binary may overlook or sidestep their individual responsibility to critically reflect on their own privilege and to challenge racial inequality and injustices in their communities (DiAngelo, 2018; Sensoy and DiAngelo, 2017). Second, this view of racism as the individual acts of 'bad' people also obscures an understanding of racism as an institutional system of oppression, which is "reflected in the policies, laws, rules, norms, and customs enacted by organizations and social institutions that advantage whites as a group and disadvantage groups of color" (Bell et al., 2016, p. 135). Institutional racism refers to the process in which one particular race's superiority and dominance over the other is confirmed and actualized within different societal and cultural organizations and domains such as education, health care, media, and law. In fact, as Miles and Brown (2003) argue, "every racism is institutional because racism is not an individual but a social creation" (p. 109). In that sense, while microaggressions, that is, "acts of disregard or subtle insults stemming from, often unconscious, attitudes of white superiority" (Bell et al., 2016, p. 136), might often be categorized as (un) harmful acts at the interpersonal level, they are rooted in institutional and structural racism. While the terms institutional, systemic, and structural racism are used interchangeably and sometimes together in different contexts, in order to avoid 'conceptual inflation' and for the sake of clarity (Miles and Brown, 2003; Darder and Torres, 2004) this book talks about racism as systemic racism that encompasses both interpersonal and institutional forms. Systemic racism, as an ideology with a "*material* foundation" (Bonilla-Silva, 2015, p. 1360, original emphasis), has an impact not only on the interpersonal level (i.e., interpersonal racism) but also on the institutional structures and social, economic, and political relations in societies at large (i.e., institutional racism) (Kubota and Lin, 2006; McIntosh, 1989).

Antiracist pedagogies in language education

Box 6.2 Reflective task

In the book entitled, *What White people can do next: From allyship to coalition*, Emma Dabiri (2021) states:

> There is for many a new linguistic timorousness, a fear that obstructs us from meeting and recognizing each other fully. It's also a distraction technique. Instead of organizing to create substantive change, we are squabbling with each other over words. These debates might feel very current, but they were happening before many of us were born. In *A Rap on Race* Baldwin and Mead discussed the same thing in the 1970s. They noted that, instead of focusing on structural change, change occurs at the level of vocabulary. (pp. 87–88)

How are you personally, collectively, and institutionally creating an inclusive and antiracist space for Black students and teachers, students and teachers of color, and ethnic minorities in your educational contexts? In what ways do you thrive to be proactively antiracist? What kind of meaningful action plans do you make to address the inherent nature of institutional racism in your schools?

Critical race theory (CRT), as a cross-disciplinary approach to antiracism, emphasizes the interwoven nature of racism within individuals, institutions, organizations, and the society at large. Emerging from around the mid-1970s to address the effects of race and racism on US laws, CRT has quickly spread to other disciplines including education. Since the first attempts to apply CRT to the field of education (Tate, 1993, 1994; Ladson-Billings and Tate, 1995), many educational scholars have adopted CRT to understand and dismantle race-based power relations, struggles, and inequities in education (e.g., DeCuir and Dixson, 2004; Dixson et al., 2017; Gillborn, 2006; Love, 2004; Lynn and Dixson, 2013; Taylor et al., 2009). CRT, in other words, has offered educators "a way to understand how ostensibly race-neutral structures in education – knowledge, truth, merit, objectivity, and 'good education' – are in fact ways of forming and policing the racial boundaries of white supremacy and racism" (Roithmayr, 1999, p. 4).

While critical race theorists present a diverse range of perspectives and approaches to dismantle racism, there are six prominent tenets of CRT that have been commonly agreed upon: counter-storytelling, the permanence of racism, Whiteness as property, interest convergence, the critique of liberalism (Cabrera, 2014; DeCuir and Dixson, 2004; Ladson-Billings, 1999; Taylor, 2009), and the intersectionality of race with sexism, classism, ableism, and other forms of oppression (Crenshaw, 1989, 1991; Jennings and Lynn, 2005; Ledesma and Calderón, 2015). Based on these six tenets, this book proposes an antiracist language pedagogy by also following Ibram X. Kendi's (2019) work on *How to be an antiracist*. According to Kendi (2019), racism can only be dismantled by antiracists, not non-racists, the difference being:

> One endorses either the idea of a racial hierarchy as a racist, or racial equality as an antiracist. One either believes problems are rooted in groups of people, as a racist, or locates the roots of problems in power and policies as an antiracist. One either allows racial inequities to persevere, as a racist, or confronts racial inequities, as an antiracist. There is no in-between safe space of "not racist." The claim of "not racist" neutrality is a mask for racism. (p. 11)

In the next sections, the following strategies will be discussed to help language educators become antiracist pedagogues who can actively fight against the normativity of Whiteness and its effects on marginalized learner groups through equitable educational experiences and institutional change:

- Accepting the permanence of racism by resisting colorblind pedagogies
- Centralizing experiential knowledge through (counter-)storytelling
- Decolonizing the language curriculum by de-normalizing Whiteness
- Dismantling administrative policies and practices that promote Whiteness
- Centering the role of political economy in antiracist pedagogy
- Adopting an antiracist, anti-capitalist, and intersectional approach to environmentalism
- Tackling racism in moment-to-moment interactions
- Developing critical consciousness as antiracist language educators

Accepting the permanence of racism by resisting colorblind pedagogies

Criticizing the claims about countries such as the UK or US being 'post-racial' or beyond racism, scholars have discussed the existence of a new form of racism that benefits from liberalism. This liberal view perceives institutional racism as something of the past, while minimizing the existence of contemporary racism at the individual level (Bell, 2016; Bonilla-Silva, 2002, 2015; Cabrera, 2014; Darder and Torres, 2004; Williams and Evans-Winters, 2005). According to Bonilla-Silva (2015), the 'new racism' has the following features:

> (1) the increasingly covert nature of racial discourse and practices, (2) the avoidance of direct racial terminology, (3) the elaboration of a racial political agenda that eschews direct racial references, (4) the subtle character of most mechanisms to reproduce racial privilege, and (5) the rearticulation of some racial practices of the past (Bonilla-Silva, 2001). (p. 1362)

Educators supporting this form of 'racism-as-prejudice' (Bonilla-Silva, 2015) often refer to *Brown* v. *Board of Education* (1954) as a landmark judgment that ended racial segregation in US schools. These sorts of progress narratives[2] that often contain success stories of people of color and women serve as an 'illusion of progress' (Sleeter and Grant, 2008). For instance, the election of Barack Obama as the first Black president of the United States[3] and policies that prohibit employment discrimination based on race, religion, sex, and national origin reinforce the idea that today's racism is limited to the acts of individuals. Any conscious attempt to engage in racetalk, therefore, may be considered 'White victimization,' 'reverse racism,' and 'reverse discrimination' (Omi and Winant, 2015; Williams and Evans-Winters, 2005). These attempts might also be responded with projection, that is, affixing the blame onto someone else – usually on to Black people, and people of color – in order to avoid responsibility and to feel better about oneself (Bonilla-Silva, 2002, 2017). As Cabrera's (2014) study with White male college students revealed:

> Demonizing, for example, the KKK functionally served as a means of seeing themselves as not racist because they did not hate people of color. This meant these racially privileged people spend the majority of their time downplaying the importance of systemic racial oppression instead focusing on how minorities are 'racist' against whites. (p. 49)

These liberal views are also associated with colorblind racism which refers to one's (claimed) intention not to notice race and/or to overlook the racial and cultural differences among groups of people in order not to appear to be racist (Bonilla-Silva, 2002, 2015, 2017). Colorblind (or ethnic-blind) racism originates from the assumption that racism takes place at individual and interpersonal levels; therefore, racist discrimination can be ended if one treats everyone equally. Focusing on the linguistic aspects and rhetorical strategies of colorblindness, Bonilla-Silva (2002) documented its language to be as follows:

> Color blind racism's racetalk avoids racist terminology and preserves its myth through semantic moves such as "I am not a racist, but," "Some of my best friends are," "I am not black, but," and "Yes and no." Additionally, when something could be interpreted as racially motivated, whites can use the "Anything but race" strategy. Thus, if a school or neighborhood is completely

[W]hite, they can say "It's not a racial thing" or "It's economics, not race." They can also project the matter onto blacks by saying things such as "They don't want to live with us" or "Blacks are the really prejudiced ones." (p. 61)

Progress narratives and colorblind ideologies help legitimize the racial order across society by preventing individuals from realizing that racism permeates through all social, economic, and political structures that privilege White people and oppress Black people, people of color, and all other ethnic minority groups who are racialized as non-White (Bonilla-Silva, 2015, 2017; DeCuir and Dixson, 2004; Gillborn, 2006; Sullivan, 2014).

Box 6.3 Reflective task

On February 3, 2020 *The Guardian* published an article with the title, 'Why liberal women pay a lot of money to learn over dinner how they're racist.' This article included a number of images of several women sitting at a dinner table, with wine glasses, salad bowls, and candles reading DiAngelo's *White fragility*. The context was described as follows:

> This is Race to Dinner. A white woman volunteers to host a dinner in her home for seven other white women – often strangers, perhaps acquaintances. (Each dinner costs $2,500, which can be covered by a generous host or divided among guests.) A frank discussion is led by co-founders Regina Jackson, who is black, and Saira Rao, who identifies as Indian American. They started Race to Dinner to challenge liberal white women to accept their racism, however subconscious. "If you did this in a conference room, they'd leave," Rao says. "But wealthy white women have been taught never to leave the dinner table."

Have you ever participated in a diversity training? Were your experiences similar to the one depicted here? What are your thoughts and feelings about Race to Dinner? What issues presented so far in this chapter can be discussed in relation to this diversity training?

Progress narratives and colorblind ideologies also end up perpetuating the hegemonic ideologies that discriminate and oppress immigrants and ethnic minorities. The main approach in educational contexts towards anyone who is not White, middle class, and a speaker of 'standard' English is the 'difference-as-deficit' approach that devalues the experiences, identities, and funds of knowledge different learner groups bring to the classroom (McKay and Wong, 2000; May and Sleeter, 2010; Mitchell, 2013; Rosa and Flores, 2021). There is a plethora of studies focusing on Latinx populations as well as Asian students in the US context, indicating the stereotypical views attributed to their identity and culture (Marx, 2009). The hegemonic deficit thinking against Latinx students not only positions them as 'lazy,' 'ignorant,' 'unintelligent,' and 'unclean' but also blames the learners, their families, and cultures for any academic failure. Asian and Asian American students, suffering from a 'perpetual-foreigner syndrome,' are asked where they are from even when they are US-born and have American accents. On the other hand, East Asian populations, often portrayed as 'model minority' or 'honorary Whites' in movies, TV shows, and books, are criticized for not speaking up for their rights against racial discrimination. These monolithic representations of Asians and Asian Americans as a homogeneous group of hardworking individuals erase the differences among Asian and Asian American students in relation to their ethnicity, social class, sexual orientation, disability, religion, etc. (Kumashiro, 2000; Lee and Kumashiro, 2005). These representations and stereotypes also create tensions between Asian populations and African American and Latinx communities, especially when they are used to promote meritocracy through a criticism of the latter two for their 'under-achievement' (Lee, 2009; Mitchell, 2013). Both the deficit thinking towards Latinx and other ethnic minorities and the model minority myth towards Asian students serve to manipulate and deepen the divide between these marginalized groups and to perpetuate White supremacy (Lee, 2006, 2009; Marx, 2009; Quach et al., 2009; Rolón-Dow, 2011).

Language educators who work with immigrant populations need to be informed about culturally relevant/sustaining pedagogies that affirm their native languages and home cultures (Ladson-Billings, 1995). Culturally sustaining pedagogies are also required to fight against colorblind ideologies and practices in classrooms, which Herrera and Rodriguez Morales (2009) refer to as educators' *colorblind non-accommodative denial* (e.g., "I don't see color, I treat all my students the same."). Race and ethnicity are central to the way individuals make sense of themselves, others, and the world around them. Colorblindness, in that sense, erases the lived experiences and identities of different learner groups by replacing them with "an illusion of sameness" (Herrera and Rodriguez Morales, 2009, p. 210). Colorblind pedagogies ignore the unique needs, interests, and funds of knowledge learners bring to the classroom. They adopt an equality-based approach that overlooks the inequitable power relations and put the blame of any academic and social failure on learners rather than educational institutions and societies. Therefore, the goal of any pedagogy should not be mainstream inclusion but a systemic inquiry into historical and institutional processes that deem these marginalized and racialized learners and their practices deficient and in need of remediation (Flores and Rosa, 2015, 2019; Rosa and Flores, 2021). Language education, as a multilingual/multicultural field, needs to move beyond "modest reforms supporting affirmation and inclusion of marginalized populations and practices" (Rosa and Flores, 2021, p. 1162) to implementing changes at institutional and societal levels in order to eradicate the underlying forces that produce such marginalization.

Centralizing experiential knowledge through (counter-)storytelling

> **Box 6.4 Problem-posing task**
>
> In their book chapter entitled, 'Toward a critical race theory of education,' Ladson-Billings and Tate (2009) argue that, "[s]tories by people of color can catalyze the necessary cognitive conflict to jar dysconscious racism" (p. 175).
>
> Whose stories are told in your language classes or in an educational context that you are familiar with? How do you think these stories perpetuate the racialization and ethnicization of groups of people? How do they contribute to the interpersonal and institutional racism in your school, community, and culture?

Storytelling, counter-storytelling, and testimonios have been widely emphasized for their role in constructing language learners' social worlds through tacit agreements, assumptions, beliefs, and norms – especially of those held by the dominant groups. While counter-storytelling refers to the process of telling the stories of marginalized and silenced groups, testimonios are critical reflections of one's own experiences and socio-political realities. This book, however, uses (counter-)storytelling as an all-encompassing term to refer to any storytelling that exposes, resists, and even deconstructs the existing majoritarian stories of privilege and hegemony. Majoritarian stories, or master narratives, refer to "the description of events as told by members of dominant/majority groups, accompanied by the values and beliefs that justify the actions taken by dominants to insure their dominant position" (Love, 2004, pp. 228–229). Perhaps the most common majoritarian stories in multilingual/multicultural educational contexts are 'race is no longer an issue in the US,' 'difference is deficit,' 'meritocracy is appropriate,' and 'English is all that matters' (Mitchell, 2013). (Counter-)storytelling has the potential to attack these "embedded preconceptions that marginalize others and conceal their humanity" (Delgado and Stefancic, 2001, p. 42). Through (counter-)storytelling, language learners can reflect on their own privileges, build empathy with marginalized populations, and "contradict the Othering process" (DeCuir and Dixson, 2004, p. 27). Majoritarian stories are not only about racial privilege but "carry layers of assumptions that persons in positions of racialized privilege bring with them to discussions of racism, sexism, classism, and other forms of subordination" (Solórzano and Yosso, 2002, p. 28). Therefore, (counter-)storytelling provides affordances for deconstructing the normalized hegemonic ideologies and essentialist narratives that perpetuate not only racism, but also classism, sexism, and other forms of oppression (Delgado and Stefancic, 2001; Lewis Ellison and Solomon, 2019). Essentialism assumes that if someone is perceived to be and categorized as

Black, then they should have shared interests, perceptions, values, experiences, and even a sense of affiliation with the larger Black community. As Miles and Brown (2003) have explained:

> People differentiated on the basis of the signification of phenotypical features are usually also represented as possessing certain cultural characteristics (such as diet, religious belief, mode of dress, language, etc.). As a consequence, the population is represented as distinctive by virtue of a specific profile of (sometimes real and sometimes imagined) biological and cultural attributes. The deterministic manner of this representation means that all who possess the signified phenotypical characteristics are assumed to possess the concomitant cultural characteristics. (p. 89)

Therefore, language educators should be cognizant of the dynamic, diasporic, and hybrid nature of diverse racial, ethnic, cultural, religious, and linguistic communities and avoid conveying fixed worldviews that would lead to stereotypes, prejudice, and racist beliefs and practices about different societies (Kubota, 2010).

(Counter-)storytelling can also allow language learners to 'name one's own reality' and 'claim one's voice' (Ladson-Billings and Tate, 1995, 2009). Through (counter-)storytelling, members of the marginalized groups could reflect on the factors and processes that resulted in their oppression and subjugation (Ladson-Billings and Tate, 2009). (Counter-)storytelling has been employed as an instructional strategy in culturally and linguistically diverse classrooms to enable multilingual and multicultural learners to express, document, and appreciate their experiential knowledge. Allowing learners from diverse linguistic and cultural backgrounds to bring in their identities, families, communities, and cultures into their classrooms through visual, aural, textual, digital, and multimodal stories, testimonios, family histories, narratives, and parables not only supports their bi/multilingual literacy development, but also validates their identities and funds of knowledge (Blackmer Reyes and Curry Rodríguez, 2012; Katz and DaSilva Iddings, 2009; Lewis Ellison and Solomon, 2019).

(Counter-)storytelling, however, may lead to the romanticization of the experiences of the marginalized groups and the dichotomization or over-homogenization of White people and people of color. Kumashiro (2000), for instance, explains how teachers can use stories – about Native Hawaiians in this case – in ways that avoid essentialism and a superficial understanding of the social inequalities:

> rather than ask, "what does this novel tell us about, say, Native Hawaiians," what if teachers were to ask, "how can this novel be used to learn more about Native Hawaiians, or about racism against Native Hawaiians, or about Native Hawaiians in the mainstream-U.S. imagination?" Rather than ask, "what do we know, based on this book, about Native Hawaiian cultures and people," what if teachers asked, "which stereotypes of Native Hawaiians does this novel reinforce, and which ones does it challenge?" Rather than ask, "according

to this book, what is it like to be Native Hawaiian," what if teachers asked, "what is not said in this book about being Native Hawaiian, and how do those silences make possible and impossible different ways of thinking about Native Hawaiian peoples and experiences?" (pp. 34–35)

(Counter-)storytelling, therefore, should be used as a pedagogical tool to develop language learners' critical literacy through which learners can examine their own positions, challenge master narratives that maintain and perpetuate the status quo in their societies, and enact social change (Martin-Beltrán et al., 2020).

Decolonizing the language curriculum by de-normalizing Whiteness

Concerned with the nature of Whiteness, Critical Whiteness Studies (CWS) aims to understand and deconstruct the taken-for-granted assumptions and day-to-day individual and institutional practices that convey what it means to be – or to not be – a White person (Delgado and Stefancic, 1997; Gillborn, 2006; Leonardo, 2002). Whiteness comes with cultural, social, and economic but unearned racial privileges and benefits in the form of an "invisible knapsack of special provisions, maps, passports, codebooks, visas, clothes, tools and blank checks" (McIntosh, 1989, p. 10). White privilege not only entails economic, political, and cultural assumptions and benefits only Whites can enjoy but also embodies "a property interest worthy of protection" (Harris, 1993, p. 1768). As a legacy of slavery, the notion of 'Whiteness as property' refers to "the idea that whiteness–that which Whites alone possess–is valuable and is property" (Harris, 1993, p. 1721). In that sense, Whiteness is normative and standard. As Delgado and Stefancic (2001) have stated, "Other groups, such as Indians [sic], Latinos, Asian Americans, and African Americans, are described as nonwhite. That is, they are defined in terms of or in opposition to whiteness—that which they are not" (p. 76).

   Whiteness as property not only permeates the school curriculum, resulting in educational disparities within and across schools, but also the decisions around who gets to have access to high-quality education and well-paid jobs. There is also a plethora of research that illustrated the ways Blacks are discriminated against at all stages of the hiring process regardless of their educational background (Bonilla-Silva, 2017; Roediger, 1991; Royster, 2003; Wilson, 2015). Royster (2003) explains the divergent pathways and unequal educational outcomes of Black and White students as resulting from "*only* their racial status and the way it situates them in racially exclusive networks during the school-work transition process" (p. 180, emphasis added).

   Achieving racial equity in language classrooms as well as in society at large demands the decolonization of the language classroom. According to hooks (2015c), decolonization refers to "an act of confrontation with a hegemonic system of thought ... a process of considerable historical and cultural libera-tion" (p. 15). As abstract as this definition may sound, there have been concrete attempts towards decolonization in educational contexts. For instance, the 2014 student-led campaign 'Why is my curriculum white?' drew attention to the Whiteness at University College London (UCL). This campaign aimed to raise awareness that UCL's curriculum "is white comprised of 'white ideas' by 'white authors' and is a result of colonialism that has normalized whiteness and made blackness invisible" (Peters, 2015, p. 641). Within language education, scholars such as Kubota and Lin (2009) also posed the following questions to enable language educators to explore Whiteness in their classrooms:

> What teaching methodologies are deemed more legitimate and what episte-mologies are they based on? What aspects of culture and society are or are not taught in a second/foreign-language course? Are any particular racial groups represented more than others? What racial images are projected in second/foreign-language textbooks and how do they influence the learners' view of the target language, target-language speaking world and their identities? (p. 14)

As discussed already in relation to (counter-)storytelling, language educators can bring in poems, short stories, and novels by Black authors, and authors of color and ethnic minorities to disrupt the Whiteness in their classrooms. However, the process of decolonizing the curriculum is not limited to the inclusion of Black authors or work by Indigenous peoples but requires an accurate representation of history. In many ESL and EFL textbooks, there is still a unit on 'The Discovery of America by Cristopher Columbus' as if there were not already hundreds, if not thousands, of societies and cultures present and thriving in the Americas at the time of his entirely accidental arrival and as if Columbus did not dominate, subjugate, brutally extract, and control the wealth and resources of Indigenous populations (M. Charles, 2019; Loewen, 2005). One particular example comes from a unit called 'The First Americans,' in the language textbook *Life* (Student's Book 1, 2nd edition) published in 2018 by National Geographic Learning (Stephenson et al., 2018). This unit includes a reading text on Indigenous populations, which may be perceived by some as a step towards decolonization. However, the text only really glosses over historical facts about different Indigenous nations while ignoring key historical events that caused these nations and peoples to become colonized (e.g., forced migration, starvation, enslavement, illegal usurpation of land and territorial wars, incarceration, biological warfare, and sexual violence). Additionally, since the unit focused on the regular simple past, the reading text reinforces this language structure and states that "In North America, the Apache, Navajo, Sioux, and other Native American groups *lived* in different areas" (Stephenson et al., 2018, p. 123, emphasis added). This is an inaccurate representation of history, as these Indigenous populations still exist and live in these areas today.[4] It is paramount that language teachers are cognizant of the hidden and no-so-hidden messages conveyed in textbooks, and that they evaluate and adapt materials in ways that will help raise their learners' critical awareness and cultivate a sense of advocacy and agency. Whiteness and the White curriculum, therefore, are not only harmful to Black students, students of color, Indigenous learners, and those from ethnic minority groups, but for *all students* who "are potentially experiencing similarly distorted versions of culture, history, and the creation and development of worldwide civilisations" (M. Charles, 2019, p. 737).

Dismantling administrative policies and practices that promote Whiteness

---

Box 6.5 Problem-posing task

In a paper entitled 'Racializing ESOL teacher identities in U.S. K-12 public schools,' Motha (2006) states, "I consider linguistic identities to be inextricable from racial identities because I believe Whiteness to be an intrinsic but veiled element of the construct of mainstream English" (p. 497).

In light of this quotation, imagine a pre-service student teacher commenting in their mid-term class evaluation in the following manner: "Faculty should be allowed to take off their masks while teaching. It's really difficult to understand them at times, especially if they have an accent or something."

In what ways do racism and native speakerism perpetuate each other?

Whiteness also permeates the broader policies and practices regarding student discipline and punishment, library resources and technology, and administrative policies and practices. According to Kumaradivelu (2016), the hegemonic power structures in language education subordinate non-native speakers by means of various political, cultural, economic, and educational relations that have stripped them of their critical consciousness and agency. *Native speakerism*, in that sense, refers to the ideology which perceives the native speaker as a representative of the West and the non-native speaker as the culturally deficient Other (Holliday, 2005). Native speakerism embodies Whiteness which is often reflected in discriminatory hiring practices based on 'unprofessional favoritism,' and the commodification of the native speaker teacher (Kumaravidelu, 2016; Park, 2015; Rivers and Ross, 2013).

Drawing on Harris' (1993) notion of "Whiteness as property," Ruecker (2011) documented how native speaker privilege has permeated recruitment policies and practices and has served as a gatekeeper to deny the Other from entry into this privileged community of practice. In fact, Holliday (2015) refers to native speakerism as a 'neo-racist ideology' for two main reasons. First, the phenotypical differences embedded in the Othering of different races are more currently replaced by culture, and cultural differences have become a euphemism for racial differences. Second, the promotion of the native-speaker brand in the ELT industry actually means Whiteness, excluding not only the so-called non-native speakers but also teachers of color who may have been speaking English from birth. Being perceived as 'the norm,' the native speaker adopted an "almost moral mission to improve the world" (Holliday, 2005, p. 13) and that "the white man's burden has been metamorphosed into the British native speaker's burden" (Phillipson, 1992, p. 179).

Native speakerism embodies Whiteness in ways that privilege not only White language teachers but also the "White" varieties. According to the ESL teachers interviewed in Amin's (1997) study, the students thought "Only White people can be native speakers of English"; "Only native speakers know 'real,' 'proper,' 'Canadian English'"; and "only White people are 'real' Canadians" (p. 580), ignoring the Indigenous populations that have lived on those lands for thousands of years before the arrival of White settlers. Creese and Kambere's (2003) article 'What colour is your English?' also underscores the ways in which 'foreign' accents in White settler contexts such as Canada intersect with the processes of racialization reproducing deficit thinking, oppression, and inequality. Questioning whether 'native speaker' means 'White,' Grant and Wong (2008) have posed the following questions:

> Why is it that White New Zealanders or Canadians or South Africans, whose accents evolved from British English, are considered "native speakers" and Blacks from the former colonies of Rhodesia (now Zimbabwe) or Trinidad are not? Why are Indian and Singapore English varieties or Native Hawaiian pidgin seen as being "incomprehensible"? TESOL scholarship on World Englishes, Black English (or AAVE), and by non-native English language professionals raises the need to address racism in language teaching. Does "native speaker" mean "White"? (p. 170)

In order to resist the hegemonic ideology of native speakerism, all language educators – native and non-native, White, Black, person of color, or ethnic minority – need to challenge the institutional policies and practices that discriminate against and oppress marginalized teachers based on their race and ethnicity. This process involves recognizing the translinguistic and transcultural identities language teachers from all racial and ethnic backgrounds bring to their classrooms and working towards more egalitarian policies and practices that evaluate language teachers on the basis of their teaching qualifications rather than their so-called native-speaker status (Jenks, 2017; Ruecker, 2011; Rudolph et al., 2015). At the classroom level, language teachers should shift their emphasis from the native-speaker model and cultural norms of (mainly) the US and the UK varieties of English to plurilingualism, hybridity, intercultural communication, and more contextually sensitive curriculum (Houghton et al., 2018).

Centering the role of political economy in antiracist pedagogy

> **Box 6.6 Problem-posing task**
> In *Capital*, Karl Marx (1990) mentions that, "[l]abour in a white skin cannot emancipate itself where the black skin is branded" (p. 414).
>
> How do race and social class and racism and classism intersect with each other in your educational context and the wider society? How can language educators fight against different forms of racism by taking a perspective of political economy?

It is no surprise that the ideology of racism is linked to – if not primarily about – political economy. The idea of different races emerged; racial hierarchies were consolidated; and race specific exploitation, marginalization, and deprivation were 'scientifically' justified because of colonialism's economic exploitation that reinforced White supremacy (Block, 2014; Bradley, 2015; Darder and Torres, 2004, 2009; Miles and Brown, 2003). Race, according to Fraser (2019), "structures the division within paid work between low-paid, low-status, menial, dirty, and domestic occupations, held disproportionately by people of colour, and higher-paid, higher-status, white-collar, professional, technical and managerial occupations, held disproportionately by 'whites'" (p. 80). As interpersonal racism has become unacceptable in the larger societies, race has started to be used as a proxy for social class (Block, 2014). Sullivan (2014) explains the ways in which intra-White class biases are linked to racism:

> one of the main ways that white class hierarchies operate is through the production and display of white middle-class moral goodness. This is achieved by establishing the moral badness of poor and lower-class white people. Lower-class white people supposedly are the retrograde white people who still believe and act in racist ways; they are the real problem, when it comes to lingering racism in our enlightened times. Knowing this, white middle-class liberals know and/or take steps to ensure that they are different in kind than the white lower class, and this process of Othering secures white liberals' status as good. *Those* white people (the lower class) are racist; we middle-class whites are not like them; therefore we are not racist. (p. 28, original emphasis)

According to Omi and Winant (2015), "neoliberalism was at its core a racial project as much as a capitalist accumulation project" (p. 211). Given this intricate and interdependent relationship between race and class, some scholars have even criticized critical race theory's sole focus on race and lack of engagement with political economy and capitalism, thus running the risk of contributing to the downplaying of socio-economic factors and the demise of class (Darder and

Torres, 2004; Delgado and Stefancic, 2001). For instance, Darder and Torres (2009), while acknowledging the intersectionality of race, class, and gender, disagree that "a host of oppressions should be afforded equal analytical explanatory power while the unrivaled force of capitalism in the world today is ignored" (p. 160). Rather, they recognize racism – as well as other forms of oppression – as central to the socio-political life of a capitalist state, and therefore, "ultimately linked to the exploitation and domination of both natural resources and human populations" (p. 164). As Darder and Torres (2004) further explain:

> The process of racialization, then, is at work in all relations in a capitalist society … Racism is one of the primary ideologies by which material conditions in society are organized and perpetuated in the service of capitalist accumulation. That is why, to repeat, the empire is not built on "race" but on a variety of ideologies (of which racism is one) that justify the exploitation and domination of populations deemed as "Other" so as to conserve the capitalist social order. (p. 101)

Thus, efforts towards dismantling racist policies and practices should extend beyond a limited understanding of racism at the individual level (i.e., good versus bad binary) to addressing institutional racism by altering the economic and political relations that benefit from the idea of different races (Miles and Brown, 2003). Instead of putting race against class and vice versa, racism and classism should be attacked in tandem through an intersectional approach since "neither can be overcome while the other flourishes" (Fraser, 2019, p. 22). The next strategy will therefore address a particular area that requires an antiracist and anti-capitalist approach: environmentalism – a topic that is widely but superficially discussed in language classrooms.

Adopting an antiracist, anti-capitalist, and intersectional approach to environmentalism

Box 6.7 Problem-posing task

In her TED Talk on *Environmental Justice*, Peggy Shepard states, "some communities don't have the wealth or the complexion for [environmental] protection" (n.a.).

According to Kendi (2019), "do-nothing climate policies" are racist since "the predominantly non-White global south is being victimized by climate change more than the Whiter global north even as the Whiter global north is contributing more to its acceleration … Human made environmental catastrophes disproportionately harming bodies of color are not unusual …" (p. 47).

Considering these two quotations above, reflect on the following questions in relation to your community, culture, or country:

- What environmental policies exist in this context?
- Who is in charge of making and executing these laws, regulations, and policies?
- Whose voice is included or silenced in the process of making these decisions?
- Who is influenced the most when faced with environmental hazards and challenges?
- Who benefits from the environmental laws, regulations, and policies, and why?
- How do race, oppression, and poverty intersect with environmental justice?

Based on your answers, consider how you might talk about environmentalism within language classrooms in this particular context.

Environmental education is a field that aims to help individuals acquire the necessary knowledge, skills, and dispositions to critically evaluate environmental issues in terms of socio-economic, cultural, and political concerns while also developing their sense of agency and advocacy to take action. Environmental issues have been quite widespread within language education especially with the emphasis on content-based language teaching (Bigelow et al., 2005; Hauschild et al., 2012; Jacobs and Goatly, 2000; Kautz, 2016) and learner-centered approaches such as experiential (Tangen and Fielding-Barnsley, 2007) and cooperative learning (Royal, 2016). Despite the prevalence of environmental topics such as climate change in language textbooks, studies have drawn attention to their often superficial environmentalism. This includes 'placeless' and 'disjointed' treatment of environmental issues such as the melting ice caps and the extinction of polar bears, which rarely involves addressing the underlying economic, cultural, and socio-political causes. Stibbe (2004), for instance, found that the causes of environmental destruction were described in terms of the most immediate physical ones (e.g., in relation to 'Acid Rain,' sulphur dioxide and nitrogen dioxide were discussed as the causes) rather than the deeper reasons (e.g., consumerism). Underscoring the textbooks' lack of attention to individual responsibility and agency when it comes to environmental issues, Stibbe's (2004) study also revealed that "the agents responsible for ecological destruction are elided by the use of nominations such as 'emissions' … or by ascribing the source of pollutants to 'car exhaust' and 'power plants' … rather than to drivers of cars or users of electricity" (pp. 244–245). Overall, environmentalism in language education has failed to adopt a critical and intersectional approach that involves in-depth discussions of the underlying causes of climate change and environmental degradation at the local and global levels. What's more, policy-level solutions which address the root causes of environmental issues (e.g., neoliberal policies) in ways that could alleviate the effects impacting low-income and racialized communities are rarely, if ever, presented. Discussing the embeddedness of nature in culture, the economy, and daily life, Harvey (2020) states:

> Capital modifies the environmental conditions of its own production but does so in the context of unintended consequences (like climate change) and against the background of autonomous and independent evolutionary forces that are perpetually re-shaping environmental conditions. There is from the standpoint no such thing as a truly natural disaster. (p. 180)

Robert Bullard, known as the father of the environmental justice movement, has extensively documented the adverse and disproportionate impacts of environmental and health threats to low-income communities and communities of color (Bullard, 1994a, 1994b; Bullard et al., 2008). *Environmental racism* was one of the early terms used to refer to "any policy, practice, or directive that differentially affects or disadvantages (whether intended or unintended) individuals, groups, or communities based on race or color" (Bullard, 1994b, p. 1037). Today, the all-encompassing term 'environmental justice' brings together race, gender, nationality, class, age, ability, and geography under a unifying, interdisciplinary and intersectional field to ensure fair, equitable, ethical, democratic, and nondiscriminatory environmental treatment and protection for all populations (Bullard et al., 2008; Kuehn, 2014). Kuehn (2014) explains this intersectionality as follows:

> oppressed people do not have compartmentalized problems—they do not separate the hazardous waste incinerator in their community from the fact that their schools are underfunded, there is no day care available for their children while they work, no sidewalks or streetlights, no water, sewerage or drainage, and no jobs (Sierra 1993). Disadvantaged communities do not separate these problems because their quality of life as a whole is suffering and the political, economic, and racial causes are likely interrelated. (p. 332)

The COVID-19 pandemic and its repercussions have been perhaps the most recent example of the indivisible, mutually dependent, and reinforcing nature of social justice, human rights, peace, and environmentalism, and the interdependence of the local and global. According to Harvey (2020), for instance, "COVID-19 is Nature's revenge for over forty years of Nature's gross and abusive mistreatment at the hands of a violent and unregulated neoliberal extractivism" (p. 205).

First observed in Wuhan, China in late 2019, SARS-CoV-2 was erroneously treated by the rest of the world "as something going on 'over there'" (Harvey, 2020, p. 189). COVID-19 quickly spread all over the world with major health-related and economic impacts especially on vulnerable and marginalized populations. It also reignited hatred towards Asians and people of Asian descent in many parts of the world but especially in the United States. Exemplified by the 45th US President Donald Trump referring to COVID-19 as 'the Chinese virus' and later 'the kung flu,' new forms of COVID-19-fueled xenophobia and racism emerged all around the world.[5]

Various antiracist, anti-capitalist, anti-colonialist, and intersectional pedagogies have been proposed to integrate environmental justice (or eco-justice) into school curricula (Andrzejewski et al., 2009; Bigelow and Swinehart, 2014; Dei, 2010; Bowers, 2002; Furman and Gruenewald, 2004; Gruenewald, 2003; Kagawa and Selby, 2010; Khan, 2009; Weber, 2009; Winograd, 2016). Scholars have particularly underlined the connections between Indigenized environmental justice, race, and capitalism. As Gilio-Whitaker (2019) has argued:

> Indigenous peoples fighting for political autonomy from the hegemony of the [United States] are fighting the forces of colonialism while simultaneously fighting capitalism – all aimed at control of land and resources – with colonialism as the precondition for capitalism. (p. 35)

From a similar perspective, Dei (2010) defines environmental education as "the possibilities of critical, anticolonial education that can help learners and local communities subvert the 'colonial/imperial order' that scripts human groups and our relations with environments" (p. 90). Bowers (2002) also suggests that any eco-justice pedagogy should include the non-commoditized, familial, and communal traditions of ethnic minorities or marginalized populations that enable face-to-face, intergenerational sharing of knowledge and skills while also ensuring their survival in economically and politically repressive environments without being too dependent on consumerism. Andrzejewski et al.'s (2009) edited book, *Social justice, peace, and environmental education*, on the other hand, adopted a more practical perspective to provide transformative standards for educators in all disciplines. Some of the environmental justice standards that relate to creating and maintaining effective learning environments include (p. 307):

- Developing holistic student understanding through participatory, experiential, accessible, and activist pedagogical practices.
- Incorporating local knowledge and ways of knowing through the study of 'place' in all its diverse forms.
- Building linguistically, culturally, and ecologically responsive and accessible learning environments.
- Cultivating a web of relationships that encompass all elements and creatures that make up the natural world in which we live.
- Developing multiple and varied forms of assessment to measure and achieve social justice, peace, and environmental education objectives.

Language educators can refer to Andrzejewski et al.'s (2009) transformative standards when discussing environmental disasters such as Hurricane Katrina in 2005, which battered the US Gulf Coast states of Louisiana, Mississippi, and Alabama, where African Americans comprise 26–36 percent of the population. Such topics draw learners' attention to the economic and environmental vulnerability of low-income and minoritized communities as well as their capacity to weather the health and other risks attendant with environmental disasters (Pastor et al., 2006). For language learners in different parts of the world, discussions can begin with local environmental disasters and then expand to global events in ways that will link their local experiences "to the experience of others in other places and to the cultural, political, economic, and ecological forces that connect people and places on a global scale" (Furman and Gruenewald, 2004, p. 62). The stories of young activists – not just Greta Thunberg, but also for instance, Canadian Indigenous activist Autumn Peltier (Anishinaabe) or Ugandan activist Leah Namugerwa – can be discussed in ways that will cultivate language learners' sense of advocacy and activism (Unigwe, 2019).

> **Box 6.8 Problem-posing task**
> To what extent do the materials/textbooks/curriculum used in your teaching context:
>
> - Create anthropocentric hierarchies which promote the idea that humans are at the center of the world – if not the masters' – and their lives are worth more than nonhuman life and biodiversity?
> - Convey consumerism through environmental issues (e.g., greenwashing)?
> - Enable learners to understand their relationship to their local and global environment in ways that would develop their critical consciousness regarding environmental justice issues?
> - Promote individual responsibility and agency in addressing environmental destruction and injustices and to promote world peace?

There are two main principles to keep in mind when discussing environmental issues in language classrooms. First, environmental education cannot be limited to classroom teaching but needs to extend beyond school walls. Place-based education that engages learners in first-hand experience of social and ecological issues can enable them to observe, appreciate, and take action to conserve the biotic and cultural diversity of their local environments and communities (Furman and Gruenewald, 2004; Winograd, 2016). Second, environmental education needs to address both local and global concerns simultaneously in ways that connect the two. According to Kagawa and Selby (2010), especially in wealthier societies, climate change education seems to be missing "an appreciation that the metaphorical North of the planet is primarily responsible for carbon buildup but that its effects are coming thickest and fastest to the peoples and societies of the South" (p. 242). While localism is essential for learners to engage with their immediate communities, it cannot be an excuse for "raising the drawbridge on others less fortunate" (Kagawa and Selby, 2010, p. 242). With these principles of environmental education in mind, the sample lesson plan[6] presented in Appendix 6.1 is designed to promote the intersectionality of peace, environment, and social justice in ways that connect the local and global.

Tackling racism in moment-to-moment interactions

Since teaching language and culture are not only interrelated processes but widely encouraged within language education, it is not uncommon to encounter racist incidents and instances of cultural appropriation in language classrooms with diverse learner groups. Cultural appropriation refers to act(s) of adopting or utilizing artifacts and features from another culture, without showing understanding, respect, and appreciation of that context. Impersonating a racial or ethnic identity through hair, clothing, and language use can be given as examples of cultural appropriation. The US holiday of Halloween, which is also celebrated in language teaching contexts in different parts of the world, is replete with examples of blatant cultural appropriation and/or overtly racist costumes. While it is part of this tradition that celebrants dress up in costumes, wearing the traditional clothing of different racial and ethnic groups (e.g., the most typical one being the 'sexy' Native American attire which ignores the violence against and the murder of Indigenous people) is considered cultural appropriation.

Language educators, therefore, need to address racist classroom incidents and instances of cultural appropriation in moment-to-moment interactions. When language educators are unprepared to tackle them, these incidents or microaggressions may go unnoticed, unaddressed, or ignored in the language classroom. As discussed in Chapter 2, teachers might avoid engaging in racetalk in order to 'remain neutral' or to not 'upset anyone,' or 'bring negativity' into their classrooms. However, addressing these incidents is not only important in order to alleviate the emotional and cognitive stress they might cause Black students, students of color, ethnic minorities, and, indeed, White students as well, but also to combat the larger social, historical, and political factors in the societies that create them. These sorts of incidents, in fact, provide teachable moments for language educators to tackle racism not only in educational contexts but also in society at large (Blum, 2008; Gooding and Gooding Jr., 2016; Kubota, 2010; Sue, 2015). According to Pollock (2004), educators' racetalk should include "questions about *how* race matters, questions that disrupt our normal scripts, unthinking statements, or muffled complaints about race" (p. 218, original emphasis).

Racial discussions or racetalk, however, can generate powerful emotional responses particularly in White students who might feel guilt, discomfort, denial, shame, anger, powerlessness, and despair. DiAngelo's (2018) best-selling book,

White fragility, depicts a myriad of defensive rhetorical moves (e.g., self-defense, denial, projection) and emotions White people utilize when asked to question and reflect upon their privilege in racial discussions. Therefore, language educators should directly address the tensions and emotions that arise as a reaction to course content to avoid disengagement and resistance that will interfere with student (un)learning. Pressure-release discussions, as cognitive and affective interventions, might help resolve potential conflicts in the language classrooms. However, conflicts sometimes may remain unresolved for ongoing discussion (Byars-Winstan et al., 2005; Tatum, 1992). Also, racetalk should be accompanied with social action projects and field experiences in order to cultivate learners' sense of agency and activism and to enable them to connect the curriculum to their lived experiences and social contexts (Ahlquist, 1991; Liggett, 2008; Tatum, 1992). Finally, language educators should also be willing to accept that mistakes might happen when talking about race (Tatum, 2017). As Pollock (2004) argues:

> Admitting that race talk can be inappropriate or inaccurate, and that mention-ing racialized populations when analyzing "problems" can risk making those populations themselves seem dangerously problematic, we can proceed with the explicit recognition that in our quests to make things better we will fail in countless small ways that we must continually repair. (p. 219)

This aspect of racetalk, therefore, requires language educators to develop their critical consciousness in ways that enable them to take responsibility and the initiative to fight against racism.

Developing critical consciousness as antiracist language educators

Language educators, regardless of their racial or ethnic background and iden-tification, need to understand the already existing race-based power relations inherent in teacher-student relationships and reflect upon their individual beliefs, assumptions, biases, and privileges in order to take an active stance towards dismantling their role in perpetuating racism in their educational contexts as well as in wider society (Ahlquist, 1991; Anya, 2021; Chan and Coney, 2020; Coles-Ritchie and Smith, 2017; Gooding, 2016; Lathan, 2014; King and Castenell, 2001; Sue, 2015). According to Matias and Grosland (2016):

> Just as people of color need curricular inclusions to understand their racial positioning in a racist structure and pedagogical strategies to learn how to decolonize the minds and increase racial empowerment, Whites need cur-ricular inclusions of Whiteness and pedagogical ways to self-interrogate their own Whiteness. By taking a corner of each side of the racial pillar, the burden of race is better distributed. (p. 161)

In addition to autobiographies and reflective papers as tools to develop teachers' critical consciousness, digital storytelling through multimedia projects has more recently emerged as a tool for reflecting upon teacher identities and experiences in order to enable them to deconstruct and dismantle the hegemony of Whiteness in language education (Matias and Grosland, 2016). Digital storytelling, which functions as a "microscopic looking glass that re-examines their own life on their own terms" (p. 157), also helps teachers decolonize the mind-sets of the racial colonizers, the White teachers, in this case. Autobiographies, reflection papers, and digital stories also benefit Black teachers and teachers of color by encouraging them to self-interrogate any ideologies of Whiteness embedded within their internalized racism. Sometimes referred to as self-condemnation (Ladson-Billings and Tate, 2009), internalized racism results from a racialized group's internalizing and accepting the negative stereotypes and the attributed inferior status regarding their racial or ethnic group. For instance, marginalized populations may believe that they are not good enough to get accepted into graduate school or become tenured faculty, rather than questioning the institutional racism inherent in these organizations. In that sense, autobiographies, reflection papers, and digital stories have the potential to help Black teachers, teachers of color, and ethnic minorities in deconstructing the way Whiteness impacts their lives and identities. Lastly, just as racism is not limited to educational contexts, nor should antiracism be. Bonilla-Silva and Embrick (2008) recommend teachers reflect on the following questions:

> do I live in a desegregated neighborhood? Do I take an active stance against racial stereotypes and racist jokes by friends, family, and co-workers? Do I support programs designed to give minorities an equal opportunity? Do I support interracial friendships, dating, and marriage? (p. 335)

Therefore, antiracist language educators should aim to extend their antiracism beyond the school walls and into their everyday experiences.

Box 6.9 Reflective task: Understanding your privilege

Tell us how you managed to get where you are in life today: your academic degree, teaching position, etc. What kind of support (e.g., financial, pastoral, collegial, friendship, family, social networks, etc.) did you receive? How equally do you think these support systems and privileges are distributed in the society you grew up in? How often do you interrogate and critically reflect upon your unearned privileges? How do you think these support systems and privileges shape your story of fighting injustices in the society or in educational contexts?

Conclusion

This chapter was influenced by two guiding principles. First, I attempted to define race, ethnicity, and racism in order to make these concepts clear to a global audience. In doing so I was informed by Miles and Brown (2003), who underline the problems around the definition of these concepts:

> *If racism is defined as politically or morally unacceptable, there must be a reasonable consensus about what it is.* A definition of racism cannot establish simple criteria for deciding whether or not a given discourse is racist (though cf. Wetherell and Potter 1992: 15–16, 69–71), but in the absence of any definition, the concept becomes meaningless, and opposition to racism is hindered. (pp. 3–4, original emphasis)

Second, I agree that race is a highly contextualized issue. There is no one single, generic form of racism, but rather multiple, diverse, and context-dependent racisms that make up the larger racist ideology in the world (Darder and Torres, 2009). I concur that race and ethnicity are socially and historically constructed, discursively perceived, and materially enacted, and, thus, discussions of race-based inequities need to be contextualized for a particular readership. Yet, this approach may result in a false sense that racism exists *only* in these societies, namely, in the US, the UK, Canada, Australia, and New Zealand, as well as the reduction of racism to acts of bigotry committed by White people against Black people and people of color. One of my former students once said racism did not exist in China, "a highly homogenous country where everyone has the same skin color." Therefore, in this chapter, I aimed to present "conceptual starting points" (Gillborn, 2006, p. 13) that can resonate with a wider global audience who can adapt the antiracist strategies presented in this book to the many forms of racism in their own contexts. I focused on critical race theory to propose instructional strategies for antiracist pedagogies in ways that can present takeaways for everyone around the world. While doing so, I kept in mind that critical race educational scholars "reject a paradigm that attempts to be everything to everyone and consequently becomes nothing for anyone, allowing the status quo to prevail" (Ladson-Billings and Tate, 1995, p. 62). My goal overall was to inform language educators about the many ways language classrooms can perpetuate racial or ethnic hierarchies across society and the ways in which language educators begin to become antiracist language educators who actively fight against these inequities and for social justice.

Notes

1. In order to indicate that race is not a biological reality but a socio-historical construct, some scholars use 'race' – in quotation marks – rather than race. This is

done to signal their rejection of the idea that human beings can be categorized into racial identities (often according to their skin color). Although I sympathize with the rationale, I have two concerns regarding this approach. First, as Miles and Brown (2003) argue, "because 'race' and 'race relations' are ideological notions which are used both to construct and negotiate social relations, the concepts that are employed to analyse that social process should reflect that fact consistently, something which is not achieved by simply placing the word 'race' inside quotation marks" (p. 92). Second, ethnicity, like race, is a problematic construct that according to this rationale would also need to be presented in quotation marks. In this book, therefore, I have avoided this approach and used both race and ethnicity without 'scare quotes.' Instead, I aimed to use a language – in this chapter as well as the rest of the book – that not only avoids legitimizing race and ethnicity but allows readers to deconstruct them.

2. In *Language before Stonewall*, Leap (2020) refers to a similar concept of triumph narratives about progress towards LGBTQ+ rights and how these narratives tend to occlude the experiences of minoritized and marginalized groups within LGBTQ+ populations.

3. According to Omi and Winant (2015), "Obama has not interceded for blacks against their greatest cumulative loss of wealth in U.S. history, the Great Recession of 2008. He has not explicitly criticized the glaring racial bias in the U.S. prison system. He has not intervened in conflicts over workers' rights—particularly in the public sector where many blacks and other people of color are concentrated. When massive demonstrations took place against public sector union-busting in Wisconsin in February and March of 2011, Obama was conspicuously silent" (p. 230). From a similar perspective, Bonilla-Silva (2015) discussed how the election of Obama "was not a miracle but a deepening of the 'new racism'" (p. 1366).

4. The discussion here comes from the materials evaluation and adaptation project completed by Kathryn DePietro, then a graduate student in the TESOL program at Middlebury Institute of International Studies at Monterey. She completed this project as part of the Language Teaching for Social Justice course offered by the author in Fall 2019. Kate currently teaches Spanish at Stevenson School in Monterey, California.

5. COVID-19 fueling anti-Asian racism and xenophobia worldwide. https://www.hrw.org/news/2020/05/12/covid-19-fueling-anti-asian-racism-and-xenophobia-worldwide

6. This lesson plan was designed by Sydney Zamudio who at the time this book was written was a graduate student in the Teaching Foreign Languages program – Arabic at Middlebury Institute of International Studies at Monterey. She completed this lesson plan as part of her project in the Language Teaching for Social Justice course offered by the author in Fall 2021. Sydney currently teaches Arabic at BelovED Community Charter School in Jersey City, NJ.

Multimedia resources

Oxford African American Studies Center
  https://oxfordaasc.com/page/lesson-plans
      The center provides lesson plans that highlight its resources along with discussion questions, supplementary reading suggestions, and a summary of the topic for lecture preparation.
Racism. It stops with me
  https://itstopswithme.humanrights.gov.au/
      Racism. It stops with me, an anti-racism campaign of the Australian Human Rights Commission, provides resources as well as a list of other anti-racist organizations for anyone interested in anti-racism work.
RACE: The power of an illusion
  https://www.racepowerofanillusion.org/
      As the online companion of the documentary *RACE: The power of an illusion*, this website provides lesson plans, materials, and other resources that can be used in classrooms to guide learners' discussion of the origins, beliefs, and consequences of race.
Racial Equity Tools
  https://www.racialequitytools.org/home
      Racial Equity Tools provides more than 3,500 tools, research reports, tips, curricular materials, and ideas for everyone working to achieve racial equity in communities, institutions, and the society at large.
The economic injustice of plastic
  https://www.ted.com/talks/van_jones_the_economic_injustice_of_plastic
      In this TED Talk, Van Jones, an American news and political commentator, author, and lawyer draws the audience's attention to the issue of recycling and how the throwaway, consumerist culture affects poor people and poor countries.

Children's books

Sorell, T. and Lessac, F. (2021). *We are still here!: Native American truths everyone should know*. Charlesbridge.
      This book's longer passages do a great job of educating readers about the history of the dispossession and displacement of Indigenous peoples by the federal government, in what is now called the United States of America.
Nyong'o, L. (2019). *Sulwe*. Simon & Schuster Books for Young Readers.
      A story about a young Black girl grappling with colorism, and her eventually finding pride and beauty in her skin.

Hannah-Jones, N. and Watson, R. (2021). *The 1619 Project: Born on the water* (illustrated by N. Smith). Kokila.

As the children's book accompaniment to the 1619 project, this book presents the pre-enslavement history and cultures of the West African people.

Robertson, D., Flett, J., and Leask, A. (2020). *Ispík kákí péyakoyak/When we were alone* (Cree and English edition). HighWater Press.

This bilingual edition of Robertson's 2015 book tells the story of the residential school system in Canada in a way that makes it easier for children to understand the deeply racist and unjust policies that led to entire generations of Indigenous children being taken from their families and communities in the name of a 'civilizing mission.'

Chapter 7

Social justice pedagogies for all gender and sexual identities

Box 7.1 Lead in
In their book chapter, 'Queering family difference to dispel the myth of the "normal,"' Marrun et al. (2020) argue:

> [Normal] is an otherizing social construct … [W]hat is considered "normal" from a societally hegemonic perspective, is not, in fact, typical for the majority. Thus, "normal" is a lie that is persistently re-told to perpetuate marginalization and minoritization of the masses for the unmerited benefit of the few; typical is the truth. (pp. 99–103)

What practices and behaviors are accepted as 'normal' in your educational teaching context and the wider community? What are the reactions towards those who are considered 'abnormal'? In what ways do these reactions marginalize and discriminate those who do not conform the standards of 'normal'? How do those individuals who are considered 'abnormal' transgress?

Introduction

We live in a patriarchal world. Although commercials and TV shows that display women in subservient roles are in many parts of the world less common or blatant than in the past, the dominance of men over women is perpetuated in more subtle ways through social media, popular culture, and the larger neoliberal discourse. A walk into the local shopping mall, main street, or downtown area or a look at media advertisements will present opportunities to see how women are objectified and held to unrealistic beauty standards (e.g., skinny mannequins, hypersexualized women in posters and billboards, commercials comparing buying a car with finding a wife). The World Economic Forum's 2020 *Global gender gap report* clearly demonstrated gender-related gaps in pay, unemployment, leadership roles, inheritance rights, property ownership, educational attainment, health, and survival across 153 countries. As lessons from the Ebola outbreak in West Africa (2014–2016), Zika, and recently COVID-19 have taught, infectious diseases are not gender-neutral but put women and girls at higher risks of exploitation and domestic and sexual violence (Meinhart et al., 2021; United Nations Population Fund, 2020). In various parts of the world, men's dominance – justified on the grounds of their alleged biological superiority – is praised, celebrated, and reinforced at the expense of women's rights and well-being. It did not take long for the Taliban, which returned to power in Afghanistan in August 2021, to backtrack on their promise to allow tens of thousands of schoolgirls to return to class for the new term, banning any schoolgirl above the age of eleven from attending school.

We live in a heteropatriarchal world. The judicial, medical, and educational systems all reinforce not only masculinity and patriarchy but also the view of gender as binary, which expects everyone to be *either* a girl/woman or a boy/man, oppressing anyone who does not conform to the norms of the gender binary (e.g., gender non-conforming, gender non-binary, or transgender). The very inequities and oppressions that concern gender identities (e.g., unequal rights, treatment, and protection; violence, harassment, and discrimination; lack of representation) are also pervasive when it comes to sexual identities (e.g., gays, lesbians, bisexuals, pansexuals).

Following the recommendations of previous studies (e.g., Catalano and Griffin, 2016; Blackburn, 2013), in this chapter I will simultaneously discuss gender and sexual identities in order to present an integrated, intersectional, and expansive approach to combatting, challenging, and dismantling sexism, heterosexism, heteropatriarchy, genderism, and trans*[1] oppression and other forms of oppression that impact the lives of lesbians, gays, bisexuals, cisgender women, and trans* and queer individuals, as well as those who are non-binary, genderfluid, and non-conforming. This chapter will discuss the following issues:

- Gender and sex as non-binary and interrelated social constructs
- The theoretical underpinnings of sex and gender: feminist and queer approaches
- Social justice pedagogies for all gender and sexual identities

Unpacking gender

Gender – traditionally understood as what it means to be masculine or feminine – is socially, culturally, and politically constructed and does not include a permanent or unitary set of characteristics. Gender is performative: Individuals *do* genders through their linguistic practices, and gender relations, roles, responsibilities, or differences change contextually and historically (Butler, 1990; Enns and Sinacore, 2005).

> **Box 7.2 Reflective task**
>
> In her oft-cited book, *The second sex*, Simone de Beauvoir (1949) states that, "[o]ne is not born, but rather becomes, a woman" (p. 273).
>
> In what ways have your upbringings constructed your gender identity and expression? To what extent is the construction of your gender identity a self-reflexive process? To what extent do you 'choose' your gender? What role have educational institutions in your society played – and continue to play – in socializing you into gender roles and expressions?

Gender socialization begins as soon as a child's biological characteristics are found out when simultaneously a child is *assigned* their gender. It is from that moment on that the unborn child is socialized into the gender binary of boy or girl starting with the question "Is it a boy or a girl?" and extending to their gifts, toys, and clothes. Postnatal gender socialization takes place at a larger and much faster scale throughout one's life span through the discourses at home, school, workplace, and the community. Gender socialization ensures that one's gender identity, expression, roles, and sexual orientation conform to particular societal and cultural expectations and remain consistent over one's lifetime. Here is an anecdotal example: A friend of mine contacted a person via email to inquire about a bike being sold online. The owner of the bike responded to her email saying that "I can bring the bike to you so that you can check it out, after I take my truck to a mechanic for a check-up." My friend told me how surprised she was, expecting a male owner, when it was a woman who brought the bike in her pick-up. The words 'mechanic' and 'truck' are associated with the world of men. It is because of her gender socialization that my friend expected a man to show up at her door after 'a visit to a mechanic with their truck.'

A related concept to gender socialization, *gender essentialism* leads individuals to evaluate their own experiences as well as those of others in terms of these binary categories of boy/man and girl/woman (Persinger and Persinger, 2016). Girls and boys – expected to play with different toys (dolls versus cars, respectively), engage in different leisurely activities (yoga/pilates versus soccer), and wear different types of clothing – are negatively evaluated, marginalized, and oppressed when they do not conform to these expectations. Gender essentialism partly derives from *biological determinism*, the assumption that biological factors – as opposed to social and environmental ones – shape the way individuals behave and express themselves. Yet, as Butler (1990) argues in *Gender trouble*, it is not because of their gender as an intrinsic essence that individuals behave in particular ways; it is their everyday actions, experiences, and performances (e.g., gestures, dress codes, speech) that construct gendered identities.

Gender socialization not only promotes a gender-binary worldview, but also reinforces genderism and patriarchy. *Genderism* refers to the ideology that expects individuals to conform to the characteristics of their assigned gender at birth in a restrictive gender-binary view that includes only man and woman. Failure to confirm to genderism leads to being perceived as 'abnormal,' 'weird,' and 'inferior,' and being stereotyped, marginalized, discriminated against, and oppressed (Catalano and Griffin, 2016). On the other hand, patriarchy is the ideology and its associated institutionalized practices that regard men as the authority figure and inherently superior (i.e., smarter, physically stronger, more capable, etc.) to women. According to Sensoy and DiAngelo (2017), patriarchy often takes the form of "a male god; the father as the head of the household; males as authority in all social realms such as law, government, religion, and culture; women as inherently inferior to men and the property of men" (p. 125). In patriarchal societies, women may internalize *misogyny* – that is, hatred and prejudice against women – and reinforce male privilege and female subordinate status. Within educational contexts, gender socialization and essentialism both mirror and influence the way a teacher approaches their students and designs their curricular activities. Unexamined assumptions and biases are quite common in educational environments where a student's behavior, outfit, and self-expression are evaluated based on 'typical' gender norms, expectations, and reinforcements. Acts of sexism (e.g., discrimination based on one's gender) and misogyny range from requiring boys/men to perform culturally prescribed forms of masculinity to a preference for male children; and from girls dropping out of school due to social pressures or lack of safety measures to sexual objectification of and violence against women (Catalano and Griffin, 2016; Kapur, 2016).

Unpacking sex

Gender is a term that is often used interchangeably and conflated with sex. Sex has been traditionally explained in terms of biological characteristics (e.g., physical, hormonal, and genetic), resulting in a binary view that individuals can either be male or female. The 'sex *equals* gender paradigm' assumes that if one has the biological characteristics of male, then *he*, as a masculine man, should dress, behave, and live accordingly, and vice versa. However, this idea of sex as a stable, intrinsic, biological construct has been contested by scholars for several reasons.

First of all, not all babies are born with biological characteristics (e.g., chromosomes, gonads, internal or external genitalia) that would categorize them as male or female. Intersex is an umbrella term for a person born with sexual or reproductive anatomy that falls outside the strict female/male binary. According to the 2017 report of Human Rights Watch (HRW), one in 2,000 people are born with differences, for which doctors historically and even today routinely and reflexively recommend surgical intervention (e.g., gender normalizing surgeries) and/or hormonal therapy in order to make a body appear more 'in line' with the sex assigned to them at birth. Many doctors nowadays advise against these surgeries on infants and young children because of their irreversible physical and psychological harm starting in infancy and lasting throughout their lives, while there are generally no urgent health risks in the first place.

Second, people have different stances regarding the spectrum of gender identities and gender expressions; that is, how they present their gender identity through their clothing, behavior, communication, and so on. Cisgender people, for instance, accept the sex they are assigned at birth according to their biological and physical characteristics and identify themselves as a girl or boy (or woman or man). On the other hand, some feel differently about their gender at different stages (i.e., genderfluid) or reject the idea of being gendered at all (Sokolower, 2016). Genderqueer, gender non-binary, and gender non-conforming refer to those who believe that gender identity is fluid and dynamic and not limited to the man versus woman gender binary. Transgender refers to those individuals whose gender identity is different from their gender assignment at birth. More people are openly transgender, identifying themselves differently from their assigned sex at birth, and/or physically transitioning from male to female (or vice versa) through hormone therapy and gender reassignment surgery. There are also individuals who express both sexes, reflecting a phenomenon sometimes called third gender or third sex. Kathoey (known as 'Ladyboys') in Thailand (Aldous and Sereemongkonpol, 2008), Inuit third gender in the Canadian Arctic (d'Anglure, 2018), Two-Spirit[2] Indigenous cultures (e.g., niizh manitoag from Anishinaabe/Ojibwe cultures, napêw iskwêwisêhot in Cree), Hijras of India,[3] or Māhū in Native Hawaiian and Tahitian cultures (Herdt, 1993) transcend how society defines the division of sex and gender roles.

The conventional understanding of sex in the 1970s as a biological construct that is 'fixed,' 'binary,' and 'scientific,' therefore, has been challenged by those who argue that sex, just as gender, is also a historically variable social construct created to categorize humans in order to make prescriptive claims about the world (Bradley, 2015, Davis and Preves, 2017; Butler, 1990; Lockhart, 2021). In fact, according to Butler (1986), the physical characteristics and behavior of human beings cannot be reduced to sex but are manifestations of their gender: "We never experience or know ourselves as a body pure and simple, i.e., as our 'sex,' because we never know our sex outside of its expression. Lived or experienced 'sex' is always already gendered" (p. 39). Butler (1990) goes on to say that "If the immutable character of 'sex' is contested, perhaps this construct called 'sex' is as culturally constructed as gender; indeed, perhaps it was always already gender, with the consequence that the distinction between sex and gender turns out to be no distinction at all" (p. 98). Similarly, Foucault's (1978) *The history of sexuality* discusses sexuality not as a natural or biological feature, but as a historically, socially, and culturally constructed category of experience. It is noteworthy that this view of sex as a social construct does not deny the existence of biological characteristics, but rather asserts that the ways in which individuals make sense of these biological features are historically, culturally, and socially constructed and are always political (Spargo, 1999).

Theorizing gender and sexual identities

Many theories and movements have been developed to support the rights and well-being of various gender and sexual identities. In the next sections, I discuss two intersectional frameworks, diversity feminism (e.g., feminists of color, antiracist feminists, lesbian feminists) and queer theory, both of which explored the experiences and oppression of marginalized gender and sexual identities in regard to age, social class, race, and ethnicity.

Diversity feminism

Various feminist theories and movements emerged in many countries over the centuries, reflecting the role of local exigencies, religions, cultures, and geographies on women's struggle for equal rights.[4] There are also others who adopted a more international and decolonized perspective, such as feminism without borders (Mohanty, 2003a, 2003b), transnational feminism (McLaren, 2017; Taylor and Zine, 2014), and global critical race feminism (Davis and Wing, 2000; Wing, 2000). Taking the United States as an example, this section aims to illustrate how feminist movements have developed and evolved to address the weaknesses of the earlier movements that ignored the complexity of women's experiences within and across different groups of race, gender, and sexuality.

The first wave feminism in the US was associated with nineteenth-century women's rights movements and the early twentieth-century suffragettes who demanded political parity and, in particular, women's right to vote. Although some of the supporters of this first wave were slavery abolitionist women, they have been widely criticized for centering on the needs of White, middle- and upper-class, Western women (Davis, 1983; Sokolower, 2016), a criticism that still prevails today (hooks, 2015a, 2015b; Phipps, 2020; Zakaria, 2021). The early waves, by arguing that all women are oppressed, implied the commonalities across women in terms of their oppressions, problems, and challenges, a phenomenon Higginbotham (1992) called as *false homogenizing* of women. As a reaction to this line of feminism, women of color and antiracist feminists underlined the multiple forms of intersecting and interlocking oppressions and, instead, argued for an analysis of differential oppression that acknowledges the particularities of issues and challenges faced by many women of color, poor women, women of different religions, and non-heteronormative women (Davis, 1983; Higginbotham, 1992; Mohanty, 2003b; Enns and Sinacore, 2005).

Second-wave feminism in the US, which took place between the 1960s and early 1980s, turned its attention to sexuality, family, and domestic violence. The second wave created an alternative platform for lesbians who could not raise their voice within the mostly male-dominated gay rights movement. Yet, lesbians interested in joining the second wave – being perceived as a "lavender herring" – were not welcome into the heterosexual feminist movement under the pretext that they would damage the feminist cause and reputation. Similar separatists' communities also existed within lesbian and gay rights movements. *Lesbian feminism* emerged out of a criticism of this second wave and argued for an analysis of the role heteronormativity plays in perpetuating patriarchy.

Heteronormativity is a hegemonic ideology that relies on the normative belief that heterosexuality (i.e., being attracted to the "opposite" sex, a female-male relationship) is the only natural form of romantic relationship. That is, anything outside of a female-male relationship is ostracized and marginalized as 'weird,' 'strange,' or even an 'illness.' Heteronormativity, however, is not only about sexual desire or sexual identities, but also relates to gender identities: women are not only expected to desire men, but also need to appear feminine in their clothing, hairstyles, behavior, and so on (Blackburn, 2013; Ng et al., 2019). As Grace et al. (2004) stated, "[hegemonic heterosexual and masculine ideologies] allow heterosexual men to maintain control by reinforcing the binary structures that value heterosexual over homosexual and masculine over feminine, linking them together inextricably" (pp. 318–319). Thus, *heteropatriarchy* as an ideology assumes and reinforces the dominance of cisgender, heterosexual males over cisgender females as well as those who are non-binary, non-conforming, and queer. While doing so, heteropatriarchy relies on institutionalized practices that permeate all social domains such as family, religion, work, leisure, law, education, and health.

Lesbian feminists who have aimed to deconstruct *compulsory heterosexuality* within feminist movements (e.g., Rich, 1980) have also worked towards a true inclusion of diverse lesbianism (e.g., lesbians of different races, ethnicities, classes, and abilities). They drew attention to, for instance, how Black lesbians were asked to choose between their racial and sexual identities and were caught in-between White supremacy and homophobia since lesbianism was seen as a White women's problem and a threat to Black nationhood (Lorde, 1984). As Catalona and Griffin (2016) mention:

> [L]esbians and gay men of color, working-class gay and lesbian people, trans* people, and bisexual people demanded recognition of their needs in lesbian and gay organizations, just as women of color and working-class women expressed their dissatisfaction with the middle-class white focus of mainstream feminist and lesbian organizations (Lorde, 1984; Moraga & Anzaldúa, 1983). (p. 196)

On the other hand, lesbian feminism has been criticized by queer theorists for stabilizing and essentializing categories of gender and sexual identities (Garber, 2001). More specifically, for queer theorists, lesbian feminists have created artificial divisions and gender configurations that further perpetuate the hierarchical man/woman dichotomy in the long run (Nelson, 1999; Enns and Sinacore, 2005).

Queer theory

As a multidisciplinary field drawing on ethnic and gender studies, sociology, anthropology, education, and psychology, queer theory aims to problematize the constructs of gender and sexuality in order to support gender fluidity, uncertainty, and flexibility. A queer understanding of gender and sexual identities means multiple gender and sexual expressions that "allow individuals to place themselves on a *queer continuum* between and beyond both heteronormative and homonormative ideals" (Neto, 2018, p. 593, emphasis added). Queer theory also involves an understanding of sexual identities that are beyond sexual attraction but as components of individuals' social identities that influence their lived experiences. In that sense, queer theory presents an intersectional approach that allows Black women to express their sexuality without having the need to choose race, gender, or sexuality as their predominant identity.

Foucault's (1978) insights regarding *normalization*, that is, "constant pressure to conform to the same model" (p. 182), has been central to queer theory. Rather than perceiving homosexuality as the form that deviates from heterosexuality, queer theory recognizes homosexuality and heterosexuality as mutually constructing each other, since "[in] order for heterosexuality to function as the normal, natural, and given, it must have its abnormal, unnatural, absent other: the homosexual" (Filax, 2006, p. 143). Queer theory, therefore, challenges the mainstream gay movement for normalizing homosexuality as natural, a phenomenon known as *homonormativity*.[5] Homonormativity, while aiming to increase the visibility and equality of gay communities, afforded "privilege to certain categories of LGBTQ identities without addressing how homophobia and transphobia intersect with oppressions based on racialization, poverty, immigrant status, and other markers of otherness" (Ng et al., 2019, pp. 52–53).

Queer theory rejects the representations of a unified, homosexual subject that is in line with White, middle-class, hetero-imitative values, and neoliberal order (Ng et al., 2019; Seidman, 1995). To illustrate: At first sight, the American TV show *Modern family* might be seen as an effort to provide an 'inclusive representation' of gay families on TV. From a queer perspective, however, *Modern family* promotes White homonormativity through a stereotypical White middle-class gay couple living in a White neighborhood, who adopt a child of Vietnamese heritage and assimilate into the larger culture and society. By conveying how ordinary – and just like everyone – White affluent gay couples are, *Modern family* not only perpetuates homonormativity but also affirms that being gay is accepted to the extent that one conforms to the social norms and values of the society – being a White upper-middle-class male in this case.

Queer can be used as a noun, an adjective, and a verb (Shlasko, 2005), though the noun form is the most complicated and contested. Queer, on the one hand, might be used as an umbrella term to refer to lesbian, gay, bisexual, and trans* identities. On the other hand, queer is employed to deconstruct these identity categories by blurring the boundaries between them.[6] Nelson (2009) describes this paradox of queer theory as follows: "The term includes all 'minority' sexual identities, while, at the same time, it troubles the very notion of sexuality as a basis of identity" (p. 22). As a verb, to queer or queering refers to the set of actions that aim to *queer* – to fragment, inquire, disrupt, break apart – normative and hegemonic discourses and relations of gender and sex as well as the larger concept of identity. As Morris (1998) states, "queer suggests a self-naming that stands outside the dominant cultural codes; queer opposes sex-policing, gender-policing, heteronormativity, and assimilationist politics" (p. 227). As an adjective, queer can be used to modify subject positions such as queer teachers and queer activism. Queer, in this case, might refer to those who identify themselves as queer as well as those who adopt queer theory to inform their teaching and activism.

Queer pedagogy and queering language education

Queer pedagogy provides educators with a perspective into what queer theory means for teaching and learning. Queer pedagogy is not a unified framework (Paiz, 2019b, 2020), nor is it about the correct method, approach, or explorations, "but rather the possibility to question our practices or notions of equality and acceptance" (Neto, 2018, p. 591). As Luhmann (1998) states, "instead of posing (the right) knowledge as answer or solution, queer theory and the pedagogy … pose knowledge as an interminable question" (p.128). In other words, a queer educator is not concerned about what knowledge to convey to students in a particular lesson but what questions can be raised – by everyone in the class – and what questions remain unexplored (Shlasko, 2005). In other words, queer pedagogy encourages learners to "ask questions about why our social world is the way that it is; who benefits from its current configuration; who is marginalized by the status quo; and what, if anything, can be done to create a more inclusive and equitable world" (Paiz, 2019b, p. 6). In that sense, queer pedagogy can be explained as a strategy towards troubling the day-to-day lived experience of school life and the impact of the overall curriculum:

> [the queer curriculum worker] digresses from mainstream "official" discourse; (b) challenges the status quo by queerly reading texts (uncovering potentially radical politics), or queering texts (points out silences or absences of marginalized groups like the Hijras and adds them to the text); (c) understands that curriculum is gendered, political, historical, racial, classed, and aesthetic; (d) sees herself or himself [or themselves] as a co-learner with student. (Morris, 1998, p. 234)

Within language education, queer pedagogy can be dated back to the work of Cynthia Nelson (1999) on gay-friendly pedagogies that aimed to make classroom instruction more relevant to those learners who identified themselves as lesbian, bisexual, and gay; and to legitimate these "subordinate sexual identities" in the long run (p. 175). Since Nelson's (1999) early work, language education scholars have been exploring what it means to queer language education and in what ways queering – that is, problematizing those hegemonic ideologies and heteronormative discourses that normalize certain identities while alienating others – would help create inclusive and thriving spaces for all gender and sexual identities (Cahnmann-Taylor et al., 2022; Curran, 2006; Nelson, 2009; Nguyen and Yang, 2015; Ó'Móchain, 2006; Paiz, 2019a).

Social justice pedagogies for all gender and sexual identities

> ### Box 7.3 Problem-posing task: Unpacking heteropatriarchy in your teaching context
> Interview three people (e.g., school administrators, teachers, students) in your teaching context or a context you are familiar with. How often do they speak up against sexist, misogynistic, homophobic, and transphobic language and behaviors they encounter in this educational context? What response(s) do they receive? What is common/different in their narratives? Based on their responses, what recommendations would you make to fight against heteropatriarchy in this context?

There are various pedagogical frameworks developed by educational scholars in order to help combat heteropatriarchy, misogyny, homophobia, cisgender-ism, and other forms of oppression concerning gender and sexual identities in educational contexts. Some of these include feminist pedagogy (Weiler, 1991); engaged pedagogy (hooks, 1994); multicultural feminist pedagogy (Enns and Sinacore, 2005; Tetreault, 2016); lesbian, gay, bisexual, transgender, and queer (LGBTQ) inclusive curriculum and pedagogy (Burdge et al., 2013; Lawrence and Nagashima, 2021; Snapp et al., 2015); gay-friendly pedagogies (Blackburn, 2013; Nelson, 1999); and queer pedagogy (Banegas and Evripidou, 2021; Nelson, 2009; Paiz, 2020; Shlasko, 2005).[7] The social justice pedagogies approach I will be presenting in this chapter draws on both queer perspectives and feminist pedagogies and underlines not only the interplay between gender and sexual identities but also their intersectionality in regard to race, ethnicity, and class. The following strategies will be discussed in this section:

- Problematizing representation and inclusion in language education materials
- Deconstructing and reconstructing family in language education practices
- Establishing inclusive and equitable classroom discourses
- Decentering Whiteness and Eurocentrism in gender and sexual identities
- Centering intersectionality of struggles within social justice pedagogies

Adopting a similar approach to what Davis (2016) calls "the intersectionality of struggles" (p. 144), this chapter overall aims to enable language educators to see sexism, heteropatriarchy, heterosexism, and trans* oppression as interlocking and intersecting systems of oppression that require the liberation of not only cisgender and heteronormative women but also women of color, women from poor backgrounds, as well as those whose gender and sexual identities transgress the status quo.

Problematizing representation and inclusion in language education materials

A plethora of studies have revealed language textbooks' role in perpetuating heteropatriarchy and sexism through images and texts that convey gender stereotypes (e.g., women in secretarial positions, girls playing with dolls versus men using hammers and screwdrivers) and bias (e.g., use of gender-biased language, unequal representation of male and female characters) (e.g., Bursuc, 2013; Lee, 2014; Ndura, 2004). These studies, to a large extent, adopted a gender-binary view, and therefore failed to draw attention to the invisibility of non-binary or trans* characters in language textbooks.

The few studies that adopted a queer lens have revealed that LGBTQ+ identities and lives remained silent and invisible in language textbooks (Gray, 2013b; Paiz, 2019a). Even when gay figures such as Elton John, Oscar Wilde, and Gianni Versace were discussed in occasional short texts, there was no mention of their homosexuality (Gray, 2013b). Representation of LGBTQ+ issues in language education materials, through films, books, or through the creation and adaptation of language textbooks, is important to validate all gender and sexual identities in language classrooms. By legitimizing and making visible various forms of identities, representation can also help deconstruct normalcy and what is considered off limits and unmentionable (Gray, 2013b; Paiz, 2017). As Burdge et al. (2013) state:

> Avoidance of LGBTQ-inclusive lessons may send a message to students that LGBTQ issues are shameful and should not be addressed. Intentional avoidance and exclusion may hinder school safety, discourage learning, and further ostracize students who are already vulnerable to harassment and bullying. (p. 10)

Thus, providing diverse representations of the LGBTQ+ leaders (e.g., including race, class, gender, dis/ability, *and* sexual orientation) in students' societies or disciplines will not only inspire them to pursue their dreams, but will help them feel validated, visible, and affirmed, and supported in school and beyond (Burdge et al., 2013; Snapp et al., 2015).

Representation and inclusion, however, should be problematized. For instance, as De Vincenti et al. (2007) indicated, when these identities were in fact present in French, Italian, and Japanese language teaching materials, they stereotyped homosexuals as diseased (e.g., HIV), and, as a result, "reinforce[d] the isolation of a social group by portraying them in a negative light" (p. 65). Cashman and Trujillo's (2018) analysis of nine Spanish-as-a-heritage-language textbooks used in the States also revealed similar findings. The inclusion of Ricky Martin, as a "good gay token," was not only exclusionary of other LGBTQ+ identities and lives, but his identity and experiences were presented as a 'controversial topic' that put LGBTQ+ identities up for debate for classroom discussion. As Nelson (2009) states, this kind of framing of LGBTQ+ related topics as controversial not only reduces potentially complex issues to two sides – one side being right and the other wrong – but also invites homophobic and transphobic comments into the language classroom.

Given the notable erasure and problematic representation of LGBTQ+ identities in language education textbooks, it is important that language educators bring in greater diversity within curricula and resources in order to affirm all gender and sexual identities. However, this form of curricular representation and inclusion has also its caveats (Britzman, 1995; Luhmann, 1998; Shlasko, 2005). First, what it means to provide an accurate representation or who qualifies as a positive role model is highly contested since queer resists definitions or essentialized characteristics. Similar to what Nelson (2009) calls the counseling approach, representation might be limited to mainstream, positive gay and lesbian characters presented in an essentialized and binary way, without troubling the foundational elements of heteronormativity at a large scale. Second, 'positive' and 'unthreatening' representations of LGBTQ+ people might just serve the purpose of reinforcing "the legitimacy of the boundaries that continue to keep some people on the outside" (Shlasko, 2005, p. 126), by homogenizing queer and trans* experiences and victimizing and pitying LGBTQ+ members (Griffin and Ouellett, 2003; Shlasko, 2005).

As Luhmann (1998) states, "a queer pedagogy exceeds the incorporation of queer content into curricula and the worry over finding teaching strategies that make this content more palatable to students" (p. 120). To avoid such essentializing and further discriminatory practices, language educators, for instance, can extend representations of trans* identities from wealthy White trans* people to trans* immigrants, trans* people with disabilities, poor trans* people, and other marginalized trans* populations (Spade, 2011). More importantly, curricular changes should shift from "a primary concern with curriculum (i.e., accurate representations) to an interest in reading practices" (Luhmann, 1998, p. 127).

According to queer pedagogy, texts – or instructional materials in this case – are not themselves queer. The inclusion of LGBTQ+ lives and experiences in the curriculum does not lead to queer readings. Quite the contrary, it might lead to assimilationist, tolerance-based practices by normalizing LGBTQ+ individuals within the mainstream society. Queer reading of a text – art, music, literature, and other multimodal forms – requires a radical perspective that challenges heteronormativity. Queer reading, in that sense, refers to the process of both incorporating texts about and from queer people and reading queerly, in other words, "to stop reading straight" (Britzman, 1995, p. 164). According to Britzman (1995), "[r]eading practices might well read all categories as unstable, all experiences as constructed, all reality as having to be imagined, all knowledge as provoking uncertainties, misrecognitions, ignorance, and silences" (p. 164). This form of queer reading has been discussed by educational scholars who drew from culturally relevant and social justice pedagogies that challenge heteronormativity and normalcy while also promoting intersectionality (Blackburn and Smith, 2010; Griffin and Oullett, 2003; Kumashiro, 2001a; Snapp et al., 2015). Blackburn (2013), for instance, raises several questions to reflect upon in relation to the various stories brought into language classrooms through films, books, and such:

> Are they stories that say there are no LGBTQQ[8] people? Or that there is one way to be LGBTQQ? Or that only white people are LGBTQQ? Or that all LGBTQQ people are victims? … What might it mean for a lesbian in your class to believe she is the only one or for a young gay man of color to believe that all gay people are white? Or for a white gay youth to hear and read only stories of queer youth suicides? … Are we telling stories that put individuals in isolation from society so that they are alone to receive either praise or blame? Or are they stories that explain how the world functions in constructing who they are so they can still assume agency but with an understanding of why they do what they do in relation to what others do? (p. 65)

In other words, queer readings – and queer pedagogy at large – is not only about deconstructing normalcy of certain gender and sexual identities, but also refusing any kind of normalization that concerns race, ethnicity, class, ableism, and so on (Luhmann, 1998).

There are several considerations when problematizing the representation and inclusion of LGBTQ+ lives and experiences in the language curriculum. First, language educators need to ensure that LGBTQ+ representation, inclusion, and queer readings run through the whole curriculum so that teachers can avoid an inoculation approach (Paiz, 2019b), that is, covering an LGBTQ+ related topic once in a semester for the sake of inclusion or for checking a box as part of a diversity training requirement. Isolated or stand-alone lessons that are often teacher or student driven rather than institutional might be further alienating rather than being inclusive (Blackburn and Smith, 2010; Schmidt, 2010; Burdge et al., 2013; Snapp et al., 2015). LGBTQ+ inclusivity is an issue that concerns all aspects of an educational curriculum – not only the instructional materials, activities, and classroom interactions, but also the assessment policies and practices as well.

Second, when discussing LGBTQ+ related issues, language educators should also avoid putting queer students into expert positions in the class to speak about their experiences, since this approach may reproduce dominant, essentializing narratives about queer identities in the long run. As Kumashiro (2001b) states, the goal should be to disrupt learners' knowledge through questions that take them beyond what they already know:

> So in a lesson on queers of color, in addition to asking, "What does this lesson tell us about queers of color," educators can ask, "How can we use this lesson to learn more about queers of color, or about the intersections of racism and heterosexism? Which stereotypes of queers of color does this lesson reinforce and which ones does it challenge? What is not said in this lesson about queers of color and how do those silences make possible and impossible different ways of thinking about queers of color?" (p. 18)

Lastly, learners' social action projects that raise awareness of and challenge heteropatriarchy should not derive from or perpetuate a simplistic and degrading perspective of seeing LGBTQ+ members "as victims in need of rescue by altruistic allies or by agents that fight against big, bad bullies" (Blackburn, 2013, p. 65). Love's (2018 [2000]) liberatory consciousness, a topic discussed more widely in Chapter 8, can inform learners' social action project in ways that enable them to unlearn any heteronormative and binary assumptions that maintain LGBTQ+ oppression in educational contexts.

Deconstructing and reconstructing 'family' in language education practices

Those who oppose discussing gender and sexual identities in language classrooms often argue that 'teachers should teach language only' or 'these discussions are not age-appropriate especially with young learners.' However, classrooms and the wider educational institutions – as microcosms of their larger societies – not only mirror but also perpetuate the existing power relations, including hierarchies that pertain to sexual and gender identities (e.g., Kapur, 2016). Perhaps one of the most telling examples of this reproductive function of education comes from the theme *family*. In addition to themes such as relationship, dating, socializing, travelling, and meeting new people, family – as one of the most-widely discussed topics in language classrooms – conveys information about the involved parties' gender and sexual identity (e.g., Cashman and Trujillo, 2018; De Vincenti et al., 2007; Gray, 2013b). Yet, the representation of family – in most language textbooks, in a variety of languages – is strictly limited to the gender-binary view, with a heterosexual couple who have two – presumably biological – children, typically a boy and a girl. By erasing all other gender and sexual identities and expressions, this heterosexual nuclear family constitutes the basis of heteropatriarchy as an economic and reproductive unit (Neto, 2018; Phipps, 2020). This is one of the reasons why gender and sexual identities are *already* part of the language education curriculum, representing cisgender, heterosexual couples while excluding same-sex parents and trans* parents, to name only two.

Coming out is yet another concern that relates to the discussion of family in language classrooms. Coming out refers to the repetitive process of and series of decisions that involve accepting and identifying with one's gender and sexual identity and sharing it voluntarily and willingly with others. Publicly declaring one's sexual or gender identity is also an act of deconstructing heteropatriarchy and heteronormativity (Enns and Sinacore, 2005). Yet, this process has been reported to be challenging especially in biracial families with Black and White parents (McCready, 2001); or for Chicanx queers who may fear that support from *la familia* (the family) might disappear (Misa, 2001); or for Asian/Pacific Island queer communities in which coming out intersects with gender, social class, and familial expectations (Varney, 2001). For instance, one of the participants in Varney's (2001) study discussed how coming out is seen as a Western process in Asian communities in the US "where you have to automatically be proud and be out to everyone" (p. 94). Discussing the topic of family, therefore, can be particularly sensitive and emotionally laden for those learners who might be in the process of coming out to their families; who might be dismissed from their families and denied family-based social-welfare benefits; or who were forced to leave their home due to domestic violence and abuse.[9]

The representations of family in language education materials convey not only nuclear heteronormative families, but also upper-middle-class White families, excluding families of color, and biracial, poor, immigrant, homeless, differently abled, and teen and single parents. For students coming from diverse family backgrounds and configurations, such representations can be demotivating, alienating, and exclusionary (Marrun et al., 2020). As Marrun et al. (2020) state:

> This can leave students feeling unwelcome and/or as if they do not belong, and further lead to students becoming labeled as "low-achievers," or worse, as "emotionally disturbed," "behaviorally disordered," and "deviant," all because of the perception that they come from "abnormal" homes, and their families are often described as "broken" and "troubled" (Chavez, 2013; Howard, 2013; Spillers, 1987; Villenas, and Deyhle, 1999). (p. 103)

Language educators need to be cognizant and inclusive of different forms of families and their life experiences by recognizing possibilities for different gender and sexual expressions with a lens "outside the imperatives of normalcy" (Britzman, 2012, p. 304). Marrun et al. (2020), for instance, present several critical questions for teachers to reflect upon in order to decenter nuclear, White, middle-class, heteronormative notions of what makes a 'normal' family:

- What are the "traditional" dominant narratives about "normal" family dynamics and how might our beliefs around those narratives impact student learning?

- What makes a family a family?
- How can schools and educators counter limited definitions of, and deficit assumptions about, students' families in order to create more educationally welcoming, affirming, and rigorous learning communities in which all students achieve academic excellence? (p. 104)

Queer reading of texts on family has the potential to encourage learners to trouble pre-existing perceptions of family; consider any implicit and unchecked assumptions related to gender and family structures; and reimagine the text from the perspective of unconventional families (Paiz, 2019a). Sleeter's (2008) conceptual framework of critical family history[10] enables learners to situate their own family and its history within the larger society and its institutionalized power relations. This framework also allows learners to reflect on their own families while also building connections with others. It is, however, important to note that whenever students are asked to share information about their own families and family relations, they should be informed in advance of that particular class with regard to how the information will be used/shared in the class and for what pedagogical purpose.

Queer reading of text is not limited to written materials only but applies to any multimodal text. For instance, the Family Diversity Project[11] is a non-profit organization that aims to eliminate different forms of oppression based on gender, sexuality, race, nationality, religion, and disability through photo-text exhibits that tour different communities and educational contexts in the US. Their online exhibit presents educators with complex images and stories of diverse families such as immigrant and refugee families, LGBTQ+ people and their families, multiracial families, as well as representations of mental illness and disability in the family. Similar multimodal resources could be useful for the inclusion of learners' diverse families and for the disruption of heteronormative and patriarchal discourses around family in the long run.

Establishing inclusive and equitable classroom discourses

In addition to redesigning and queering their curriculum, language educators need to employ inclusive and equitable instructional strategies that provide a physically and psychologically welcoming environment for all students (Persinger and Persinger, 2016). This process also involves creating classroom discourses that will help their learners perform their gender and sexual identities in linguistically appropriate ways in another language and to communicate with each other in ways that are respectful and understanding (Cahnmann-Taylor and Coda, 2019; Cashman and Trujillo, 2018; Moore, 2016; Paiz, 2019a; Sadker and Zittleman, 2016). This is mostly because the linguistic and cultural practices that take place in the language classroom portray a certain worldview, and therefore construct certain identities as 'normal' and 'natural,' while silencing, policing, and marginalizing others. That is to say, classroom discourses about gender and sexual identities "do not passively reflect social realities but actively constitute those realities, and the social inequities associated with sexual diversity are not just described with language but produced through it" (Nelson, 2009, p. 51).

Studies have revealed the inequitable interaction patterns and the gendered nature of classroom interactions, favoring male students over females (e.g., Sadker and Zittleman, 2016), as well as the heteronormative assumptions embedded within teachers' classroom behavior (e.g., Liddicoat, 2009). In Liddicoat's (2009) study, the Spanish language learners who implicitly or explicitly performed their lesbian and gay identities during classroom activities were perceived by the classroom teacher as having a problem of linguistic competence, which led to the correction of gendered form from masculine to feminine when the student was in fact referring to his boyfriend. This sort of (un)conscious policing of learners' gender and sexual identities through corrective feedback may not be easily identified without a careful look into actual teacher-student interactions (e.g., Liddicoat, 2009; Paiz, 2017, 2020). The heteronormative discourses in the classroom, however, are not limited to teacher-student interactions but may also include student-student interactions (e.g., homophobic comments). These anti-queer instances can be used by language educators as teachable moments in order to problematize heterosexuality as the norm and to help learners begin to deconstruct their unexamined assumptions about gender and sexual identities (Curran, 2006; Rhodes and Coda, 2017; Rhodes, 2019). According to Curran (2006), deconstruction, from a queer perspective, refers to:

> Unpacking discourses that would ordinarily be taken for granted within mainstream contexts ... This involves identifying binaries, absences, presumptions, hierarchies and practices of marginalization, concerning how particular groups (i.e., heterosexuals and homosexuals) are positioned, or position themselves, within discourses. (p. 92)

Box 7.4 Reflective task

Which one(s) of the strategies in the checklist below do you adopt to establish inclusive and equitable classroom discourses for all gender and sexual identities? What other strategies can you think of? Add as many as you like to this checklist to create your own.

A – Unlearn heteronormative assumptions (i.e., all students are heterosexual and/or monosexual) that have an impact on classroom interaction:

E.g., Avoid arranging students into binary groups of girls and boys. Group students in terms of their month of birth, their astrological sign, favorite sports and season, etc.

E.g., Avoid asking students to describe their husband/wife or their ideal/current partner that might force them to come out. Be mindful when asking personal questions about their lives in general.

B – Convey openness and acceptance of all gender and sexual identities through your verbal and non-verbal behavior:
E.g., Present your personal pronouns and offer them the opportunity to do so for themselves.

E.g., In your classroom guidelines, include pronouncing names and using pronouns correctly.

C – Establish turn-taking norms and practices for equitable classroom participation:
E.g., Provide two or three ice-cream sticks to everyone. Every time a learner takes a turn, they turn in one of their sticks, indicating the remaining turns they have for the rest of the class.

E.g., Be mindful of teacher wait time. Provide enough time for students to respond to questions and prompts, and also to ask questions themselves. Allow students to have 'think time' before responding.

E.g., Encourage discussing sensitive topics while allowing zero tolerance for discriminatory and stereotypical language use and behaviors.

D – Avoid promoting stereotypes around gender and sexual identities:
E.g., In group work, avoid assigning secretarial roles (e.g., note taker) to female identifying students and rotate tasks across different group members.

E.g., Use gender-neutral language and/or texts, or point out gendered language in texts.

E.g., Avoid gendered job assignments such as asking male-identifying students to move desks and tables for group tasks and female identifying students to hand out papers or help clean up.

Based on the previous studies that examined heteronormative classroom discourses (e.g., Bursuc, 2013; Meyer, 2010; Persinger and Persinger, 2016; Enns and Forrest, 2005; Sadker and Zittleman, 2016; Widodo and Elyas, 2020), the following checklist in Box 7.4 is designed to help language educators critically analyze their classroom interactions in order to dismantle heteropatriarchy in their classrooms and educational institutions. While the checklist in Box 7.4 is presented as part of a reflective task, it can also be used for classroom observation and peer feedback.

Decentering Whiteness and Eurocentrism in gender and sexual identities

According to the 2020 state-sponsored homophobia report by the International Lesbian, Gay, Bisexual, Trans and Intersex Association (ILGA; Mendos et al., 2020), there are still sixty-nine UN member states that criminalize homosexuality.[12] While the death penalty is implemented for consensual same-sex activity in Iran, Northern Nigeria, Saudi Arabia, Somalia, and Yemen, it is a legal possibility in Afghanistan, Brunei, Mauritania, Pakistan, Qatar, and United Arab Emirates. Homosexuality is still seen as a mental disorder in some countries, and conversion therapy, which aims to 'cure' gay, lesbian, and transgender people with 'appropriate medical intervention,' is still endorsed and practiced (e.g., in Israel, Indonesia, Malaysia). Even in countries where same-sex relationships are not criminalized (e.g., Turkey), there is still high stigmatization and violence towards non-heterosexual and non-cisgender people, with limited protection laws and inequitable health services (Mendos et al., 2020). Given this grim picture, scholars drew attention to the importance of contextual factors while talking about gender and sexual identities,[13] while some even recommended not discussing these issues at all in countries where homosexuality is illegal.

Within language education, De Vincenti et al. (2007) discussed the potential linguistic and cultural challenges while addressing sexual identities in French, Italian, and Japanese classrooms in Australia. While the Romance languages such as French and Italian have a gendered grammar (e.g., gendered vocabulary, suffixes attached to nouns to mark their gender), the linguistic context with Japanese is quite different and poses its own idiosyncratic challenges for queering language classrooms:

> [Japanese] has quite a strong codification of masculine/feminine language use in vocabulary (e.g. in the choice of words for 'me' and 'you'), intonation and the use of sentence final particles. At the intermediate level, students are taught that the use of *wa* (a sentence final particle) by females serves to soften the tone of an utterance, and female students may be encouraged to use it. At the beginner level, however, students are taught that *watashi* means I/me and is used by both males and females, but *boku* is used only by males and only when speaking with colleagues or people below the speaker in the social hierarchy. Students may also be taught other pronouns and that the overuse of *watashi* by males indicates femininity. (p. 69)

Ó'Móchain's (2006) study, on the other hand, focused on EFL classrooms in Japan where queer-identifying people might feel a disconnection between Japaneseness and queerness due to the Western-dominated images of homosexuality. While De Vincenti et al. (2007) called for case studies that examine the linguistic and contextual challenges for queering language education for languages other than English, Ó'Móchain (2006) recommended language educators to use narratives of local, queer-identifying individuals as contextually appropriate materials for classroom discussions in order to facilitate meaningful communication and the recycling of language that would contribute to learner language development. Language learners can engage in similar tasks to the one presented in Box 7.5 and relate these narratives to their own experiences in ways that problematize dominant notions of normalcy rooted in their own geographical and socio-historical exigencies.

And just as Whiteness has been a central criticism of the mainstream feminist movement, queer scholars such as Mayo (2016), challenged the potential Whiteness within the term queer:

> Who is excluded if we privilege visible or legible differences? How does the pressure to be out in a certain way rely on particular culturally specific forms of understanding identity or generationally specific forms of political engagement? Where do other forms of difference appear if the central term is queer and implies "White?" (p. 144)

Underlining the need for opening up "conversations about ongoing decolonial struggles and the relationships between sexuality, gender, colonization, and decolonization" (p. 70), Cherokee scholar Qwo-Li Driskill (2010) drew attention to the need for queer studies that take into consideration the present colonial realities of the Native Two-Spirit/LGBTQ people in the United States and Canada. Two-Spirit critiques share commonalities with queer critiques in terms of challenging heteropatriarchy and the policing of gendered and sexualized bodies. However, rooted in Native histories, politics, and nationalist, decolonial struggles, Two-Spirit critiques position Indigenous gender and sexual identities within Indigenous land, community, and history. According to Driskill (2010):

> The stance that we are – and should be – an integral part of our communities, that our genders and sexualities are something that actually are "normal" within traditional worldviews, marks Native Two-Spirit/queer politics as very separate from non-Native movements. Being a part of our nations and communities is actually an antiassimilation stance against colonial projects – such as boarding/residential schools and forced Christianization – that have attempted to assimilate Native people into non-Native culture and tried to eradicate Indigenous sexualities and gender systems. Two-Spirit critiques call into question, then, how radical queer politics replicate colonial taxonomies and realities even as they attempt to disrupt them. (p. 83)

Therefore, language educators, when having discussions around gender and sexual identities in relation to particular contexts, need to keep in mind the potential Whiteness and Eurocentrism in feminist and queer movements, since these discussions might circulate 'us versus them' ideologies that further lead to the Othering of certain societies and cultures. Colonialist and Orientalist assumptions consider gender and sexual imparities as a problem of the "Other" – more often so the Muslim world. They also position women of color waiting to be saved from men of color by their White sisters, which is just another form of the White feminist savior complex (Mohanty, 2003a; Sensoy and DiAngelo, 2017; Zakaria, 2021; Zine and Taylor, 2014). This problematic 'us versus them' dichotomy relies on the assumption that "examples of sexism … occur 'over there'—in non-White, non-Western contexts—examples of sexism 'over here' are usually situated in the past" (Sensoy and DiAngelo, 2017, p. 129), and, therefore, views Western women as liberated and Muslim women as oppressed and marginalized. In other words, White feminist perspectives regarding the struggles of Black women, women of color, women of different ethnic backgrounds, Indigenous women, and transgender women might further perpetuate a gendered, sexualized, capitalist, and colonial order. As Rafia Zakaria (2021) states in her book, *Against White feminism*:

> By highlighting Brown and Black and Asian women suffering trauma as the "usual," their victimhood stemming from their cultures, while suffering white women are portrayed as an aberration, a glitch, white culture, including the feminism that has sprung from it, asserts itself as superior. (p. 6)

Drawing on the kidnapping of 276 Nigerian schoolgirls in 2014 by the group commonly known as Boko Haram, Phipps (2020) discussed how the hashtag #BringBackOurGirls started by Abuja-based lawyer Ibrahim Abdullahi, received Western empathy and engagement in the form of feel-good posts about the brutalized schoolgirls 'over there' and colonial demands such as Western military intervention; and "when the girls were not rescued or returned, most Western feminists moved on" (p. 89). In a similar vein, the feminist movements in some parts of the world, such as Brazil, have been found to be Eurocentric, failing to reflect the impact of colonialism and neocolonialism on women's problems (e.g., racial violence, health issues) in these countries (Walters, 2005).

The 'us versus them' ideologies around the oppression and marginalization of women of color not only ignore the colonial histories of these cultures and contexts but also superficially gloss over the current exigencies of the so-called civilized societies. Today, reports of the Russian invasion of Ukraine that began in late February 2022 have documented the widespread use of sexual violence against Ukrainian women and girls by Russian forces as a weapon of war for genocide through forced impregnation.[14] In the US, rape has been a colonialist, capitalist weapon of domination and oppression not only during the age of slavery – for the purpose of putting "Black women in their place," but also during the Vietnam War against Vietnamese women and girls who were "singled out as victims of terrorism by a sexist military force governed by the principle that war was exclusively a man's affair" (Davis, 1983, p. 24). On the other hand, femicide or feminicide (i.e., the intentional killing, disappearing, and threatening of girls and women) seems to be more common in the United States (with 2,991 women killed in 2019) than in Turkey (with 474 women), a significant difference even accounting for the fact that the US is four times larger in population than Turkey.[15] As I write these words, debates and protests are taking place in the United States over the Supreme Court's highly contentious overturning of *Roe* v. *Wade* – which means the demise of abortion as a federal right in the US, an outcome with possible repercussions at the global level.[16]

Box 7.5 Problem-posing task

Step 1:

- Interview a professor/teacher/student/friend in your educational context and report their observations and experiences regarding LGBTQ+ issues and LGBTQ+ inclusive pedagogy, or
- Interview a self-identifying LGBTQ+ member in your educational context and report their observations and experiences regarding LGBTQ+ issues and LGBTQ+ inclusive pedagogy.

Please make sure that you adhere to the following steps to minimize the ethical concerns involved in interviews:

- Before the interviews, please tell your participant(s) about the reasons behind this interview and receive their formal or informal consent for participation.
- Make sure you are informing them about if and how you are recording the interview (audio, video, note-taking), how you will store the data, and what information will be shared with whom and in what ways.
- Avoid any identifying information about the individual you have interviewed in your report. Use pseudonyms instead of real names.

Step 2: Discuss their responses in relation to the following questions:

- How safe is this educational context for LGBTQ+ students and teachers?
- What can be done to provide more inclusive and equitable pedagogies to LGBTQ+ students and teachers in this particular context?

Step 3: Create a multimodal representation of your findings. This could be a life story map, a graphic organizer, a picture collage, and so on. Share this multimodal product with your colleagues or students to raise awareness of LGBTQ+ issues in this context.

Given the importance of current socio-historical exigencies of different societies and cultures for social justice pedagogies, language educators might benefit from a feminist solidarity model that "requires understanding the historical and experiential specificities and differences of women's lives as well as the historical and experiential connections between women from different national, racial, and cultural communities" (Mohanty, 2003a, p. 522). For Mohanty (2003a), these pedagogies must be "attentive to the micropolitics of context, subjectivity, and struggle, as well as to the micropolitics of global economic and political systems and processes" (p. 501). Therefore, language educators not only need to be cognizant of this 'us versus them' binary that reinforces racism, classism, and other forms of oppression but also actively work towards anti-Orientalist, anti-colonialist, and anti-capitalist pedagogies. Resistance, according to Mohanty (2003b), "lies in self-conscious engagement with dominant, normative discourses and representations and in the active creating of oppositional analytic and cultural spaces" (p. 196). Thus, any anti-Orientalist, anti-colonialist, and anti-capitalist pedagogy should work towards developing "counternarratives to the clichéd images of Muslim women [and other women of color] represented through victim-centered tropes" (Zine and Taylor, 2014, p. 12). This process includes bringing about new readings of all sorts of multimodal texts that could potentially disrupt dominant discourses around Muslim women and other women of color while also making space for new articulations of all marginalized women's lives and experiences. Engaging in critical literacy, as discussed in Chapter 4, is essential for anti-colonial education that "requires deconstructing [hegemonic] frames and developing resisting forms of reading as well as defiant pedagogy and praxis that actively works against colonial and Orientalist imaginaries" (Zine, 2014, p. 195).Topics such as environmental justice and human rights could enable language educators to build those connections as well as to indicate possible disjunctures across different cultures, with emphasis on mutuality and common interests and with an outlook towards agency and resistance.

Centering intersectionality of struggles within social justice pedagogies

As discussed in Chapter 1, Crenshaw (1991) developed the notion of intersectionality as a criticism of unidimensional frameworks that focused solely on sexism or racism. This notion was much needed then – and is still needed now – to draw attention to the experiences of Black women, who were in the crosshairs of both. According to hooks (2015b), "Racism has always been a divisive force separating black men and white men, and sexism has been a force that unites the two groups" (p. 159). In other words, unidimensional frameworks that focus only on gender or race "can only benefit white women who are not oppressed by race or Black men who are not oppressed by gender" (Phipps, 2020, p. 50).

And while Crenshaw is widely credited for coining and popularizing the term, intersectionality has built upon the voices and efforts of Black women who resisted against interlocking forms of oppression. "Ain't I a woman?" – which later gave bell hooks the title of her 2015 book, was taken from an 1851 speech by Sojourner Truth at the Women's Rights Convention in Akron, Ohio.[17] The Combahee River Collective, formed in Boston in 1974 by a group of Black lesbian feminists, released a statement in 1977 explaining their intersectional work as follows:

> we are actively committed to struggling against racial, sexual, heterosexual, and class oppression, and see as our particular task the development of inte-grated analysis and practice based upon the fact that the major systems of oppression are interlocking. The synthesis of these oppressions creates the conditions of our lives. As Black women we see Black feminism as the logical political movement to combat the manifold and simultaneous oppressions that all women of color face. (Combahee River Collective, 2017 [1977], p. 20)

More recently, publications have come out discussing how White women, by weaponizing '[White] women's safety' continue to perpetuate systems of coloni-alism, neoliberalism, racism, and patriarchy over Black women and women of color (Eisenstein, 2019; Hamad, 2019; Phipps, 2020; Taylor, 2017). For instance, Allison Phipps' (2020) book, *Me, not you,* focuses on how the #MeToo movement begun by a Black woman activist, Tarana Burke, has been led by middle-class White feminists who have focused on gaining power and success within the exist-ing hierarchical structures rather than dismantling it. Similarly, Ruby Hamad's (2019) *White tears/Brown scars*, discusses how the protection of White women has been predicated upon White supremacy and consequently on Black death:

> ... The white feminist battle is not one that aims to dismantle the [racial and gendered] hierarchy but merely seeks to ensure that white women join white men at its helm by agitating only against those limitations imposed on their sex ... But it is a patriarchy they themselves have just ensured will continue, because their weaponised tears are a form and function of it ... By keeping the old structures in place, white women's innocence and virtue serve as the front line of white civilisation. (p. 72)

Sexual assault and rape were not only weapons of war used against enslaved Black women, but also targeted Indigenous women as well. For Indigenous pop-ulations, therefore, fighting against sexual violence also means fighting against colonialism and capitalist expansion. In a similar way, ecofeminists who study the intersections of feminism and environmental justice discussed the various ways in which climate change, natural resource extraction, and hyper-exploitation exacerbated gender inequality and sexual violence (e.g., 'sex for fish trade' in Malawi, Kenya). It is widely documented that the loss of lands, territories, and resources, and forced immigration in Native/Indigenous North America, Africa, Latin America, and Asia Pacific, have put Indigenous women at disproportionately much higher risk of sexual violence than their non-Indigenous counterparts (Murphy-Oikonen et al., 2022; Perkins, 2017; Tosh and Gislason, 2016; United Nations, 2014). As Phipps (2020) explains:

> [First Nations, Chicana and Native American feminists, and feminists of the South Asian diaspora] argued that while white women were bearers of the imperial order, Indigenous women were seen as bearers of the counter-imperial order, which justified their rape and murder and the murder of their children. They exposed how indigenous men and people who did not conform to bourgeois binary gender (for instance, hijras in South Asia and people who are now called Two Spirit in Native American cultures) were also sexually humiliated, victimized, mutilated and killed. (p. 53)

Just as mainstream feminist movements have been criticized for being Eurocentric, White, class biased, and heterosexist (e.g., Davis, 1983; hooks, 2015a, 2015b; Phipps, 2020), marginalized queers have also criticized the mainstream gay, lesbian, and queer movements.

The experiences of trans* women – especially trans* women of color from poor backgrounds – have been underlined for the disproportionate levels of violence, unemployment, homelessness, and engagement in survival sex work (Human Rights Campaign, 2020; Ritchie, 2017). *Transmisogynoir*, which targets Black trans* women, is a term that reflects this intersection of misogyny, transphobia, and anti-Blackness, as evidenced by Cece McDonald's story (Johnson, 2013). As an African American transfeminine woman, Cece McDonald survived a vicious attack outside a bar in Minneapolis, Minnesota that began with racist and transphobic epithets being hurled at her and ended with her imprisonment for defending herself. Alicia Garza, who co-founded Black Lives Matter (BLM) along with Patrisse Cullors and Ayo Tometi has also underlined BLM's emphasis on the intersectionality of race, gender, and sexuality as "a tactic to (re)build Black liberation movement" (n.a.). Criticizing those movements that benefitted from BLM but failed to acknowledge their own work as queer Black women, Garza (2014) argues that:

> When you design an event/campaign/et cetera based on the work of queer Black women, don't invite them to participate in shaping it, but ask them to provide materials and ideas for next steps for said event, that is racism in practice. It's also hetero-patriarchal. Straight men, unintentionally or intentionally, have taken the work of queer Black women and erased our contributions. Perhaps if we were the charismatic Black men many are rallying around these days, it would have been a different story, but being Black queer women in this society (and apparently within these movements) tends to equal invisibility and non-relevancy.

In an attempt to address the inequalities and oppressions faced by queer identities in tandem with racism, Loutzenheiser (2001) has proposed a queered, antiracist pedagogy in order to "disrupt the essentializing call for the primacy of race that is often inherent in U.S. incarnations of multicultural education" (p. 198). Similarly, hooks (2015b) argued that:

> … feminism is not simply a struggle to end male chauvinism or a movement to ensure that women will have equal rights with men; it is a commitment to eradicating the ideology of domination that permeates Western culture on various levels–sex, race, and class, to name a few–and a commitment to reorganizing U.S. society so that the self-development of people can take precedence over imperialism, economic expansion, and material desires. (p. 299)

In a similar vein, Hamad (2019) has called on mainstream feminism to dismantle the Whiteness embedded within the movement so that feminism can become "a truly global project aimed at bettering the lives of all women emerge, be those women white or of colour, trans or cis, not women at all but non-binary, poor or middle class, disabled, neurodivergent" (p. 86).

Scholars have also underscored the separatism between feminist and transgender movements, due to the former's emphasis on female-bodied women that perpetuates a transphobic discourse. Halberstam (2018), for instance, calls for a combined struggle that "wage[s] battle against the violent imposition of economic disparity and forcefully oppose[s] a renewed and open investment in white supremacy and American imperial ambition transacted through the channels of globalization" (p. 126).

Lastly, drawing on Davis' (2016) intersectionality of struggles, Phipps (2020) raises the following questions:

> What would happen if the white women at the forefront of #MeToo listened to and learned from Black women, both trans and cis, at the forefront of prison abolition? Or if activists against sexual harassment in universities and other institutions joined forces with sex workers' unions and organizations supporting migrant labourers? What would a campaign against trafficking look like, if it was also a campaign against the exploitation of nature? How might we put the fight against sexual violence alongside battles for the essentials of social reproduction, such as water and cleaner air? (p. 162)

In sum, language educators need to be thoughtful and engaged in reflecting upon similar questions that highlight the intersectionality of struggles when discussing gender and sexual identities in their classrooms in order to fight against the hegemony of capitalist heteropatriarchal White supremacy and Eurocentrism in educational contexts as well as society at large.

Box 7.6 Problem-posing task

The media and popular culture are overflowing with stories of domestic violence, harassment, child brides, sexism, homophobia, and transphobia. Check out the following TED Talks from courageous women in Saudi Arabia, India and Nigeria:

A Saudi woman who dared to drive:
https://www.ted.com/talks/manzl_al_sharif_a_saudi_woman_who_dared_to_drive

Why I defend women's inheritance rights:
https://www.ted.com/talks/leila_seth_why_i_defend_women_s_inheritance_rights

Chimamanda Ngozi Adichie's TED Talk: Why everyone should be feminist:
https://www.ted.com/talks/chimamanda_ngozi_adichie_we_should_all_be_feminists

- What are your thoughts and feelings about the talks you have seen? Which parts have stood out for you?
- What do the stories presented in each talk have in common? Are they similar to/different from the feminist stories you have heard of before? How?
- In what ways do the stories represent the power relations in your society?
- In what ways do the stories represent the intersectionality of struggles?
- What conclusions can be drawn based on these talks in relation to gender and sexual identities in your society?
- In what ways can these stories be used for social justice language education?

Conclusion

In this chapter, I simultaneously discussed gender and sexual identities in order to present an intersectional approach which also addressed racial and ethnic identities as well as social class. Following Davis' (2016) call for intersectional struggles, I aimed to draw connections between sexism, misogyny, heteropatriarchy, heterosexism, and trans* oppression as interlocking and intersecting systems of oppression that require the liberation of *everyone*, not just cisgender and heteronormative women, but also women of color, women from poor backgrounds, trans* and queer people, and many others whose gender and sexual identities transgress the status quo. There are, however, two main issues that remain unaddressed in this chapter but are worth mentioning for further exploration.

First, although coming out has been mentioned in this chapter in relation to the discussion of family-related issues in language classrooms, how LGBTQ+ learners and teachers come out in educational contexts, what risks, challenges, and vulnerabilities are involved, and how language educators can support this process has not been discussed. The literature is still limited to studies that explored the discursive processes of learners' coming out in the language class-room (Liddicoat, 2009) or those that relied on anecdotal, introspective data to discuss the fears queer teachers face when making decisions about coming out (Ó'Móchain, 2006). Autoethnographies from LGBTQ+ language teachers who are in the process of coming out to their colleagues, students, and their families would help language educators understand this process from a queer teacher's perspective, while discourse analytic approaches to classroom interaction can shed light on what coming out means in the language classrooms for queer learners.

Second, there are various risks, challenges, and vulnerabilities involved when it comes to discussing gender and sexual identities in educational contexts. While I talk about some of these issues in Chapter 8, one deserves atten-tion here – that is, "the unearned privileges granted to people based on their assumed heterosexuality" (Young, 2009, p. 111). Assumed heterosexuality as a privilege for a cisgender, heterosexual teacher includes, for instance, the ability to talk about the gender of their partner in the classroom and teaching a cur-riculum that perpetuates the dominance of heteronormativity. Being allowed to discuss gender and sexual identities in the classroom with their students is also a privilege of one's assumed heterosexuality since these teachers are less likely to be accused by parents or other stakeholders for 'having an agenda' to 'convert' or 'indoctrinate' their learners. Perhaps one question language educators can reflect upon is: *How comfortable am I in discussing gender and sexual identities in my classes and is it because of any unearned privileges I have?* The field of language educa-tion certainly needs more autoethnographies and classroom-based research that will challenge these assumptions and stereotypical perspectives by bringing in the voices of classroom teachers we are less likely to hear from. Social justice pedagogies that aim to provide equitable, inclusive, and transformative education to all gender and sexual identities are certainly the responsibility of all language educators and cannot be put solely on the shoulders of LGBTQ+ educators (Paiz, 2019a; MacDonald et al., 2014; Meyer, 2007). Challenging institutionalized systems of oppression such as sexism, heteropatriarchy, homo-phobia, and trans* oppression requires everyone to work collaboratively to deconstruct normalcy and other hegemonic ideologies that harm us all.

Notes

1. In order to reflect the non-binary nature of sex and gender, many have started to use trans* (spelled out *trans asterisk* or *trans star*), as an inclusive and gender non-confirmative term to refer to those who are transgender, agender, genderqueer, Two-Spirit, non-binary, genderfluid, gender non-conforming, third gender, and bigender (Catalano, 2015; Johnson, 2013; Halberstam, 2018; Killermann, 2012, 2017; Tompkins, 2014; Steinmetz, 2018). Added to the *Oxford English Dictionary*, trans* is also used to describe a person who identifies themselves in more than one of these categories.
2. According to Driskill (2010), Two-Spirit "indicates the presence of both a feminine and a masculine spirit in one person" (p. 72).
3. Hijras are a group of peoples who live in India as devotees (followers) of the goddess Buhuchara Mata. These devotees initiate sacred rituals during the births of males and marriages. Hijras also serve as sex workers. It may be difficult for Westerners, and even some Easterners, to associate priesthood with sex work, but in this particular sect of Indian culture priests as sex workers do exist. Moreover, these priests/sex workers are "intersexed and eunuchs … they are neither male nor female, man or woman. At a more esoteric level, the hijras are also man plus woman, or erotic and sacred female men" (Nanda, 1996, p. 373).
4. See, for instance, Walters' (2005) chapter on feminists across the world for a summary of feminist movements in Latin America and in Muslim countries.
5. I have to note here that even establishing homonormativity may be a challenge in some cultures and societies, especially in those countries and jurisdictions where same-sex relationships are criminalized, and even punished with the death penalty.
6. Hereafter, I will be using queer in this broader sense to refer to lesbian, gay, bisexual, and transgender people, and anyone else whose sexual and gender identity transgresses normalized discourses and the status quo.
7. It is also important to make a distinction here between LGBT-inclusive pedagogies and queer pedagogies. According to Blackburn (2013), although the LGBTQ-inclusive pedagogies acknowledge the lived experiences of largely marginalized groups of LGBT students in schools, coming from a positivist and essentialist perspective, it falsely dichotomizes learners as those who are LGBT and those who are not, Othering the former and excluding those who are questioning their sexuality and gender or those who are genderfluid. On the other hand, coming from poststructuralist and critical perspectives, queer pedagogy calls into question any essentialized body of knowledge and identities.
8. Blackburn (2013) uses LGBTQQ as an inclusive term to refer to lesbian, gay, bisexual, queer, and questioning (one's sexual or gender identity).

9. According to a 2021 report published by akt – a Manchester-based charity organization that supports LGBTQ+ young people aged 16–25 who are facing or experiencing homelessness in the UK – 24 percent of the homeless young population identifies as LGBT, and 77 percent of those believed coming out to their parents was the main factor. In the United States, according to a national survey carried out with 26,161 participants, LGBT youth had a 120 percent higher risk for homelessness compared to their heterosexual and cisgender counterparts (Morton et al., 2017).

10. Christine Sleeter (2022). Critical Family History. http://christinesleeter.org/critical-family-history/

11. Family Diversity Project's Exhibit: Love Makes a Family. https://familydiv.org/exhibits/love-makes-a-family/

12. Human Dignity Trust (2022). *Map of countries that criminalise LGBT people.* https://www.humandignitytrust.org/lgbt-the-law/map-of-criminalisation/

13. Readers can see Kjaran and Sauntson's 2020 edited volume, *Schools as queer transformative spaces: Global narratives on sexualities and genders*, for classroom-based research across nine countries: Iceland, South Africa, Brazil, Australia, China, Spain, Croatia, the UK, and Chile.

14. Rape has reportedly become a weapon in Ukraine. Finding justice may be difficult. https://www.npr.org/2022/04/30/1093339262/ukraine-russia-rape-war-crimes

15. Femicides in the US: The silent epidemic few dare to name. https://www.theguardian.com/us-news/2021/sep/26/femicide-us-silent-epidemic

16. US supreme court abortion reversal would be global 'catastrophe' for women: https://www.theguardian.com/global-development/2022/may/18/us-supreme-court-abortion-reversal-would-be-global-catastrophe-for-women

17. Sojourner Truth's speech given in 1851 at the Women's Rights Convention in Akron, Ohio. https://blogs.loc.gov/headlinesandheroes/2021/04/sojourner-truths-most-famous-speech/

Multimedia resources

Gay, Lesbian and Straight Education Network (GLSEN)
   https://www.glsen.org/
      Founded by a group of teachers in 1990, GLSEN provides research reports and resources that help support schools, communities, families, and educators to create safe spaces for LGBTQ+ students.
Human Rights Campaign (HRC) Foundation's Welcoming Schools
   http://www.welcomingschools.org/
      Human Rights Campaign's bias-based bullying prevention program provides lesson plans, booklists, and resources for educators to create LGBTQ+ and gender inclusive schools.

The Safe Zone Project
  https://thesafezoneproject.com/
    The Safe Zone project provides educational resources as well as links to
    other organizations and networks for effective LGBTQ+ awareness and
    allyship.

Children's books

Richardson, J. and Parnell, P. (2005). *Tango makes three* (illustrated by H. Cole). Simon and Schuster.
    Based on a real story that took place in New York City Zoo, this book is
    about two penguins who create a non-traditional family.
Newman, L. (2016). *Heather has two mommies* (illustrated by Laura Cornell). Candlewick.
    This story is about Heather who is asked about her daddy on her first day
    at school.
Munsch, R. (2018). *The paper bag princess* (illustrated by Michael Martchenko). Annick Press.
    Reversing the stereotypical gender roles, this book tells the story of Princess
    Elizabeth who embarks on a journey to save her prince.
Fierstein, H. (2002). *The sissy duckling*. Simon and Schuster.
    This story is about Elmer who does what he *likes* rather than what others
    think he *should* do.
Axel, B. (2012). *Goblinheart: A fairy tale* (illustrated by Terra Bidlespacher). East Waterfront.
    Brett Axel uses 'fairy' and 'goblin' in lieu of 'female' and 'male' to describe
    the physical transition of a youngster named Julep to live as a goblin.

Part III

Conclusion

Chapter 8

The rough and yet traversable road ahead

Box 8.1 Lead-in

As discussed widely in this book, many inequalities and forms of oppression observed in schools are deeply rooted in the power relations that exist within other institutional structures (e.g., health care, the economy, the criminal justice system) in society more widely. As Hawkins (2011) has rightly put it, "a stand-alone approach to 'fixing' schools" is unlikely to affect substantive change" (p. 103).

What are some challenges that await language educators who endorse social justice language education? What are some remaining concerns or questions that are not addressed in this book in relation to transforming language classrooms for social justice?

Introduction

Teaching for social justice is a difficult, emotional, perennial journey. It requires language educators not only to have the necessary knowledge, skills, and dispositions but also to have agency, advocacy, perseverance, and a positive outlook in the face of potential challenges, backlash, and criticism. This chapter, therefore, aims to introduce language educators to some of the challenges they might encounter while teaching for social justice and enable them to overcome these through the following strategies:

- Countering ideological indoctrination with critical consciousness
- Having difficult conversations with parents and other stakeholders
- Acknowledging the existence of worldly concerns and pain in the language classroom
- Problematizing 'tolerance and empathy,' 'giving voice,' and 'empowering learners'
- Altering safe spaces with brave, risky, and vulnerable communities

- Bridging the digital divide across diverse populations, languages, and geographies
- Redefining the meaning of allyship
- Designing assessment *for* learning in social justice education

Countering ideological indoctrination with critical consciousness

Perhaps the most widely held concern among educators as well as other stakeholders including parents regarding social justice education is indoctrination – getting one's learners to think in a certain way or imposing one's own political agenda onto their learners. This concern derives from the assumption that schools and educational programs are 'neutral' entities that provide equal opportunities for all learners. However, as mentioned in Chapter 2, schools, through their selective tradition of school knowledge, hidden curriculum, and other socialization of practices, maintain the social, cultural, economic, and political order across society. The goal of transformative pedagogies such as critical pedagogy and social justice education, therefore, is to disrupt this reproductive function of schooling by cultivating learners' critical consciousness. However, this process does not mean educators will impose "their view of reality on their students, ultimately leaving learners with a language of critique but no ability to employ the critical ontologically or extend it beyond its particulars" (Carpenter and Mojab, 2017, p. 19). Instead of enabling their learners to view the world in a particular way, transformative, anti-oppressive teachers help them analyze and evaluate their own lives and experiences and explore what is unsaid and what is unthinkable (Kumashiro, 2000). As Giroux (2007) states:

> In spite of the right-wing view that equates indoctrination with any suggestion of politics, critical pedagogy is not simply concerned with offering students new ways to think critically and act with authority as agents in the classroom; it is also concerned with providing students with the skills and knowledge necessary for them to expand their capacities both to question deep-seated assumptions and myths that legitimate the most archaic and disempowering social practices that structure every aspect of society and to take responsibility for intervening in the world they inhabit. Education is not neutral, but that does not mean it is merely a form of indoctrination. (p. 2)

In that sense, social justice language education should embody "a healthy skepticism about power" (Giroux, 2007, p. 1), starting with the power of the classroom teacher and moving to institutions, governments, and hegemonic ideologies. Critical inquiry and critical agency, therefore, allow learners to understand, analyze, and pose questions about the social, cultural, political, and economic realities that influence their lives and to work towards transforming them (Leistyna, 2007).

Having difficult conversations with stakeholders

There may be several internal and external pressures teachers might face when discussing social justice issues in their classes: prescribed pacing guides by governments or schools, assessment policies, political mandates, and possible backlash from governing institutions could all potentially impact "how far outside the classrooms [teachers] are willing to venture for social justice and action" (Boyd, 2017, p. 107). The podcast *Southlake* presents the challenges faced by the school board, staff, students, and parents in the eponymous Texas town, following a video showing high school students chanting the N-word. *Southlake* not only provides insights into the intricacies of one school's journey towards antiracism – and gender inclusion – but also ties it to the national crusade against critical race theory fueled by the 45th President of the Unites States of America, Donald Trump. Language educators need to be aware of the local exigencies of their teaching context as well as the larger political contexts that have an impact on their institutions and communities, and be ready to articulate the rationale behind their anti-oppressive, decolonizing, inclusive, social-justice oriented pedagogy to the many stakeholders involved.

Boyd (2017) provides several strategies for informing parents about one's social justice pedagogies. For instance, weekly emails about course readings and discussions will not only keep them informed about what takes place in the classroom but also might facilitate further conversations at home. Holding events for parents to explain particular social justice themes and ways in which parents can talk about difficult subjects with their children will also help position them as potential allies. During these events, parents can be asked to engage in activities that will underline the importance of diversity, equity, and inclusion in educational settings. For instance, the paper-folding activity presented by the U.S. Institute of Peace[1] asks everyone to close their eyes and follow a very simple set of instructions for paper folding. The many products participants end up with are then discussed to enable them to problematize their 'truths' and to consider that the same experience might lead to multiple interpretations, underlining the role of learner diversity in education.

Despite these measures, criticisms and backlash could still occur, especially when discussing gender and sexual identities. Replacing a heterosexual family photo with one of two mothers might receive backlash from both conservative and liberal parents. The criticisms might revolve around "My son is too young to learn about sexuality"; "It is the parents' role to talk about these issues"; and "I wish you would *only* teach language." These concerns should be welcome by language educators since they may lead to conversations that will enable parents to understand the role language education plays in perpetuating and maintaining the status quo in the world. Acknowledging their concern and appreciating the opportunity to explain one's rationale for a particular material or an activity would help establish communication and transparency between teachers and parents. These meetings, then, can serve to explain one's goal as, certainly, not to indoctrinate but to raise learners' awareness (e.g., of different families in this case, such as LGBTQ+ families, single mother/father families, and parents or children with disabilities) and to create a more inclusive and equitable environment for *all* learners. Finally, providing real-life examples can establish the rationale for social justice pedagogies in the language classroom. Sasha Fleischman, an agender teen wearing a skirt, was set on fire by another teenager while riding the bus in Oakland, California, causing second- and third-degree burns on her legs. Also depicted in the non-fiction book, *The 57 bus* by Dashka Slater (2017), the tragic story of Sasha[2] can be shared with parents to illustrate the ways in which ignoring social justice issues in educational settings might lead to hate crimes and acts of violence even among young people. As mentioned earlier, underlining the role of the parents in having these conversations with their children will not only position them as allies but also help build bridges between teachers, learners, and their parents, which is essential for social justice language education.

Acknowledging the existence of worldly concerns and pain in the language classroom

The criticisms such as "teachers should remain neutral" and "they shouldn't bring politics into their classrooms" are often followed by arguments such as "talking about worldly concerns might be harmful to some learners" and "language education should be fun." As discussed extensively in this book, teaching is a political act with no off switch. Teachers – knowingly or unknowingly – circulate hegemonic ideologies and contribute to social injustices every day through their daily actions, routines, classroom activities, materials, and so on. Both language teachers and learners negotiate their many gendered, sexual, class-based, and racialized identities on a daily basis, not just with each other but also with the rest of the world. Additionally, social justice is not something educators *bring* to the classroom: educational contexts are imbued with social injustice(s), which manifests itself through physical and mental suffering, hardships, pain, and trauma. According to Giroux (2007), classrooms that allegedly avoid social issues and human suffering to 'protect the young kids' remain in the dominant group's comfort zone and perpetuate the current cultural, economic, social, and institutional practices. Representing "an unworldly counterpart to the gated community," this form of education is nothing but a "flight from self and society" (Giroux, 2007, p. 4). Assuming that language learners, their families, and communities do not suffer from homophobia, xenophobia, racism, colorism, classism, ageism, and ableism derives from a privileged status and a sense of entitlement to a supposed, though virtually impossible pain-free existence that turns a blind eye to the many forms of oppression that exist in the world. As Ennser-Kananen (2016) argues:

The White European/American way of erasing pain from education, in effect, erases the identities of individuals and groups who experience it with the objective of maintaining pain-free, convenient instruction, education, and life-styles. From this erasure arises an obligation, especially for White European educators, to counter silences with stories of cultural conflict and pain. (p. 559)

Social justice language education, in that sense, offers language learners "a mirror, a tool kit, and a window" (Chubbuck, 2010, p. 205) into their identities, lives, experiences, and communities. This is mostly because any pedagogy that does not situate itself in learners' societies, institutions, cultures, and identities will fail to develop their critical consciousness and instead create self-interested individuals who do not care about the needs and experiences of others. As Macedo and Bartolomé (2014) mention, "educators who refuse to transform the ugliness of human misery, social injustices and inequalities; invariably become educators who, as Sartre (1967) so poignantly suggested, 'will change nothing and will serve no one, but will succeed only in finding moral comfort in malaise' (pp. xxiv–xxv)" (p. 33).

Social justice language education, therefore, not only draws on a pedagogy of pain but also a pedagogy of hope. A *pedagogy of pain* takes painful conversations as a foundation for learner engagement with sensitive issues; as a tool to enable everyone in the classroom to question truths, realities, comfort zones, and frames of reference; and as an outlet for "creating possibility for humane responses to inhumane experiences" (Ennser-Kananen, 2016, p. 561). In a similar vein, a *pedagogy of hope* utilizes pain as a catalyst to dismantle systems of domination, imperialism, racism, sexism, and classism (hooks, 2003).

Box 8.2 Problem-posing task

Read a national or international report on a critical theme of your choos-ing. First, summarize the key points of this report: Who released the report? What is it about? What are the important findings? Second, reflect upon how this report reflects the core concepts and issues discussed in this book: What forms of oppression and discrimination intersect in this report? Lastly, relate this report to your educational context or a context you are familiar with: To what extent do the findings of this report resonate with the experiences and identities of the learners in this context? How could this report be used in language classrooms? How could language learners use this report to carry out a social action project in their communities?

Talking about potentially triggering, unsettling, and painful subjects will be challenging in language classrooms with diverse language groups who might be discriminated against, marginalized, displaced, and traumatized. Providing trigger warnings, having counseling and student services in the class to present the resources available to the students in case needed, and providing differenti-ated instruction (e.g., an alternative activity for those students who may not want to engage with the material at all) will make students feel supported and, thus, help alleviate some of the challenges. Engaging in supportive yet accountable conversations with other colleagues and professionals will also establish a broader community of practice and better equip teachers to talk about these subjects in empathetic, responsible ways in the classroom with learners.

Problematizing 'tolerance and empathy,' 'giving voice,' and 'empowering learners'

'Cultivating tolerance and empathy,' 'giving voice,' and 'empowering learners' are quite common phrases to come across in many academic publications on social justice and multicultural education. However, these phrases have been criticized for falling short as transformative goals within social justice education and for positioning minority and marginalized groups as 'the Other,' 'the inferior,' and 'the colonized' (e.g., Cabrera, 2014; Ellsworth, 1989; Macedo and Bartolomé, 2014). For instance, as Macedo and Bartolomé (2014) have argued, it is problematic for language teachers to assume that English-only policies can 'give voice to the voiceless' and 'empower learners' since:

> [V]oice is not something to be given by those in power, for if you have the power to give voice, you also maintain the power to take it away … For most immigrants and other subordinated groups in the United States, coming to voice represents a process through which they come to know what it means to be at the periphery of the intimate and yet fragile relationship between the colonizer and the colonized. It also means that the colonized becomes fully aware that voice is not something to be given by the colonizer. Voice is a human right. Voice is a democratic right. (p. 25)

Kumashiro (2000) also cautions against "building empathy" which often takes the form of teaching about the Other. Empathy can provide a starting point to discuss different identities and experiences, but cannot be the panacea for anti-oppressive, equitable, and social justice pedagogies since "the root of the oppression does not reside solely in how individuals think about, feel towards, and treat another" (p. 35). Empathy needs to be accompanied with active intention: the intention to abandon and to work against one's own privileges and to get involved in – and initiate action for – social change and transformation.

Diversity programs and other initiatives that aim to promote tolerance in order to decrease the racial bias on college campuses and in other workplaces can be mentioned here as an example. As Cabrera (2014) states, "one tolerates a headache or a baby on the airplane that keeps crying. Tolerance does not imply an analysis of racial oppression" (p. 34). Also, teaching cultural tolerance is a privileged act that "not only eclipses real opportunities for the development of mutual respect and cultural solidarity, but it also hides the privilege and paternalism inscribed in the proposition 'I will tolerate you even though your culture is repugnant'" (Macedo and Bartolomé, 2014, p. 26). Therefore, teaching tolerance towards others may not do anything but maintain the status quo in which "the Other is differentiated from and subordinated to the norm" (Kumashiro, 2000, p. 35).

These catch phrases uttered as transformative goals also underline the role of language as a political act – a topic that was widely discussed in Chapter 3. The words, utterances, and other non-verbal and multimodal semiotic resources language educators use all imply meanings about the world and systems of oppression they are raised in and educated to be a part of. They not only mirror teachers' identities, upbringing, and life experiences but position them and the people they interact with in their communities. And although voice, tolerance, empowerment, and empathy are important concepts within social justice education, language educators should go beyond cultivating their learners' empathy and tolerance to appreciating and building on differences for social transformation and change. This can only be achieved by challenging and eradicating the deeply ingrained political, cultural, social, and educational hierarchies and unearned privileges that are inherent in hegemonic ideologies. As Audre Lorde (1984) mentions, "Difference must be not merely tolerated, but seen as a fund of necessary polarities between which our creativity can spark like a dialectic. Only then does the necessity for interdependency become unthreatening" (pp. 177–178).

Altering safe spaces with brave, risky, and vulnerable communities

Box 8.3 Reflective task

In *Pedagogy of the oppressed*, Paulo Freire (2005b) argues that:

[W]e teachers should be constantly asking questions of ourselves and of our students, to create a spirit in which we are certain by not being certain of our certainties. To the extent that we are not quite sure about our certainties, we begin to "walk toward" certainties. (p. 17)

In what ways can language educators create virtual or in-person learning spaces that help challenge language learners' certainties and cultivate uncertainties about identity, culture, social norms, and values in their own and also different communities?

Creating a safe space or a safe zone for diverse language learners is widely recommended in many social justice books and anti-oppressive pedagogical frameworks for establishing trust and equitable relationships within the class-room (Cyprès, 2016; Gayle et al., 2013; Grant and Agosto, 2008; Jean-Marie et al., 2009; Kumashiro, 2000; Wesely et al., 2016). A safe space, *in principle*, involves allowing all voices to be heard; and all ideas to be shared, expressed, and discussed comfortably without the fear of being ridiculed or judged. A safe space is not only important for facilitating discussions around race, ethnicity, gender, and sex in the language classroom but also for welcoming and affirming various learner identities. However, a safe space, *in reality*, might prevent both teachers and students from asking troubling questions that help everyone go beyond a superficial touch upon issues in order to avoid discomfort and tension in the classroom. Drawing on Britzman's (1998) work on unlearning, Kumashiro (2000) suggests that human beings have an unconscious desire to learn anything that affirms their identities and resist any knowledge that "reveals our complicity with racism, homophobia, and other forms of oppression" (p. 43). Hence, instead of promoting the idea of a safe space where the dominant group of learners and teachers would feel comfortable with their privileges and positionalities, several scholars, including myself, propose that it is in fact vulnerable, risky, and brave spaces that should be encouraged for social justice pedagogies (Bender-Slack, 2015; Henry, 1994; hooks, 1994; Kumashiro, 2000).

According to hooks (1994), the way educators conceptualize safe space "usu-ally translates to mean that the professor lectures to a group of quiet students who respond only when they are called on" (p. 39). Teachers also often use the idea of a safe space as a pretext to remain neutral in difficult classroom conversations, and this neutrality only serves the dominant groups while harming those who are marginalized (hooks, 1994). As Henry (1994) states, "to be able to speak of safety in the 'belly of the beast' reveals class and race privilege" (p. 2). In other words, educators who seek to create a safe space in their classrooms might be maintaining the normalized ideologies (e.g., heterosexism) by creating a safe environment for some students (e.g., straight) and not so much for others (e.g., gay). The safe spaces might be further alienating and marginalizing students of color who may withdraw from classroom interaction, an outcome that "deprives everyone, including White students, of opportunities to engage in the critical dialogue they need to become agents of change" (Villegas and Davis, 2008, p. 599). Additionally, safe spaces might ignore the intersectionality of learner identities, and instead essentialize learners based on their race, gender, or sexual-ity. Kumashiro (2001b), therefore, poses the following questions in order to underline the importance of intersectionality within safe spaces:

> Educators need to ask, "When developing safe spaces, supportive programs, and resources, who is the other that these spaces, etc., are for? If they target queers, do they ignore racism, and in the process, ignore queers of color? ... Similarly, we need to ask, "When implementing progressive pedagogies, what differences are being affirmed? If they target racial difference and racism, do they ignore ways that conceptualizations of 'race' are already (hetero)

sexualized, and thus, complicit with heterosexism? ... Finally, we need to ask, "Even when we try to be inclusive of queers of color, do we succeed in reaching them? Who makes use of the safe spaces? Who feels affirmed by the progressive pedagogies?" (p. 17)

Keeping intersectionality in mind, language educators should work towards establishing a vulnerable, risky, and brave community of practice in which both teachers and learners are encouraged to take risks and become comfortable with being uncomfortable. In fact, enabling a safe space and teaching for social justice might contradict each other since safety is all about security, protection, and a tendency to avoid taking risks, while social justice work requires examining the power relations and inequalities in a society and "constructing empowering alternatives" (Bender-Slack, 2015, p. 192). As Allen (2015) claims, "All spaces of learning are 'risky' because as Britzman (2003) contends what is educative makes us anxious" (p. 767). Thus, any anti-oppressive education, "must involve learning to be unsatisfied with what is being learned, said, and known" (Kumashiro, 2000, p. 43).

The learning spaces language educators create for their learners should also encourage them to be brave; brave enough to learn, unlearn, challenge, and be challenged. Instead of allowing learners to *say whatever they think*, language classrooms need to encourage them to *say whatever they think while also being aware that some of those things might be challenged or confronted, and to welcome these challenges as opportunities for further learning and growth*. As Edelsky and Johnson (2004) put forward:

> Safety implies that students will be able to voice genuine (not merely acceptable) interpretations, some of which may, to the teacher's dismay, promote *in*justice and *in*equity—e.g., children saying that boys should not play with dolls or girls with trucks because God doesn't like that. The teacher has to protect all interpretations, has to work mightily not to punish students for their positions (which often reflect what their parents think). At the same time, the teacher has to make sure that *any position can be interrogated even as it is protected*. (p. 132, original emphasis)

Safety, in that sense, does not mean that language learners will sit comfortably with their biases, stereotypes, and ideologies but being ready to feel discomfort in ways that will help them unlearn these. Discomfort within social justice language education is not only unavoidable, but also potentially productive for learning and unlearning. As Henry (1994) describes, learning and teaching about "difference" – and about sexism, classism, and racism – requires educational terrains that are "political, dangerous, and 'unsafe'" (p. 1).

Being vulnerable is equally important for language teachers if they are committed to working with their students to understand their worlds from their own lenses and perspectives (Agnello, 2016) As hooks (1994) suggests:

Professors who expect students to share confessional narratives but who are themselves unwilling to share are exercising power in a manner that could be coercive. In my classrooms, I do not expect students to take any risks that I would not take, to share in any way that I would not share. When professors bring narratives of their experiences into classroom discussions it eliminates the possibility that we can function as all-knowing, silent interrogators. It is often productive if professors take the first risk, linking confessional narratives to academic discussions so as to show how experience can illuminate and enhance our understanding of academic material. (p. 21)

Social justice educators who work towards troubling those identities and knowledge that help maintain the status quo need to create a not-so-safe space in their classrooms where both learners and teachers anticipate discomfort and vulnerability but also the courage to find ways to have difficult and complex conversations that lead to learning and unlearning. Discomfort and uncomfortable dialogue "is a precursor to deeper understanding and growth" (Darling-Hammond et al., 2002, p. 3). In other words, "The goal is not final knowledge (and satisfaction), but disruption, dissatisfaction, and the desire for more change" (Kumashiro, 2000, p. 34). Boler's (1999) *pedagogy of discomfort*, in that sense, is helpful to unpack what it actually means to have 'discomfort-free' and 'safety-zones' in educational settings. A pedagogy of discomfort has the potential to enable language educators as well as language learners to "uncover and question the deeply embedded emotional dimensions that frame and shape daily habits, routines, and unconscious complicity with hegemony" (Zembylas, 2015, p. 166).

Redefining the meaning of allyship

Box 8.4 Reflective task

What does it mean to be an ally for all learners in your educational context and who is an ally?

In what ways do you provide allyship to language learners in your classrooms and the larger school context? To what extent does your allyship address multiple and intersectional forms of oppression?

An ally has been traditionally defined as a member of the dominant social groups who is "working to end the system of oppression that gives them greater privilege and power based on their social-group membership" (Broido, 2000, p. 3). It is, however, problematic to define allyship in this traditional sense for two reasons. First, dominant groups' intention to help – which sometimes take the form of entering a community with a set of preconceived ideas about what the community needs – reflects and reinforces not only unequal power relations but also a savior complex (e.g., White savior complex) (Bell, 2016). Second, this traditional understanding of allyship fails to take into account the complex, overlapping, multiple, and intersecting nature of identities, and might lead to a binary model of 'us versus them,' or 'oppressor versus oppressed' (Catalano, 2015). Therefore, allyship should be defined *across* and *within* identities in order to go beyond virtual equality and bring about social, political, and economic change (Catalano, 2015; Love, [2000] 2018).

Love's (2018) liberatory consciousness, which includes four actionable steps of awareness, analysis, accountability, and action, can be implemented in language classrooms in ways that redefine allyship. Taking the issue of gender and sexual identities, for instance, awareness means unlearning heteronormative and binary assumptions about learners' gender and sexual identities and acknowledging and affirming the LGBTQ+ identities in language classrooms. This sort of critical awareness supports both an individual and institutional analysis of norms, policies, behaviors, and practices that maintain LGBTQ+ oppression in educational contexts.

With critical awareness comes a realization of complicity, since "if education is complicitous, then there are no innocent bystanders" (Shlasko, 2005, p. 128). Accountability, in that sense, means welcoming criticism about one's own unacknowledged oppressive socialization and being open to unlearn any unearned privileges. Accountability requires everyone to go beyond providing minimal support or establishing virtual equality to taking responsibility in dismantling the oppressive systems that impact all marginalized groups (e.g., Catalano, 2015; Filax, 2006). An ally or an accomplice might be supporting the struggle while playing safe; it is being a comrade in action that means being "fully in it or of it" (Eisenstein, 2019, p. 17).

There are several strategies language educators can take to implement Love's (2018) framework of liberatory consciousness for allyship. First, language educators can facilitate student reflections about their life experiences and emotions through journals, autobiographies, and multimodal creative expressions. Similarly, role plays, storytelling, and dramatizations enable language learners to empathize with the characters they read about and understand different positions and life exigencies. Regardless of the activity adopted, language educators should emphasize that *the personal is political*; that is, the personal experience and the larger socio-cultural and political structures in the larger societies are interdependent. Encouraging learners to consider their own experiences as well as those of marginalized groups in light of the existing socio-political, economic, and historical realities will help validate all identities and life exigencies and lead to more concrete explorations for social action (Enns and Forrest, 2005).

Through reflections, workshops, and intentional conversations language educators can determine what actions can be taken to challenge and transform the oppressive and exclusionary policies and practices (e.g., creating LGBTQ+ inclusive policies and practices) and how to put them into practice. For instance,

Woodford et al.'s (2014) study examined the LGBT ally training programs in twenty higher education institutions that belong to the Consortium of Higher Education LGBT Resource Professionals[3] in the US. The results revealed that the ally training programs helped participants understand LGBT-related vocabulary and definitions; raised their awareness of personal biases and LGBT oppression; but lacked developing their skills to embrace advocacy and as a result left them as passive bystanders in the fight to challenge heterosexism in institutional practices.

As discussed in Chapter 4, social action projects and immersive learning activities such as field trips can be facilitated to cultivate learners' capacity for social change. Inviting guest speakers from community organizations (e.g., domestic violence shelters or rape-counseling centers) will not only support community building but also foster learners' enthusiasm to fight systemic oppression and marginalization. Student-run social action projects such as organizing a "Day of Solidarity" have various affordances for students who create multimodal texts (e.g., posters, school displays) to raise awareness through facts and statistics about homophobia, definitions of key words, resources, and so on (Young, 2009). These kind of social action projects, therefore, have the potential to not only help language learners develop their critical literacy skills to understand multiple perspectives, experiences, and identities but also cultivate a sense of social action among learners who become active participants to end oppression and marginalization in their schools and communities.

Designing assessment *for* learning in social justice education

It is not only common practice in the field but also highly recommended in many language teacher education books that teachers write learning objectives or outcomes that convey 'observable' and 'measurable' behaviors, often following Bloom's taxonomy (Bloom, 1956; Glynn et al., 2014; Martel, 2022; Shrum and Glisan, 2009). It is, therefore, no surprise that one of the most commonly asked questions in relation to social justice language education relates to whether (and if so, how) to assess social justice objectives. *How can we, as language educators, know if language learners have unlearned their privileges? How can we make sure awareness leads to social action? How can we assess transformation and social change? And in general, how can we come to terms with assessment in social justice language education, when we are strictly trained to* "delineate what [we] want students to understand, plan a lesson to get them there, and then address whether they indeed came to this understanding" (Kumashiro, 2000, p. 39)?

Language education has witnessed an increased interest in alternative forms of assessment that is more participatory, dialogic, and democratic. Democratic assessment (Shohamy, 2001), critical language testing (Shohamy, 1998, 2017), antiracist assessment (Accurso and Mizell, 2020), assessment within a social justice curriculum (Gylnn et al., 2014), and critical pedagogy (Crookes, 2013; Davies, 2010; Keesing-Styles, 2003; Leistyna, 2007; McNamara and Ryan, 2011) are only some of the egalitarian frameworks that aim to involve both learners and teachers in the assessment process, rather than conveying a one-way, banking mode of teacher-to-student knowledge transmission. Scholars who work at the intersection of race, language, and education have also argued for assessment policies and practices that confront the standards for White middle-class native speakerism (Flores and Rosa, 2015).

The tendency to adopt assessment practices that rely on an objective, rational, and positivist approach has also contributed to the tyranny of high-stakes tests in language education (Cheng, 2014; Hamp-Lyons, 1997; Kunnan, 2014, 2018; Lynch, 1997; Shohamy, 2006, 2017). Drawing on Foucault's *Discipline and punish* (1979), Shohamy (2017) discusses how "tests serve as means for maintaining hierarchies and normalizing judgment. They can be used for surveillance, to quantify, classify, and punish. Their power lies in that they can lead to differentiation among people and for judging them" (p. 444). High-stakes tests, therefore, have been under scrutiny in terms of not only their fairness, ethical use, and impact on learners' lives but also as a human rights issue concerning their use in the selection of immigrants prior to entry or for full citizenship after arrival (Kunnan, 2009, 2021; McNamara and Roever, 2006; McNamara and Shohamy, 2008; Milani, 2008; Shohamy, 2009; Schupbach, 2009).

In order to protect test takers and minimize the power of tests, Shohamy (2017) recommends several strategies such as implementing dynamic assessments; building learners' and teachers' assessment literacy; offering test accommodations; utilizing formative, inclusive, and multilingual assessments; designing tests that take into account the developments in English as a lingua franca; and addressing people's full language repertoire. According to Shohamy (2001), "such approaches change the balance of power between tester and test-taker and assumes that the tester is no longer the 'know it all' who owns all knowledge … adopting democratic principles along such lines implies that the act of testing is a mutual effort between testers and test-takers" (pp. 378–379). Additionally, teaching to the test, that is, informing language learners about the tests and test-taking strategies – if absolutely necessary – should be in the spirit of pedagogy (i.e., assessment *for* learning) and in ways that engage learners in an interdisciplinary and ideological examination of how tests are created, how they operate, whose values are behind them, and whose knowledge is assessed (Leistyna, 2007; Shohamy, 2017).

Other forms of classroom-based assessment that will challenge the power of tests include differentiated assessments, peer and self-assessments, shared grading and contracts, and process-based approaches, to name a few. Differentiated assessment provides learners with the freedom and flexibility to choose the assignments they would like to complete as well as the level of performance/the grade they would strive to achieve. Group projects, contracts, pass/fail courses are also some of the assessment techniques that can be used in the social justice classroom (Weiler, 1991). Self-assessment and peer-assessment reduce the power of the teacher in the evaluation process. Shared grading can also be used where half of the grade comes from the teacher's evaluation while the other half is determined by learners themselves through self-evaluation. Process writing can also be listed as an egalitarian approach where learners write multiple drafts to demonstrate knowledge and competency in language use, receive feedback, and have a chance to incorporate what makes sense in terms of feedback and argue against what does not.

Nevertheless, in addition to language and content objectives, social justice language education, as discussed in Chapter 3, consists of social justice objectives that encompass not only newly attained knowledge, skills, and dispositions but also a reflective process of unlearning one's privileges, biases, and stereotypes, which may not – and one might argue *should not* – be assessed. As Kumashiro states (2000), "one's identities, experiences, privileges, investments, and so forth always influence how one thinks and perceives, what one knows and wills not to know" (p. 39). Apple's (2019) comparison of scientific and ethical talk is relevant here to break down the dichotomy between objective and subjective considerations of learning:

> Scientific and technical talk in advanced industrial societies has more legitimacy (high status) than ethical talk. Ethical talk cannot be easily operationalized within an input-output perspective. And, finally, "scientific" criteria of evaluation give "knowledge," while ethical criteria lead to purely "subjective" considerations. (p. 38)

Social justice language education can bridge this gap between 'objective' and 'subjective' knowledge – and contest these terms – through holistic learning which refers to the integration of learners' cognition, feeling, and experiences. Holistic learning opposes the binary categories of learning and feeling by making "connections between *objective* textbook learning, self-awareness, and personal growth" (Enns and Forrest, 2005, p. 13, original emphasis). This approach enables learners to make meaning in relation to their own realities and subjective experiences as well as those of marginalized groups. Enns and Forrest (2005), therefore, recommend the use of journals, autobiographies, creative expression (writing and musical work), and drama activities (role plays, storytelling) for holistic learning so as to enable reflection and self-awareness as well as to build empathy by taking on the identity of another person. Social justice language education, overall, recommends forms of assessment that validate and accommodate all learner identities and experiences while also providing equitable opportunities to present their academic, social, cultural, and emotional gains.

Bridging the digital divide across diverse populations, languages, and geographies

Although some might claim that technology – including the internet – is a neutral tool in individuals' lives, the complicity of digital technologies in perpetuating the existing ideologies in the larger societies is widely documented (Fouch, 2006; Fuchs, 2014; Kolko, Nakamura, & Rodman, 2000; McLaren and Jandrić, 2020; Noble, 2018). According to Bali (2018), "[d]igital tools are largely Western products, dominated by American and Western European interests; as such, they can somewhat colonize the spaces and networks depending on them, including by making the 'other' invisible or tokenized, if not silenced or oppressed" (p. 17). Safiya Umoja Noble's (2018) book, *Algorithms of oppression*, documents the myriad ways online search engines such as Google foreground Whiteness and White privilege, while marginalizing and suppressing the experiences, knowledges, and histories of Black people and people of color. Just as with textbooks and other instructional materials, digital tools are cultural artifacts and economic commodities and eliminating the digital divide should be part of the efforts to decolonize the language education curriculum.

The imperative use of technology during the COVID-19 pandemic has confirmed that access to and use of technology is "rooted in people's history, beliefs, and identities" (Bangou and Wong, 2009, p. 172). The pandemic, however, not only mirrored but also exacerbated the systemic inequities all around the world, deriving from the intersection of sexism, classism, racism, ableism, and linguicism. Several reports illustrated the digital divide and the income-based disparities among Asian, White, Hispanic, and Black households in the US – where the latter two lagged far behind when it came to computer availability and internet connectivity during the pandemic (Ong, 2020; Pew Research Center, 2021). Examining the digital literacy and access/use of instructional technologies in multi-ethnic Russia, the study by Gladkova et al. (2020) similarly revealed the intersection of ethnicity and place of living: Russians as the ethnic majority living in big cities had a higher level of digital capital. Bennett et al.'s (2020) research also underlined how the lack of governmental and institutional support for Indigenous-specific issues during the COVID-19 era widened the digital and educational gap between Indigenous and non-Indigenous Australians, "setting back efforts to increase Indigenous participation and embrace Indigenous epistemologies in Australian higher education" (pp. 1–2).

The previous research on the digital divide mostly focused on different learner groups' material access to technology through a comparison of their haves and the have-nots. However, the achievement gap between learner groups will not close by simply providing technological devices to those who do not have them as they may not have the requisite knowledge, skills, and support to use them (Bangou and Wong, 2009; Gorski and Clark, 2003; Selwyn, 2004; van Dijk, 1999). Instead, establishing digital equity requires a look into social, psychological, cultural, economic, and political reasons that exacerbate the divide and contribute to the institutional forms of oppression (Gorski and Clark, 2003; Selwyn, 2004).

Digital equity, which underscores the intersection of equity, social justice, and instructional technologies, refers to "making the table more inclusive and open, narrowing any form of discrimination within a society and removing any forms of barriers that prevent ... socially disadvantaged groups [from accessing and enjoying] the benefits new digital technologies may offer" (Ragnedda, 2020, p. 88). The following questions by Gorski (2009) can help language educators reflect on how their use of instructional technology relates to digital equity:

> *Who has the easiest, most consistent access to these resources? How are educators using technology differently with different populations of students? Who stands to gain the most – economically, politically, and so on – from the growing urgency to technologize schools and classrooms? What are the equity and social justice implications of this educational technology craze?* (pp. 349–350, original emphasis)

Nevertheless, the increased use of instructional technology does not mean better educational outcomes for all learners. Instructional technologies should be utilized for inclusive and non-discriminatory instructional practices, equitable learning opportunities, and culturally responsive/sustaining pedagogies (DePietro et al., in press; Gorski, 2009; Hall et al., 2020; Ortaçtepe Hart, in press). Understanding the already existing digital practices of language learners would enable educators to bring instructional technologies into their classrooms in ways that sustain and develop their skills for educational benefits (Tichavakunda and Tierney, 2018). Language educators who aim to resist technological oppression in their educational institutions need to work towards diminishing deficit-oriented thinking about racialized learner groups, and instead affirm, embrace, and bring into the curriculum "students' counter-stories, communities, and digital lives" (Lewis Ellison and Solomon, 2019, p. 239).

Box 8.5 Problem-posing task

When the COVID-19 pandemic hit the world early in 2020, schools all over the world moved to online education in an effort to continue their educational programs. In your educational context (or in a context you are familiar with), what kind of measures were taken in order to address the digital divide between students who did not have a computer and/or internet access at home and those who did? Were there any state and school-level initiatives that aimed to develop the digital skills and knowledge of all learners and their families to prepare them for online education? What (further) actions are yet to be taken to achieve digital equity in this context?

Looking ahead

Before concluding this book, I would like to draw attention to three issues that have not been addressed in detail in this book but further publications on social justice language education need to delve into. The first of these issues relates to implementing social justice language education at the program or school level in ways that will expand individual efforts to the institutional level (i.e., connecting language program administration to social justice language education). The research on teacher leadership for transformative, social justice pedagogies calls for not only teachers but also educational leaders, curriculum designers, and policy makers who are committed to providing more equitable educational opportunities for their learners and to achieving social change (Henderson and Kesson, 1999; Henderson and Gornik, 2007; Lopez and Olan, 2021; Simmonds, 2017). There is, however, little research on how social justice education crosses path with teacher leadership and program administration. Carlisle et al. (2006), for instance, proposed a framework for schools to examine different domains in schooling (e.g., school-community relations; learning, teaching, and working climate; resource management practices) in terms of the following five principles: inclusion and equity; high expectations; reciprocal community relationships; a systems-wide approach; and direct social justice education and intervention. Even more limited within the field of language education, social justice leadership frameworks have also been proposed in relation to dual language (DeMatthews and Izquierdo, 2016, 2017) and English as a second language (ESL) programs (Theoharis and O'Toole, 2011). More explorations are needed regarding what social justice leadership looks like within language program administration: *What are some challenges and opportunities awaiting language program administrators and curriculum leaders engaging with social justice? In what ways can language program administrators and curriculum leaders support individual teacher efforts? What role do they play in relation to addressing parents, students, and other stakeholders' concerns regarding social justice education?* These are only some of the questions to be considered to ensure that social justice language education is successfully implemented at the school level rather than remaining within the walls of a classroom.

Second, social justice teacher education research has been criticized for educating White teachers for diverse teaching contexts, while failing to address the needs of teachers of color and/or ethnic minorities, who are expected to "use their first-hand knowledge about the cultural background and everyday life experiences of students of color to help them build bridges to learning" (Villegas and Davis, 2008, p. 584). Having to explain how injustices work in their own lived experiences while also challenging racism, sexism, genderism, xenophobia, classism, and ableism is a difficult task for teachers of color, minority ethnic teachers, trans* teachers, teachers from a lower social class, teachers with a disability, and so on. Therefore, the field of language education needs more stories, counter-stories, testimonios, and narratives from all marginalized groups of teachers and teachers who do not fit into the 'norms' of what their communities or families prescribe for them. *How do they teach for social justice? What unique challenges are involved? How do they relinquish their authority, for instance, in the class, when they are already deemed 'inferior' in their societies? How do they incorporate their identities as well* *as those of their learners into social justice education? What does it mean for them to have brave and vulnerable learning communities that engage in difficult conversations? How can teacher education programs prepare teachers of color, minority ethnic teachers, trans* teachers, teachers from a lower social class, and teachers with a disability for their journey that is potentially filled with barriers, inequities, and backlash?*

Third, the role of emotions for social change has been widely underscored by scholars of feminist and queer theory (Ahmad, 2017; Lorde, 1984; Phipps, 2020; Quinlivan, 2019), critical race theory (Dixson et al., 2017), and social justice education (Howard and Aleman, 2008; Papa et al., 2016; Sensoy and DiAngelo, 2017). As Raymond Williams' (1977) account of *structures of feeling* makes clear, emotions are not only situational, but are also part of individuals' frames of reference through which they make sense of the world: They are "thought as felt and feeling as thought" (p. 132). Emotions are, therefore, a source of knowledge about the world and can inform language educators about the various hegemonic ideologies, cultures, and discourses of power in language classrooms (Chinn, 2012; Garvey, 2017; Lorde, 1984; Moore, 2020; Nelson, 2009). As Ahmad (2014) puts it:

> Emotions tell us a lot about time; emotions are the very 'flesh' of time … Emotions show us how histories stay alive, even when they are not consciously remembered; how histories of colonialism, slavery, and violence shape lives and worlds in the present … Emotions also open up futures, in the ways they involve different orientations to others … Justice is not simply a feeling. And feelings are not always just. But justice involves feelings, which move us across the surfaces of the world, creating ripples in the intimate contours of our lives. Where we go, with these feelings, remains an open question. (p. 202)

No doubt teaching is an "emotionally layered experience" (Chinn, 2012, p. 19). Teachers' and learners' feelings, emotions, subjective realities, and personal experiences have been traditionally devalued while the objective, rational, and cognitive have been ingrained into the school curricula. And although the field of language education has increasingly paid attention to the role of emotions and the affective domain in teaching/learning processes (Benesch, 2012, 2017; De Costa et al., 2018; Kocabas-Gedik and Ortaçtepe Hart, 2020; West, 2021; Zembylas, 2003, 2005) several questions remain unexplored. *What role do emotions play within social justice pedagogies? How can emotions be transferred into advocacy and social action? In what ways can emotions help create a more socially just world?*

A lot has changed in the world since I started working on this book in 2019. For starters, COVID-19 was not then a familiar term in any language, and online education was not an option for most. The process of revising these chapters has proved particularly challenging, as I have looked to update the global events discussed to take into account rapidly shifting developments (e.g., the Russian

invasion of Ukraine, the abortion ban in the US). Given how the world is changing and how social issues are evolving – while their underlying dynamics remain
in many ways the same – it has been difficult – and was perhaps unrealistic – to
achieve a sense of closure with this book. I feel that there is still so much I need
to discuss to be able to ever complete this book, and so much I need to know. As
Baldwin ([1980] 2021) states:

> The irreducible price of learning is realizing that you do not know. One may
> go further and point out – as any scientist, or artist, that the more you learn,
> the less you know; but that means that you have begun to accept, and are even
> able to rejoice in, the relentless conundrum of your life. (p. 1641)

This book, in that sense, is my humble attempt to help language educators
address the hegemonic, harmful, and limiting ideologies that are inherent in language education – and in their very languages and daily lives. My hope is that this
book will be a starting point of a journey towards anti-oppressive, transformative,
decolonizing pedagogies that center diversity, inclusion, equity, and social justice
in language classrooms, schools, and society at large.

Notes

1. This paper-folding activity is adapted from the U.S. Institute of Peace. Details of
    the activity can be found here: https://www.usip.org/public-education-new/
    paper-folding-activity
2. The details of the incident can be found here: https://www.sfchronicle.com/
    news/article/The-teen-who-was-set-afire-on-the-bus-the-lives-12292082.php
3. The Consortium of Higher Education LGBT Resource Professionals: https://
    www.lgbtcampus.org/

Multimedia resources

Learning for social justice
  https://www.learningforjustice.org/
      Previously known as Teaching Tolerance, which was founded in 1991,
      Learning for Social Justice provides educational resources on various issues,
      including coronavirus racism, for educators, young people, caregivers, and
      community members in order to foster shared learning and reflection.
Clint Smith – The Danger of silence
  https://www.ted.com/talks/clint_smith_the_danger_of_silence
      In this five-minute TED Talk, Clint Smith, the author of the best-selling
      book entitled, *How the word is passed*, talks about finding the courage to speak
      up against injustices.

Southlake

https://www.nbcnews.com/southlake-podcast

The podcast *Southlake* tells the story of the challenges a school district in Texas faced, following a video showing high school students chanting the N-word.

Center for Digital Storytelling

http://storycenter.org

Center for Digital Storytelling provides a platform to share stories that can help community building to create a just world.

Children's books

Woodson, J. (2018). *The day you begin*. Nancy Paulsen Books.

A great book reminding readers that, instead of getting wrapped up in measuring themselves against others, everyone is unique, and diversity should be celebrated.

Little People, BIG DREAMS (created by Maria Isabel Sánchez Vegara)

Little People, BIG DREAMS provides a list of biography series which include names such as Rosa Parks, Maya Angelou, Martin Luther King, Frida Kahlo, and Greta Thunberg. The books have also been translated into more than twenty languages around the world including Spanish, French, German, and Japanese. The website – https://littlepeoplebig dreams.com/ – also includes worksheets and teachers' guides for each book that can be used for language teaching purposes.

Appendices

Intersectionality of struggles

Description

Below is the real-life story of Pavo (pseudonym), an Iraqi immigrant who escaped from her country to live in Turkey. This story is compiled by Busra Polat, based on her interview with Pavo, as part of the Social Justice in ELT project. Carried out by Dr. Deniz Ortaçtepe Hart and Dr. Adnan Yılmaz between 2018–2022 and funded by the US Embassy in Ankara/ US State Department, this project aimed to develop pre-service language teachers' capacity to teach for social justice. This is a shortened version of her original story, but the language is kept more or less the same to accurately represent her work in this book. Readers should proceed with caution as the content presented in this story could be triggering for past trauma and may lead to an emotional experience.

Pavo's story

I was born in Basra, Iraq, in 1992. Thankfully, in Basra I never had to face traumatic issues due to the wars or commotions since it was mostly in Baghdad. I was safe and not safe at the same time. I was raised in a religious family like most of the families in Iraq. And just like any other family, we had our own issues. My father has always been angry with himself, with us, and literally with everything on this earth. Domestic violence has always been a part of our lives since I can remember. We assume that the reason why he turned out to be like this was that his father used to treat him the way he treated us.

I used to define myself as 'religious' or 'a believer,' but after everything I had been through I honestly have lost my faith in God and in everything else. During my teenage years, I discovered who I am, knowing that I would never be accepted neither in this family nor in this country. There was a female writer who wrote about a group of terrorists who would kill the girls that defend or even talk about equality, freedom, or anything they were against. One day, as this writer was about to step out of her car to go to the supermarket, a man shot her in the head three times. Even though there was a CCTV camera nearby showing who the suspect was in detail, this man got away with this cruel crime. Since he was a part of that terrorist group, he knew he was untouchable. It is hard be a woman in these lands who wants freedom and equality, and just be ourselves whether gay or straight.

While I was growing up, I didn't have access to the internet, and I didn't have someone that I could talk about this to. At that time, I only knew that there was something different about me. As well as feeling strange, I was also feeling scared due to what my religion orders about people who are gay. All I could think was "If I do something vicious, God will punish me, so I should be like all the other girls around me." This was also the time when I had completely lost my faith. Once, my father was beating my sister, and I was praying in the room because that was the only thing I could do. I would go down on my knees and beg God to make all this stop. His reason to beat her to death again was that he thought her clothes were tighter than they were supposed to be even though they were apparently not. While she was being beaten, I had burst into tears and prayed with every beat of my heart. No matter how terrified I was, I worked up the courage and went into the room because I was worried about my sister's life. What I saw was my sister lying on the floor, her face and her body were covered in blood. I tried to push my father as hard as I could, but I was just too weak for him, and he was too strong for me. In the end, both my sister and I had been beaten all over again. We wouldn't know what to do because we were neither strong enough to stop him nor were we brave enough to call the police as they were going to tell us to solve it by ourselves because it is a private family issue. In Iraq, it is legal to kill a girl if she is having an affair with a boy.

After a while, I took my time, and I finally understood that being a lesbian was not something evil. I was just like anybody else. I didn't have this knot in my stomach and fear in my heart anymore. Then it dawned on me that I'd always been like this, and you don't get to choose who you love, and you can't blame yourself for the way you feel. I was only ten years old when I found this out. I had my first date when I was 14. There was this girl who came to my home, and this was actually the time when I had my first kiss. My mom stepped into my room, and it became such a huge deal, and she was extremely mad at me. She didn't talk to me for five months. She told my sisters about what happened and ordered them to keep their eyes on me. My mom didn't say a word to my dad knowing that he would probably kill all of us for what happened. I even went to college. I know it is such an unexpected and open-minded act from such a narrow-minded and abusive father. He didn't send us to college because he cared for us. He only did it, so he could show off to his family and his entire entourage with his educated children.

My sisters hated me only because I was the exact opposite of them. I would do whatever I wanted to without caring about what others would perceive of me. Even though she never admitted it, my older sister was jealous of me going out, meeting friends, and taking off my hijab. Wearing hijab in Iraq is not mandatory; if your family allows you to take it off, you can. When I finished college, I started working immediately. My father was not okay with the idea of his daughters working because his mindset was "Finish your school, then go and wait for your future husband." My sister did as he said, but she's not happy at all because her husband is no different from my father. He also had beaten us even though he had no right to do that. He even tried to rape me one day while I was at their home. Without hesitating, I told my mom, but she said "It's your problem. You shouldn't have gone to your sister's house and sat down next to him." Even though I was badly hurt by her reaction I knew why she said what she said and that's a whole other story that I would like to keep to myself.

Although my father did not want us to work, I found this fantastic company where my father visited and approved it as a place I could work. I needed to save money as much as I could to run away. Everything around me was just too much and I felt as if there was no air for me to breathe. I knew I would never live my life in a way I wanted to in that kind of place. I remember once I took so many pills to end my life, but it was such a failure that I ended up in a hospital. At that time my mom had enough of me and my two sisters, who hate me badly because of who I am, had been threatening me with telling my father every little detail about my life. That was the moment I knew I had to leave. I already had planned most of the things such as money, passport, and where I would go. My preference for the destination was Turkey because it was near and easier since the process of visa wouldn't take much time. After I got my passport, I started packing little by little. I didn't take much with me anyway, I wasn't getting ready for a vacation after all.

The night before I left was a complete nightmare. My brother started acting weird, and you could see how suspicious he was. I could not sleep much and woke up at 5 a.m. All of my family members are such heavy sleepers, that's why they did not hear a thing. The driver was a man who knew me and my family. In spite of suspecting something was not right, he didn't ask or say anything. Deep down, he knew what I was about to do because he knew my family enough to know that they would not let me go to the airport on my own at 5 a.m. in the morning.

Everything worked out as I planned. I got on the plane and finally arrived in Turkey. I got some help from some Iraqi friends to settle down. Sometimes, it breaks my heart that I may never see my mom again as long as my father is in our lives. After I left, my father emailed me and said: "I'm ashamed of you. I hope you will die. Because if you didn't I will find you and I will kill you." There are no words to explain how much this hurts but it is what it is. For now, all I want is to be who I am without being judged and build my own life. I also wish this for everyone who is fighting this hard battle to have their human rights which would be to love who they want to.

Appendix 2.1

Developing learners' critical literacy through problem-posing education

Building upon earlier frameworks of problem posing (e.g., Wallerstein, 1987; Wallerstein and Auerbach, 2004; Wink, 2011) as well as critical literacy (Janks, 2010) and multiliteracy (Cope and Kalantzis, 2000), the following critical framework aims to help language teachers implement problem-posing education in language classrooms in order to develop their learners' critical literacy. This framework is based upon the interpretation of multimodal texts through linguistic, visual, audio, gestural, and spatial modes of meaning. Language educators can use this critical framework to develop their learners' critical literacy through problem-posing education.

Step I: Describe the situation
- What do you see in this text?
- How would you describe what you see?
- What features of this text resonate with you?

Step II: Identify the problem
- What's happening in this text?
- What do you think people in this text are thinking, doing, and feeling?
- What might be the problem/challenge that people are facing in the context presented in the text?

Step III: Personalize
- How does this context and problem/challenge relate to your lives and your community?
- Have any of you experienced this problem/challenge in your lives/community? If you don't mind sharing, what was the experience (e.g., what happened to who, when, where, why)? How did you feel about it? What did you do?

Step IV: Analyze social context
- What might be some of the reasons this problem/challenge exists in your communities or cultures?
- How does this problem/challenge relate to larger social, political, historical, and economic processes in your society?
- To what extent is this a shared problem in your society, and why?
- How might other problems/challenges be connected to this one?

Step V: Develop strategies for action
- How can we link the problem to the previous issues we discussed in this course?
- What can we do as a class about this problem? How can we apply what we have learned into our lives and communities?
- What would be some alternative possibilities for social action?

Appendix 4.1

Lesson plan template[1,2]

School/Institution:
Grade/Level:
Language:
Course:

Rationale statement
Briefly provide information on the significance of the topic, your own positionality in regards to selecting this particular topic, shaping pedagogical frameworks etc. In short, explain why and how your language learners will study this topic in your classroom.

Objectives

Content objectives	Language objectives
Social justice objectives	

Procedures

Pre-activities: Brief description	Timeframe	Objective(s) targeted
During activities: Brief description	Timeframe	Objective(s) targeted
Post-activities: Brief description	Timeframe	Objective(s) targeted

Materials
List here any authentic and multimodal materials you will use in this lesson plan.

Formative assessment
Describe how you will monitor student learning throughout the lesson.

Differentiation
Describe if you will be differentiating course content, activities, or assessments according to learner needs, interests, and developmental levels.[3]

Reflection
If you get a chance to teach this lesson plan, reflect on the strengths and weaknesses of your lesson. How did it go? What would you do differently? Alternatively, use the checklist below to discuss this lesson's strengths, weaknesses, and affordances for student learning and potential threats/pitfalls.

Lesson plan review checklist

       ✓ Yes   ✗ No   NA (Not applicable)

_____ Are there language, content, and social justice objectives?

_____ Do the activities, materials, and tasks align with/support the learning objectives?

_____ Are there problem-posing, reflective, text analysis, and action-oriented activities?

_____ Are there any authentic and multimodal texts used?

_____ Do group/pair tasks foster negotiation of meaning and discussion of ideas?

_____ Does the lesson promote an equitable perspective towards different identities and cultures?

_____ Does the lesson encourage learners to investigate social, economic, and political issues?

_____ Does the lesson reflect multiple perspectives in ways that challenge the status quo?

_____ Does the lesson include topics related to students' backgrounds and concerns related to their lives and communities?

_____ Is differentiation used? If not, how could it be incorporated?

_____ Is there a formative assessment plan? If not, how could it be added?

Notes

1. This lesson plan template has been modified by the author from the classic lesson plan template used at the Middlebury Institute of International Studies at Monterey.
2. Some readers might find this format of lesson planning highly institutionalized, top down, and linear. Another concern might be that the lesson plan may not reflect any unplanned, student-led unlearning, or a pedagogy of discomfort (discussed in Chapter 8). While acknowledging these concerns, I also believe that in many teacher education programs this is the format language teachers are trained (and in some cases constrained) to follow, and they will continue to do so in their teaching contexts. Therefore, I have decided to use this template to show readers the possible integration of language, content, and social justice objectives and to present how activities, materials, and formative assessment can be designed to further such integration. Using this template does not mean that language teachers need to follow the lesson plan strictly and adaptions should be made as needed.

3. A good reference for differentiated instruction is Carol Ann Tomlinson and Jay McTighe's (2006) book, *Integrating differentiated instruction & understanding by design.*

Appendix 4.2

A critical framework for material evaluation and adaptation

Building on the previous frameworks for material evaluation and adaptation (e.g., Allen, 2006; Daniel, 2016; Gray, 2013a), this critical framework provides a starting point for language educators to examine their language teaching materials. This is not an exhaustive list and should be used and adapted in relation to one's own pedagogical purposes, contexts, learners, curriculum, and the wider community.

Part I: Describe the material, the context, and learners
- Which book/unit/material/text are you evaluating?
- What are its learning goals?
- What is the target population (e.g., age, educational level, language proficiency, language background, educational or professional goals, reasons to learn the language, etc.)?

Part II: Evaluation of the material
2.1 Evaluating the material from the teacher's perspective
- What is my take on this material as the teacher? Is it different from the author's intention?
- Do I understand/know why this material was created?
- What do I know about my students' lives that I can bring to the conversation while teaching this material?
- How can I prepare myself to be able to guide my students through the material?

2.2 Evaluating the material from the students' perspectives
- Is the material:
  - appropriate for my student population?
  - culturally relevant, affirming, and sustaining?
  - reflective of and appealing to their identities and life experiences?

- Does this material address a topic that might be perceived differently by people coming from a different social class, race, ethnicity, immigration status, etc.?

2.3 Evaluating the material in terms of praxis
- What implicit or explicit biases does this material bring to the conversation, if any?
- Does this material privilege some of my learners while discriminating others?
- Are there any biased and stereotypical statements/images/representations?
- Is there anything in this material that is culturally inappropriate and offensive?
- Whose reality is foregrounded and whose is backgrounded?
- Whose voice is heard and whose is silenced?
- What view of the world is being presented and promoted?
- Whose culture is represented and in what ways?
- What does the language used in this material say about whose identities are included and whose are excluded?
- How would different stakeholders (i.e., parents, learners, administrators) in my teaching context react to this material?

Part III: Adaptation
- What kind of social justice objectives can I add to the existing learning goals?
- How can I supplement content with any relevant and necessary information and additional perspectives?
- How can I encourage a critical analysis and discussion of the written and oral texts as well as images?
- How can I integrate authentic materials that will challenge the existing status quo and hegemonic ideologies in schooling and the larger context?
- How can the material provide more accommodation for multimodality and multiliteracies (e.g., visual, audio, spatial, gestural, digital, and dramatic)?
- How can I engage my students in an investigation of the larger social, economic, and political issues?
- What kind of problem-posing questions can be asked in relation to this material?
- How can I encourage my students to ask crucial, thought-provoking questions?
- How can I adapt the material in ways that represent different cultures and multiple perspectives in a non-essentialist way?
- How can the material include a more equitable perspective with regard to different identities and cultures?

Appendix 6.1

Sample lesson plan on environmental justice

Name: Sydney Zamudio
Theme: Food, Access, and Identity in Occupied Palestine

School/Institution: Middlebury Institute of International Studies at Monterey
Grade/Level: Intermediate high (ACTFL)/ B1/B2 (CEFR)
Language: Arabic
Course: 300-level, four-credit Arabic course (nine students), 75 minutes/lesson

Teacher Positionality: I engage with the subject of Palestine and Palestinians' right to self-determination as a White American with no ethnic ties to the region. This lesson plan does not attempt to make discursive truth claims about good or bad, right or wrong. This lesson plan endeavors to highlight one aspect of the lived experiences of Palestinians and lift up their voices. The lesson plan is designed for the EDUC 8545A: Language Teaching for Social Justice on which I was enrolled in Fall 2020, as part of my TFL Arabic degree at Middlebury Institute of International Studies at Monterey.

Rationale statement

Palestine has undergone significant changes throughout its long history, both demographic and environmental. In the last century, these environmental changes have taken on a colonial dimension (Qumsiyeh and Abusarhan, 2020). In what has been named the Environmental Nakba as a call-back to the 1948 exodus of over 700,000 Palestinians from their homes known as the Nakba, the building of illegal settlements in the West Bank and the intensifying land and sea blockades in Gaza have dramatically minimized access to arable land and clean drinking water and by extension impacted Palestinians' ability to lead dignified lives and make a steady living for their families (Qumsiyeh and Abusarhan, 2020). As a result of restrictions on movement and travel, Palestinian villages and cities have become disconnected, leading to diverse kitchens, uses of natural resources, and foods. This lesson plan endeavors to humanize an often very fraught and polarized issue by unpacking the ways in which access to land and resources impacts the foods we eat and share with others, and by extension the stories and aspects of identity that we share with others.

If needed, this lesson plan can be adapted to a hybrid or fully online context. I also envision this lesson plan as one day in one section of a larger thematic unit in an entire course focusing on social justice in the Arab World. Students will have familiarity with social justice related terms and concepts and will be comfortable discussing identities and privileges. It is established from the beginning of this unit in particular that I am not ethnically tied to the land of historic Palestine. It is also established that this lesson is not about the politics of occupation, conflict, right/wrong, etc., but rather the experiences of people who live in a context where they have unequal access to resources as a result of unequal access to power and legitimacy in a specific space.

Objectives

Students will be able to:

Content objectives (COs)	Language objectives (LOs)
A. recognize communal creativity and collaboration as a result of lack of access to resources B. discuss unique aspects of Palestinian cuisine C. make connections between Palestinian cultures, identities, and experiences and those of other communities	D. present their ideas to and negotiate concepts with a group E. express their personal identities through food as a representation of culture F. use key vocabulary related to food, cooking, and resources

Social Justice Objectives (SJOs)
G. bring under-represented, or perhaps even new, perspectives into uncomfortable conversations H. express curiosity about the history and lived experiences of others I. examine the intersection of access to resources and innovation in identity expression

J. examine what modern-day colonialism can look like in the
    Arabic-speaking world and the spheres of life it can impact
K. question the existing status quo behind political, social, and
    economic power dynamics

Materials
- Poster paper, pens, whiteboard
  - If online: Zoom room, share screen capabilities, access to shareable
    Google Doc or OneDrive file
- Video: 4:35, الطباخة الفلسطينية (English subtitles available). https://www.
  youtube.com/watch?v=1uI0zCtQw_4
- Podcast: 4:03, Olive trees in the Holy Land are in trouble. https://
  theworld.org/media/2021-11-09/olive-trees-holy-land-are-trouble
- *The Land of Sad Oranges* by Ghassan Kanafani (a short story)

References
Qumsiyeh, M. B. and Abusarhan, M. A. (2020). An environmental Nakba:
    The Palestinian environment under Israeli occupation. *Science for the
    People*, 23(1).
Royal, D. (2016). We are all environment educators (whether we know it
    or not). In L. Jacobs and C. Hastings (Eds.), *Social justice in English language
    teaching* (pp. 279–290). TESOL Press.

Procedures

Pre-activities: 16 minutes total	Timeframe	Objective(s) Targeted
Greetings and Check-in **Warm Up Activity: Mindmap**	1 minute	
• Ask the students to divide themselves into groups of three and find a space in the room to work. Provide each group with a piece of poster paper and a pen	15 minutes total	Activating Schema
• Ask students to write الأكل العربي (Arab food/cuisine) in the center of their poster paper *(can be done on a whiteboard or on Zoom in shared slides with editing access in breakout rooms depending on context)*	(8 in group, 7 sharing all together)	LO: D, F SJO: G, H, I

Pre-activities: 16 minutes total	Timeframe	Objective(s) Targeted

• Instruct students to create a mind-map of their associations with Arab food/cuisine and provide prompting questions orally, as needed:
  • What comes to mind when you think of Arab cuisine?
  • What ingredients are common?
  • Where do the ingredients come from?
  • Why are some ingredients more common than others?
  • Who traditionally prepares the meals in Arab culture?
  • How are some of the dishes prepared?
• Ask the groups to share their mind-maps out to the class and explain the connections made		

During Activities: 47 minutes	Timeframe	Objective(s) Targeted
Video and Think, Pair, Share: 1. Hand out worksheet (see Appendix 5.1a) with the prompting questions. Instructor introduces video and gives students two minutes to read the questions. 2. Watch the video on Palestinian cooking and access to ingredients with students twice (first time at .75 speed with Arabic subtitles, second time at normal speed with subtitles) 3. Have students go back into their groups of three and ask them to discuss their original mindmaps in light of what they learned in the video and the prompting questions. Students share any changes they would make to the group.	27 minutes 1. 2 minutes 2. 10 minutes 3. 15 minutes (8 in groups, 7 sharing all together)	CO: A, B, C LO: D, E, F SJO: G, H, I

Pre-activities: 16 minutes total	Timeframe	Objective(s) Targeted

Podcast and Individual Action Plan:
1. Use students' familiarity with Arabic root letter system to generate the following key terms/phrases from their roots
   • Harvest – حصاد
   • Olive Press – معصرة زيتون
   • Pruning – التشذيب
   • To restrict – التقييد
2. Listen to podcast one time and discuss the questions on the handout as a group in Arabic
3. Students work independently, brainstorming ideas for personal action plans inspired by what they learned in the video and podcast and begin to create future goals for implementing social justice in their work (can take the form of a poster, call to action paper, newspaper article, or something more creative like a song or poem)
	20 minutes
	
	1. 5 minutes
	
	2. 10 minutes
	
	3. 5 minutes
		CO: A, C
		LO: D, E, F
		SJO: G, H, I, J, K

Post-activities: 12 minutes	Timeframe	Objective(s) Targeted
Introduce the Homework: Direct students to procedures written on class handout 1. Students will read Ghassan Kanafani's short story, *The Land of Sad Oranges* • After reading, students will reflect on and answer the questions on the handout in Appendix 6.1a in their journals. (Students keep a journal throughout the semester. It can either be written or audio recorded.)	4 minutes in class Approx. 2.5 hours of asynchronous work	CO: A, C LO: F SJO: G, H, I, J, K

Pre-activities: 16 minutes total	Timeframe	Objective(s) Targeted
2. After reading *The Land of Sad Oranges*, complete the action plan started during class • Note any new thoughts, perspectives, or goals after reading the short story		
Ticket to Leave: **See Appendix 6.1a** Direct students to handout and explain that they can choose from one of two prompts: Option 1: Students reflect on today's topic by answering the following questions in 2–3 sentences each: *******this can be done either via writing or students can step outside and record a short oral reflection and then send it to me*******	8 minutes (students can leave when turned in)	**Option 1:** CO: C LO: E, F SJO: I

Option 2: Students make their own mindmap specific to الأكل الفلسطيني (Palestinian food) similar to our warm-up exercise reflecting on the following topics:
   • What do you know about Palestinian food?
   • What can you add to your prior knowledge after class today?
		Option 2:
		CO: A, B
		LO: D, E, F
		SJO: G, H, I, J

Formative assessment strategy
Throughout the lesson, I will move from group to group (or breakout room to breakout room) listening to their ideas, monitoring their interaction with the materials, and answering any questions. I will be stopping throughout class and asking students to relay concepts or terms in their own words to check for understanding. I will also be collecting their ticket to leave before the class period ends which will provide a lot of formative assessment data on their engagement with the topic along with writing or speaking skills, depending on the prompt they choose.

Differentiation

First, students are able to select their own groups for our warm-up activity. They will ideally divide into three groups of three, but if some would rather work as a pair, that is fine as well. We will watch the video the first time at 0.75 speed with subtitles. Our subsequent viewing will be at normal speed, but the subtitles will stay. Students can relate personal experiences to course content in several different ways; they can draw on their experiences in the Arab world, or the cultures of the communities they are a part of in their personal lives, differentiating by content. Finally, the ticket to leave and action plan are differentiated by product and process, as students keep a journal that can be written or spoken/recorded and the ticket to leave has two options for students to choose from.

Reflection

Please discuss this lesson's strengths, weaknesses, and affordances for student learning and potential threats/pitfalls

This lesson plan engages with a rarely discussed aspect of Palestine's occupation: food and natural resources as they relate to identity. I am very concerned with the potential for dehumanization and essentialization in only discussing struggles and hardship as they relate to social (in)justice. This lesson plan validates the hard realities in Occupied Palestine without focusing solely on conflict, violence, and sorrow. I see this as a strength. A weakness, however, is that the lesson might not be intimately connected with students' lives. Royal (2016) argues that environmental justice, as woven into the language classroom, should connect to our students' lives and I feel like this lesson could have a little bit more of that.

A massive pitfall and potential threat to learning that I need to highlight is discussing Palestine in any form. This is a threat on a few different levels. First, there may be students not willing to engage on the subject at all, which could derail the entire class. My hope here would be that the thematic unit has been scaffolded in such a way that my learners understand my goals as an instructor. In discussing Palestine in the language classroom, my goal as an instructor is to highlight that the Palestinian struggle and resistance is ongoing in its anti-colonial and anti-apartheid efforts.

Second, teaching about Palestine in America has ramifications for the instructor ranging from accusations of anti-Semitism to loss of livelihood. I hope I am steadfast in my dedication to centering Palestinian realities in the classroom and providing a space for Palestinian voices to be uplifted, even if on the small scale of a language class. While I do not want fear of those potential ramifications to impact the intellectual honesty I engage in with my students, this is easier said than done.

Any further thoughts on this lesson plan?
I have also been thinking a lot about conversations we have in social justice circles and how Palestine is, or is not, included in those conversations. Very frequently, I hear people say something to the effect of, "I cannot talk about Palestine until I know my facts. I don't want to say anything until I know what I am talking about." And the more I think about it, the more I realize that we don't do this with any other subject in the social justice space. We do not know everything about race, class, gender identity, sexual identity, (dis)ability, the list goes on, and yet we discuss these topics knowing that we will inevitably be wrong at some point and learn something that expands our thinking. The fear/silence/hesitancy to discuss Palestine drives home the power of American education, policy, and discourse in our daily lives. I also fundamentally believe that one cannot support Black liberation for example in America and simultaneously stay silent, or neutral, on the oppression that Palestinians face under a regime of settler colonialism. I realize that not everyone is on the same page as me with that and we are all on our own journeys with respect to social justice and Palestine. I am certainly not an expert, but after all is said and done, I hope my lesson plan begins to push the needle just slightly and challenges people to talk about Palestine, even if we don't know everything. I certainly am still learning, and that is okay.

Appendix 6.1a

Class handout (English) (see Appendix 6.1b for the Arabic handout)

Arabic Studies Department at MIIS
Food, Access, and Identity in Occupied Palestine
Name: _____ Date: _____

Part One – Watching the video
Read the following questions before viewing the video. You will discuss these questions in groups, so it is not necessary to answer them here.
1. The chef argued that food could be used as a tool of oppression. How so? Do you agree?
2. According to the chef, who holds the knowledge of Palestinian food? How has politics and history influenced this?
3. What did you learn about Palestinian identity from the foods discussed?
4. To the extent that you feel comfortable participating, are you aware of any ways food can be a marginalizing force in society?
5. The chef discussed a poisonous plant that can become edible when handled properly. Can you make any connections between this knowledge and your own cultures? For example: home remedies, botany, ancestral knowledge?

Part Two – Podcast and personal action plans
Read the following questions before listening to the podcast.
1. Discuss the following question as a whole class: After watching the video and listening to the podcast, what have you learned about the relationship between food, access, and identity in Palestine? To the extent you feel comfortable sharing, how have you seen these spheres intersect in your own life or in your experiences in the region?
2. Use the space below to work independently and create your own action plan to implement what you have learned into future engagement with Palestine and the Arab world more broadly.

Part Three – Ticket to leave

Choose between the following two prompts and turn in before leaving.

1. On a separate piece of paper or via voice recording, reflect on today's topic by answering the following questions in 2–3 sentences each:
   - What ingredients or dishes are meaningful to your family or in your cultural context?
   - What do you hope to share with people from outside your community when you eat these foods or meals with them?
2. On a separate piece of paper, create a mindmap for Palestinian food, similar to our warm-up exercise. Use the following prompts as needed:
   - What do you know about Palestinian food?
   - What can you add to your prior knowledge after class today?
   - How do history, politics, and access impact Palestinian food?

Part Four – Homework

1. Read Ghassan Kanafani's short story, *The Land of Sad Oranges*. After reading, reflect on and answer the following questions in your journal:
   - What role did the environment and/or natural resources play in Kanafani's story?
   - What shapes can resistance take?
   - What are your takeaways from Kanafani's story in relation to the work you hope to do in the Middle East in the future?
2. After reading *The Land of Sad Oranges*, complete the action plan you started during class. This action plan can take many forms (e.g., a poster, call-to-action paper, newspaper article, poster, or something more artistic like a song or poem. Be creative!) and should be approximately one page in length. Note any new thoughts, perspectives, or goals after reading the short story.

Appendix 6.1b

Class handout (Arabic)

قسم اللغة العربية في معهد ميدلبري
الغذاء والوصول والهوية في فلسطين المحتلة

اسم: ———————   تاريخ: ———————

الجزء الأول – مشاهدة الفيديو: اقرأوا الأسئلة التالية قبل أن نشاهد الفيديو. ستناقشون الأسئلة في المجموعات الأصلية فليس من الضروري أن تجيبوا عليها هنا.

١. تجادل الطباخة بأنه يمكن استخدام الطعام كأداة للقمع. كيف؟ هل توافق/ين معها أم لا؟

٢. بالنسبة للطباخة مَن يملك معرفة بالطعام الفلسطيني؟ كيف أثرت السياسة والتاريخ على هذه المعرفة؟

٣. ماذا تعلمتم عن الهوية الفلسطينية من الأطعمة التي تمت مناقشتها؟

٤. إلى الحد الذي تشعرون فيه بالراحة في المشاركة، هل أنت على دراية بأي طرق يمكن أن يكون بها الطعام قوة مهمشة في المجتمع؟

٥. ناقشت الطباخة نباتًا سامًا يمكن أن يصبح صالحًا للأكل عند معالجته بشكل صحيح. هل تستطيعون أن تجدوا أي روابط بين هذه المعرفة وثقافاتكم؟ مثلًا: العلاجات المنزلية وعلم النبات ومعرفة الأجداد؟

الجزء الثاني -- البودكاست وخطة العمل الخاصة: اقرأوا الأسئلة التالية قبل أن نسمع إلى البودكاست

١. ناقشوا هذه الأسئلة كمجموعة كاملة:
أ. ماذا تعلمتم عن العلاقة بين الغذاء والوصول والهوية في فلسطين من الفيديوهات والبودكاست؟ إلى الحد الذي تشعرون فيه بالراحة في المشاركة، كيف رأيتم هذه المجالات تتقاطع في حياتكم الخاصة أو في تجاربكم في المنطقة؟

٢. استخدموا المساحة أدناه لبدء تبادل الأفكار للموجه التالي:

لقد عبرتم عن هدفكم بالعمل في العالم العربي في المستقبل. بعد سماع قصة عمل الفلسطينيين معًا لشراء معصرة زيتون إيطالية ، ما هي الطرق التي ستستخدم بها امتيازاتك للارتقاء بأهداف المجتمع والعمل مع السكان الأصليين لجعل الوصول إلى الغذاء والموارد أمرًا عادلاً؟

الجزء الثالث – تذكرة الخروج:

الاختيار الأول: على ورقة منفصلة أو من خلال تسجيل صوتي، فكروا في موضوع اليوم من خلال الإجابة على الأسئلة التالية في جملتين إلى ثلاث جمل لكل منها:

١. ما المكونات أو الأطباق ذات المغزى لعائلتك أو في سياق ثقافتك؟
٢. ما الذي تأمل أن تشاركه مع أشخاص من خارج مجتمعك عندما تتناول هذه الأطعمة أو وجبات الطعام معهم؟

الاختيار الثاني: في ورقة منفصلة، قم بإنشاء خريطتك الذهنية الخاصة بالطعام الفلسطيني مع مراعاة الأسئلة التالية:

١. ماذا تعرف عن الطعام الفلسطيني؟
٢. ما الذي يمكنك إضافته إلى معرفتك السابقة بعد الفصل اليوم؟

الجزء الرابع – الواجب:

١. اقرأوا أرض البرتقال الحزين لغسان كنفاني. بعد القراءة، أجيبوا عن الأسئلة التالية في دفتركم اليومي:

ما الدور الذي لعبته البيئة والموارد الطبيعية في القصة؟
ما الأشكال التي يمكن أن تتخذها المقاومة؟
ما هي مقتطفاتك من قصة كنفاني فيما يتعلق بالعمل الذي تأمل القيام به في الشرق الأوسط في المستقبل؟

٢. بعد القراءة، أكملوا خطة العمل التي بدأتها في الصف. دوّن أي أفكار أو وجهات نظر أو أهداف جديدة بعد قراءة القصة القصيرة.

References

Abdollahzadeh, E. and Baniasad, S. (2010). Ideologies in the imported English textbooks: EFL learners and teachers' awareness and attitude. *Journal of English Language Teaching and Learning, 2*(217), 1–17.

Abu-Shomar, A. (2016). Critical pedagogy and post-colonial education. In A. Darder, P. Mayo and J. Paraskeva (Eds.), *International critical pedagogy reader* (pp. 17–26). Routledge.

Accurso, K. and Mizell, J. D. (2020). Toward an antiracist genre pedagogy: Considerations for a North American context. *TESOL Journal, 11.*

Adams, M. (2016). Pedagogical foundations for social justice education. In M. Adams, L. A. Bell, D. J. Goodman and K. Y. Joshi (Eds.), *Teaching for diversity and social justice* (3rd Ed.) (pp. 27–54). Routledge.

Adams, M. and Joshi, K. Y. (2016). Religious oppression. In M. Adams, L. A. Bell, D. J. Goodman, and K. Y. Joshi (Eds.), *Teaching for diversity and social justice* (3rd Ed.) (pp. 255–298). Routledge.

Adams, M., and Zúñiga, X. (2016). Getting started: Core concepts for social justice education. In M. Adams, L. A. Bell, D. J. Goodman, and K. Y. Joshi (Eds.), *Teaching for diversity and social justice* (pp. 95–130). Routledge.

Adams, M., Hopkins, L. E., and Shlasko, D. (2016). Classism. In M. Adams, L. A. Bell, D. J. Goodman, and K. Y. Joshi (Eds.), *Teaching for diversity and social justice* (pp. 213–255). Routledge.

Agnello, (2016). The dispositions of teachers as researchers: A call to action. In M. F. Agnello and W. M. Reynolds (Eds.), *Practicing critical pedagogy: The influences of Joe L. Kincheloe* (pp. 29–38). Springer.

Ahlquist, R. (1991). Position and imposition: Power relations in a multicultural foundations class. *Journal of Negro Education, 60*(2), 158–169.

Ahmad, S. (2014). *The cultural politics of emotion* (2nd Ed.). Edinburgh University Press.

Ahmad, S. (2017). *Living a feminist life.* Duke University Press.

akt (2021). *The LGBTQ+ youth homelessness report.* https://www.akt.org.uk/report

Aldous, S. and Sereemongkonpol, P. (2008). *Ladyboys: The secret world of Thailand's third gender.* Maverick House.

Alim, H. S. (2005). Critical language awareness in the United States: Revisiting issues and revising pedagogies in a resegregated society. *Educational Researcher, 34*(7), 24–31.

Alim, H. S., Rickford, J. R., and Ball, A. F. (2016). *Raciolinguistics: How language shapes our ideas about race.* Oxford University Press.

Allen, L. A. (2006). The moral life of schools revisited: Preparing educational leaders to "build a new social order" for social justice and democratic community. *International Journal of Urban Educational Leadership, 1*, 1–13.

Allen, L. (2015). Queer pedagogy and the limits of thought: Teaching sexualities at university. *Higher Education Research & Development, 34*(4), 763–775.

Alptekin, C. (1993). Target-language culture in EFL materials. *ELT Journal, 47*(2), 136–143.

Alptekin, C. (2002). Towards intercultural communicative competence in ELT. *ELT Journal, 56*(1), 57–64.

Alsup, J. and Miller, S. (2014). Reclaiming English education: Rooting social justice dispositions. *National Council of Teachers of English, 46*, 195–215.

Althusser, L. (2001). *Lenin and philosophy and other essays* (translated by Ben Brewster). Monthly Review Press.

American Association for Applied Linguistics (AAAL) (2022). *Social justice listserv.* https://www.aaal.org/aaal-and-social-justice-listserv

American Association of Colleges for Teacher Education (2019). *Education students and diversity.* https://aacte.org/resources/research-reports-and-briefs/education-students-and-diversity-a-review-of-new-evidence/

American Council on the Teaching of Foreign Languages (ACTFL) (2022). *Critical and social justice approaches.* https://www.actfl.org/connect/special-interest-groups/critical-and-social-justice-approaches

Amin, N. (1997). Race and the identity of the nonnative ESL teacher. *TESOL Quarterly, 31*(3), 580–583.

Andrzejewski, J., Baltodano, M. P., and Symcox, L. (Eds.) (2009). *Social justice, peace, and environmental education: Transformative standards.* Routledge.

Antony, M. G. (2013). "Thank you for calling": Accents and authenticity on NBC's outsourced. *Journal of Intercultural Communication Research, 42*(2), 192–213.

Anya, U. (2021). Critical race pedagogy for more effective and inclusive world language teaching. *Applied Linguistics, (42)*6, 1055–1069.

Anyon, J. (1981). Social class and school knowledge. *Curriculum Inquiry, 11*(1), 3–42.

Anyon, J. (2011). *Marx and education.* Routledge.

Apple, M. W. (1990). The text and cultural politics. *The Journal of Educational Thought, 24*(3A), 17–33.

Apple, M. W. (1992). The text and cultural politics. *Educational Researcher, 21*(7), 4–11.

Apple, M. W. (2006). *Educating the right way: Markets, standards, God, and inequality* (2nd Ed.). Routledge.

Apple, M. W. (2019). *Ideology and curriculum.* Routledge.

Apple, M. W. and Christian-Smith, L. (1991). *The politics of textbook.* Routledge.

Appleby, R. (2016). Researching privilege in language teacher identity. *TESOL Quarterly, 50*(3), 755–768.

Auerbach, E. (1995). The politics of the ESL classroom: Issues of power in pedagogical choices. In J. Tollefson (Ed.), *Power and inequality in language education* (p. 933). Cambridge University Press.

Auerbach, E. (2000). When pedagogy meets politics: Challenging English only in adult education. In R. D. Gonzales with I. Melis (Eds.), *Language ideologies: Critical perspectives on the official English movement* (Vol. I) (pp. 177–204). NCTE and Lawrence Erlbaum.

Auerbach, E. R. and Burgess, D. (1987). The hidden curriculum of survival ESL. In I. Shor (Ed.), *Freire for the classroom: A sourcebook for liberatory teaching.* Boynton/Cook Publishers.

Avineri, N. and Martinez, D. C. (2021). Applied linguists cultivating relationships for justice: An aspirational call to action. *Applied Linguistics, 42*(6), 1043–1054.

Avineri, N., Graham, L. R., Johnson, E. J., Riner, R. C., and Rosa, J. (Eds.) (2019). *Language and social justice in practice.* Routledge.

Badwan, K. (2021). *Language in a globalised world: Social justice perspectives on mobility and contact.* Springer.

Baecher, L., Farnsworth, T., and Ediger, A. (2014). The challenges of planning language objectives in content-based ESL instruction. *Language Teaching Research, 18*(1), 118–136.

Baldwin, J. ([1980] 2021). *The price of the ticket: Collected nonfiction 1948–1985*. Beacon Press.

Bale, J. (2015). Language policy and global political economy. In T. Ricento (Ed.), *Language policy and political economy* (pp. 72–96). Oxford University Press.

Bali, M. (2018). The "unbearable" exclusion of the digital. In D. Kim and J. Stommel (Eds.), *Disrupting the digital humanities*. Punctum Books.

Ball, A. F. (2000). Empowering pedagogies that enhance the learning of multicultural students. *Teachers College Record, 102*, 1006–1034.

Ball, S. J. (2012). Performativity, commodification and commitment: An I-Spy guide to the neoliberal university. *British Journal of Educational Studies, 60*(1), 17–28.

Banegas, D. L. and Evripidou, D. (2021). Introduction: Comprehensive sexuality education in ELT. *ELT Journal, 75*(2), 127–132.

Banegas, D. L. and Gerlach, D. (2021). Critical language teacher education: A duoethnography of teacher educators' identities and agency. *System, 98*.

Bangou, F. and Wong, S. (2009). Race and technology in teacher education: Where is the access In R. Kubota and A. Lin (Eds.), *Race, culture, and identities in second language education: Exploring critically engaged practice* (pp. 158–`175). Routledge.

Banks, J. A. (1995). Multicultural education: Historical development, dimensions and practice. In J. A. Banks and C. A. M. Banks (Eds.), *Handbook of research on multicultural education* (pp. 3–24). Macmillan.

Bartolomé, L. I. (1994). Beyond the methods fetish: Toward a humanizing pedagogy. *Harvard Educational Review, 64*(2), 173–194.

Bartolomé, L. I. (2010). Daring to infuse ideology into language-teacher education. In S. May and C. Sleeter (Eds.), *Critical multiculturalism: Theory and praxis* (pp. 47–60). Routledge.

Baugh, J. (2011). Power, social diversity, and language. In R. Mesthrie (Ed.), *The Cambridge handbook of sociolinguistics* (pp. 17–27). Cambridge University Press.

Bell, L. A. (2016). Theoretical foundations for social justice education. In M. Adams, L. A. Bell, D. J. Goodman, and K. Y. Joshi (Eds.), *Teaching for diversity and social justice* (pp. 3–26). Routledge.

Bell, L. A., Funk, S. M., Joshi, K. Y., and Valdivia, M. (2016). Racism and white privilege. In M. Adams, L. A. Bell, D. J. Goodman, and K. Y. Joshi (Eds.), *Teaching for diversity and social justice* (pp. 133–182). Routledge.

Bender-Slack, D. (2015). Talk texts, arts teachers negotiate language social justice teaching. *English Education, 42*, 181–203.

Benesch, S. (2012). *Considering emotions in critical English language teaching: Theories and praxis*. Routledge.

Benesch, S. (2017). *Emotions and English language teaching: Exploring teachers' emotion labor*. Routledge.

Bennett, R., Uink, B., and Cross, S. (2020). Beyond the social: Cumulative implications of COVID-19 for first nations university students in Australia. *Social Sciences & Humanities Open, 2*, 1–5.

Beyogle, R. (2014). Language contact and language attitudes in two Dagara-speaking border communities in Burkina Faso and Ghana. In E. C. Zsiga, O. T. Boyer, and R. Kramer (Eds.), *Languages in Africa: Multilingualism, language policy, and education*. Georgetown University Press.

Bigelow, B. (1997). The human lives behind the labels: The global sweatshop, Nike, and the race to the bottom. *Phi Delta Kappa, 79*(2), 112–119.

Bigelow, B. and Swinehart, T. (Eds.) (2014). *A people's curriculum for the Earth: Teaching climate change and the environmental crisis*. Rethinking Schools.

Bigelow, M., Ranney, S., and Hebble, A. M. (2005). Choosing depth over breadth in a content based ESOL program. In D. Kaufman and J. Crandall (Eds.), *Content-based instruction in primary and secondary school settings* (pp. 179–193). TESOL Press.

Blackburn, M. V. (2013). Learning to tell a pedagogical story about heteronormativity. In P. C. Gorski, K. Zenkov, N. Osei-Kofi, and J. Sapp (Eds.), *Cultivating social justice teachers: How teacher educators have helped students overcome cognitive bottlenecks and learn critical social justice concepts*. Stylus.

Blackburn, M. V. and Smith, J. M. (2010). Moving beyond the inclusion of LGBT-themed literature in English language arts classrooms: Interrogating heteronormativity and exploring intersectionality. *Journal of Adolescent & Adult Literacy, 53*, 625–634.

Blackmer Reyes, K. and Curry Rodríguez, J. E. (2012). Testimonio: Origins, terms, and resources. *Equity & Excellence in Education, 45*(3), 525–538.

Blake, B. E. (2016). A broken arch, a broken bridge, and a broken promise: Using Kincheloe's critical pedagogy concepts to teach about race in an urban graduate school classroom. In M. F. Agnello and W. M. Reynolds (Eds.), *Practicing critical pedagogy* (pp. 121–130). Springer.

Block, D. (2007). Language education and globalization. In S. May and N. H. Hornberger (Eds.), *Encyclopedia of language and education* (2nd Ed.) (pp. 31–43). Springer.

Block, D. (2012a). Class and SLA: Making connections. *Language Teaching Research, 16*(2), 188–205.

Block, D. (2012b). Commentary: Transnational South Korea as a site for a sociolinguistics and the distinction of global elites. *Journal of Sociolinguistics, 16*(2), 277–282.

Block, D. (2014). *Social class in applied linguistics*. Routledge.

Block, D. (2018). *Political economy and sociolinguistics: Neoliberalism, inequality and social class*. Bloomsbury Academic.

Block, D. and Gray, J. (2018). French language textbooks as ideologically imbued cultural artefacts: Political economy, neoliberalism and self-branding. In S. Coffey and U. Wingate (Eds.), *New Directions for research in foreign language education* (pp. 115–131). Routledge.

Block, D., Gray, J., and Holborow, M. (Eds.) (2012). *Neoliberalism and applied linguistics*. Routledge.

Bloom, B. S. (1956). *Taxonomy of educational objectives, Handbook I: The cognitive domain*. Longman.

Blum, L. (2008). Racial incidents as teachable moments. In M. Pollock (Ed.), *Everyday antiracism: Getting real about race in school* (pp. 236–241). The New Press.

Boler, M. (1999). *Feeling power: Emotions and education*. Routledge.

Bonilla-Silva, E. (2002). The linguistics of colorblind racism: How to talk nasty about Blacks without sounding "racist." *Critical Sociology, 28*(1–2), 41–64.

Bonilla-Silva, E. (2015). The structure of racism in color-blind, "post-racial" America. *American Behavioral Scientist, 59*(11), 1358–1376.

Bonilla-Silva, E. (2017). *Racism without racists*. Rowman & Littlefield Publishers.

Bonilla-Silva, E. and Embrick, D. G. (2008). Recognizing the likelihood of reproducing racism. In M. Pollock (Ed.), *Everyday antiracism: Getting real about race in school* (pp. 334–336). The New Press.

Bori, P. (2018). *Language textbooks in the era of neoliberalism*. Routledge.

Bori, P. (2021). Neoliberalism and global textbooks: A critical ethnography of English language classrooms in Serbia. *Language, Culture and Curriculum, 34*(2), 183–198.

Bourdieu, P. (1977). The economics of linguistic exchanges. *Social Science Information, 16*(6), 645–668.

Bourdieu, P. (1984). *Distinction: A social critique of the judgement of taste*. Harvard University Press.

Bourdieu, P. (1986). The forms of capital. In J. Richardson (Ed.), *Handbook of theory and research for the sociology of education* (pp. 241–258). Greenwood.

Bourdieu, P. (1990). *The logic of practice*. Stanford University Press.

Bourdieu, P. (2005). *The social structures of the economy*. Polity.

Bourdieu, P. and Passeron, J. C. (1991). *Language & symbolic power*. Polity Press.

Bowers, C. A. (2002). Toward an eco-justice pedagogy. *Environmental Education Research*, *8*(1), 21–34.

Boyd, A. S. (2017). *Social justice literacies in the English classroom: Teaching practice in action*. Teachers College Press.

Boylan, M. and Woolsey, I. (2015). Teacher education for social justice: Mapping identity spaces. *Teaching and Teacher Education*, *46*, 62–71.

Bradley, H. (2015). *Fractured identities: Changing patterns of inequality* (2nd Ed.). Polity.

Brantmeier, E. J. (2011). Towards mainstreaming critical peace education in US teacher education. In C. S. Malott and B. Porfilio (Eds.), *Critical pedagogy in the twenty-first century: A new generation of scholars* (pp. 349–376). Information Age Publishing.

Britzman, D. P. (1995). Is there a queer pedagogy? Or, stop reading straight. *Educational Theory*, *45*(2), 151–165.

Britzman, D. P. (1998). *Lost subjects contested objects: Toward a psychoanalytic inquiry of learning*. State University of New York Press.

Britzman, D. P. (2012). Queer pedagogy and its strange techniques. *Counterpoints*, *367*, 292–308.

Britzman, D. P., Santiago-Válles, K., Jiménez-Múñoz, G., and Lamash, L. M. (1993). Slips that show and tell: Fashioning multiculture as a problem of representation. In C. McCharth and W. Crichlow (Eds.), *Race, identity, and representation in education*. Routledge.

Broido, E. M. (2000). The development of social justice allies during college: A phenomenological investigation. *Journal of College Student Development*, *41*(1), 3–18.

Bruthiaux, P. (2008). Dimensions of globalization and applied linguistics. In P. Tan and R. Rubdy (Eds.), *Language as commodity: Global structures, local marketplaces* (pp. 1–30). Continuum.

Bruthiaux, P. (2015). Language education, economic development, participation in the greater Mekong subregion. In T. Ricento (Ed.), *Language policy and political economy* (pp. 145–161). Oxford University Press.

Bullard, R. D. (1994a). The threat of environmental racism. *Natural Resources & Environment*, *7*(3), 23–26, 55–56.

Bullard, R. D. (1994b). Environmental racism and invisible communities. *West Virginia Law Review*, *96*(4), 1037–1050.

Bullard, R. D., Mohai, P., Saha, R., and Wright, B. (2008). Toxic wastes and race at twenty: Why race still matters after all of these years. *Environmental Law*, *38*(2), 371–412.

Burdge, H., Snapp, S., Laub, C., Russell, S. T., and Moody, R. (2013). *Implementing lessons that matter: The impact of LGBTQ-inclusive curriculum on student safety, well-being, and achievement*. San Francisco, CA: Gay-Straight Alliance Network and Tucson, AZ: Frances McClelland Institute for Children, Youth, and Families at the University of Arizona.

Bursuc, G. C. (2013). Achieving gender equality in teaching and learning: Identifying problems and searching for solutions. *Linguaculture*, *2013*, 64–73.

Butler, J. (1986). Sex and gender in Simone de Beauvoir's second sex. *Yale French Studies*, *72*, 35–49.

Butler, J. (1990). *Gender trouble*. Routledge.

Butler, J. E. (2001). Transforming the curriculum: Teaching about women of color. In C. A. McGee Banks and J. A. Banks (Eds.), *Multicultural education: Issues and perspectives* (4th Ed.) (pp. 174–193). Wiley.

Byars-Winston, A. M., Akçali, Ö., Tao, K. W., Nepomuceno, C. A., Anctil, T. M., Acevedo, V., Benally, N., and Wilton, G. (2005). The challenges, impact and implementation of critical multicultural pedagogies. In C. Z. Enns and A. L. Sinacore (Eds.), *Teaching and social justice: Integrating multicultural and feminist theories in the classroom* (pp. 125–142). American Psychological Association.

Cabrera, N. L. (2014). Exposing whiteness in higher education: White male college students minimizing racism, claiming victimization, and recreating white supremacy. *Race Ethnicity and Education, 17*(1), 30–55.

Cahnmann-Taylor, M. and Coda, J. (2019). Troubling normal in world language education. *Critical Inquiry in Language Studies, 16*(2), 107–129.

Cahnmann-Taylor, M., Coda, J., and Jiang, L. (2022). Queer is as queer does: Queer L2 pedagogy in teacher education. *TESOL Quarterly, 56*(1), 130–153.

Cammarata, L. (2016). *Content-based foreign language teaching: Curriculum and pedagogy for developing advanced thinking and literacy skills.* Routledge.

Canagarajah, S. (1993). American textbooks and Tamil students: Discerning ideological tensions in the ESL classrooms. *Language, Culture, and Curriculum, 6,* 143–156.

Canagarajah, S. (1999). *Resisting linguistic imperialism in English teaching.* Oxford University Press.

Canale, G. (2016). (Re)Searching culture in foreign language textbooks, or the politics of hide and seek. *Language, Culture and Curriculum, 29*(2), 225–243.

Carlisle, L. R., Jackson, B. W., and George, A. (2006). Principles of social justice education: The social justice education in schools project. *Equity and Excellence in Education, 39*(1), 55–64.

Carpenter, S. and Mojab, S. (2011). *Educating from Marx: Race, gender, and learning.* Palgrave Macmillan.

Carpenter, S. and Mojab, S. (2017). *Revolutionary learning: Marxism, feminism, and knowledge.* Pluto Press.

Casey, Z. A. (2021). *Encyclopedia of critical whiteness studies in education.* Brill Sense.

Cashman, H. and Trujillo, J. A. (2018). Queering Spanish as a heritage language: Contesting heteronormativity in the SHL curriculum and making LGBTQ identities visible in the classroom In K. Potowski (Ed.), *The Routledge handbook of Spanish as a heritage language* (pp. 124–141). Routledge.

Catalano, D. C. J. (2015). Beyond virtual equality: Liberatory consciousness as a path to achieve trans* inclusion in higher education. *Equity & Excellence in Education, 48*(3), 418–435.

Catalano, D. C. J. and Griffin, P. (2016). Sexism, heterosexism, and trans* oppression. In M. Adams, M., L. A. Bell, D. J. Goodman, and K. Y. Joshi (2016). *Teaching for diversity and social justice* (3rd Ed.) (pp. 183–212). Routledge.

Chan, E. L. and Coney, L. (2020). Moving TESOL forward: Increasing educators' criticalconsciousness through a racial lens. *TESOL Journal, 11*(4).

Charles, M. (2019). Effective teaching and learning: Decolonizing the curriculum. *Journal of Black Studies, 50*(8), 731–766.

Charles, Q. (2019). Black teachers of English in South Korea: Constructing identities as a native English speaker and English language teaching professional. *TESOL Journal, 10*(4), 1–16.

Cheng, L. (2014). Consequences, impact, and washback. In A. Kunnan (Ed.), *The Companion to language assessment* (pp. 1–16). John Wiley & Sons.

Chinn, S. E. (2012). Once more with feeling: Pedagogy, affect, transformation. *Transformations: The Journal of Inclusive Scholarship and Pedagogy, 22*(2), 15–20.

Cho, J. (2017). *English language ideologies in Korea: Interpreting the past and present.* Springer.

Chomsky, N. (1998). *Profit over people: Neoliberalism and global order.* Seven Stories Press.

Christian, M. (2019). A global critical race and racism framework: Racial entanglements and deep and malleable Whiteness. *Sociology of Race and Ethnicity, 5*(2), 169–185.

Chubbuck, S. M. (2010). Individual and structural orientations in socially just teaching: Conceptualization, implementation, and collaborative effort. *Journal of Teacher Education, 61,* 197–210.

Clarke, J. and Clarke, M. (1990). Stereotyping in TESOL materials. In B. Harrison (Ed.), *Culture and the language classroom* (pp. 31–44). Modern English Publications and the British Council.

Cochran-Smith, M. (2000). Blind vision: Unlearning racism in teacher education. *Harvard Educational Review, 70*(2), 157–190.

Cochran-Smith, M. (2004). *Walking the road: Race, diversity, and social justice in teacher education.* Teachers College Press.

Cochran-Smith, M. (2010). Toward a theory of teacher education for social justice. In A. Hargreaves, A. Lieberman, M. Fullan, and D. Hopkins (Eds.), *Second international handbook of educational change* (pp. 445–467). Springer.

Cochran Smith, M., Feiman-Nemser, S., McIntyre, D. J., and Demers, K. E. (Eds.) (2008). *Handbook of research on teacher education: Enduring questions in changing contexts.* Routledge.

Cochran-Smith, M., Barnatt, J., Lahann, R., Shakman, K., and Terrell, D. (2009a). Teacher education for social justice: Critiquing the critiques. In W. Ayers, T. M. Quinn, and D. Stovall (Eds.), *Handbook of social justice teacher education* (pp. 625–639). Routledge.

Cochran-Smith, M., Shakman, K., Jong, C., Terreli, D. G., Barnatt, J., and Mcquillan, P. (2009b). Good and just teaching: The case for social justice in teacher education. *American Journal of Education, 115*, 347–377.

Coffey, S. (2013). Communicating constructions of Frenchness through language course-books: A comparison. In J. Gray (Ed.), *Critical perspectives on language teaching materials* (pp. 137–160). Palgrave.

Coles-Ritchie, M. and Smith, R. R. (2017). Taking the risk to engage in race talk: Professional development in elementary schools. *International Journal of Inclusive Education, 21*(2), 172–186.

Collen, I. (2021). *Language trends 2021.* British Council.

Collins, J. (2006). Where's class in second language learning? *Working Papers in Urban Language & Literacies, 41*, 1–9.

Combahee River Collective ([1977] 2017). The Combahee River Collective statement. Reprinted In K.-Y. Taylor (Ed.), *How we get free: Black feminism and the Combahee River Collective* (pp. 20–32). Haymarket Books. (Original work published in 1977.)

Cone, J. (2012). *Martin & Malcolm & America: A dream or a nightmare.* Orbis Books.

Coney, L. (2016). The first step toward social justice: Teacher reflection. In C. Hastings and L. Jacob (Eds.), *Social justice in English language teaching* (pp. 11–24). TESOL International Association.

Cook, V. (2003). Materials for adult beginners from an L2 user perspective. In B. Tomlinson (Ed.), *Developing materials for language teaching* (pp. 275–290). Continuum.

Cope, B. and Kalantzis, M. (2000). Introduction: Multiliteracies: The beginnings of an idea. In B. Cope and M. Kalantzis (for The New London Group) (Eds.), *Multiliteracies: Literacy learning and the design of social futures* (pp. 3–8). Routledge.

Cope, B., Kalantzis, M., and Group, T. N. L. (Eds.) (2000). *Multiliteracies: Literacy learning and the design of social futures.* Routledge.

Coulmas, F. (1992). *Language and economy.* Blackwell.

Council of Europe (2018). *Better education for better democracies.* https://www.coe.int/en/web/education/home/-/asset_publisher/9JxkQQFIKSBa/content/council-of-europe-la unches-the-cefr-companion-volume-with-new-descriptors?inheritRedirect=false

Cowie, C. (2007). The accents of outsourcing: The meanings of "neutral" in the call centre industry. *World Englishes, 26*, 316–330.

Creese, G. and Kambere, E. N. (2003). What colour is your English? *The Canadian Review of Sociology and Anthropology, 40*(5), 565–573.

Crenshaw, K. (1989). Demarginalizing the intersection of race and sex: A Black feminist critique of antidiscrimination doctrine, feminist theory and antiracist Politics. *University of Chicago Legal Forum, 1*(8), 139–167.

Crenshaw, K. (1991). Mapping the margins: Intersectionality, identity politics, and violence against women of color. *Stanford Law Review*, *43*(6), 1241–1299.

Crookes, G. (2009). The practicality and relevance of second language critical pedagogy. *Language Teaching*, *43*(3), 333–348.

Crookes, G. (2013). *Critical ELT in action: Foundations, promises, praxis*. Routledge.

Crookes, G. V. (2021a). Critical language pedagogy: An introduction to principles and values. *ELT Journal*, *75*(3), 247–255.

Crookes, G. V. (2021b). Introduction to the special issue on critical language pedagogy. *Educational Science*, *11*, 694–698.

Crookes, G. V. (2022). Critical language pedagogy. *Language Teaching*, *55*, 46–63.

Cudd, A. (2006). *Analyzing oppression*. Oxford University Press.

Cummins, J. (2000). *Language, power and pedagogy: Bilingual children in the crossfire*. Multilingual Matters.

Cummins, J. (2009). Multilingual education for global justice: Issues, approaches, opportunities. In T. Skutnabb-Kangas, R. Phillipson, A. K. Mohanty, and M. Panda (Eds.), *Social justice through multilingual education* (pp. 19–35). Multilingual Matters.

Cummins, J. and Davison, C. (Eds.) (2007). *International handbook of English language teaching*. Springer.

Curran, G. (2006). Responding to students' normative questions about gays: Putting queer theory into practice in an Australian ESL classroom. *Journal of Language, Identity, & Education*, *5*, 85–96.

Curtis, A. and Romney, M. (Eds.) (2006). *Color, race, and English language teaching: Shades of meaning*. Lawrence Erlbaum.

Cyprès, A. T. (2016). Leading is teaching: Real-life ways to connect theory to practice and address issues of social injustice in school culture. In R. Papa, D. M. Eadens, and D. W. Eadens (Eds.), *Social justice instruction: Empowerment on the Chalkboard* (pp. 65–74). Springer.

Dabiri, E. (2021). *What White people can do next: from allyship to coalition*. Penguin Books Limited.

Da Cruz, J. Z. (2017). *Social justice-oriented teaching in the English language classroom*. M.Ed. Thesis in Teaching in Upper-Secondary School. University of Iceland.

d'Anglure, B. S. (2018). *Inuit Stories of being and rebirth: Gender, Shamanism, and the third sex* (translated by P. Frost). University of Mantitoba Press.

Daniel, M. C. (2016). Critical pedagogy's power in English language teaching. In C. Hastings and L. Jacob (Eds.), *Social justice in English language teaching* (pp. 25–38). TESOL Press.

Darder, A. and Torres, R. D. (2004). *After race: Racism after multiculturalism*. New York University Press.

Darder, A. and Torres, R. D. (2009). After race: An introduction. In A. Darder, M. P. Baltodano, and C. Torres (Eds.), *The critical pedagogy reader* (pp. 150–166). Routledge.

Darder, A., Baltodano, M. P., and Torres, C. (Eds.) (2009). *The critical pedagogy reader*. Routledge.

Darder, A., Mayo, P., and Paraskeva, J. (Eds.) (2016). *International critical pedagogy reader*. Routledge.

Darling-Hammond, L., French, J., and Garcia-Lopez, S. P. (2002). *Learning to teach for social justice*. Teachers College Press.

Darvin, R. and Norton, B. (2014). Social class, identity, and migrant students. *Journal of Language, Identity & Education*, *13*(2), 111–117.

David, E. J. R. and Derthick, A. O. (2018). *The psychology of oppression*. Springer.

Davies, A. (2010). Test fairness: A response. *Language Testing*, *27*(2), 171–176.

Davis, A. (1983). *Women, race, and class*. Random House.

Davis, A. (2016). *Freedom is a constant struggle: Ferguson, Palestine, and the foundations of a movement.* Haymarket Books.

Davis, A. and Wing, A. K. (2000). *Global critical race feminism.* New York University Press.

Davis, D. R. (2010). Standardized English: The history of the earlier circles. In A. Kirkpatrick (Ed.), *The Routledge handbook of World Englishes* (pp. 17–37). Routledge.

Davis, G. and Preves, S. (2017). Intersex and the social construction of sex. *Contexts, 16*(1), 80.

De Beauvoir, S. (1949). *The second sex.* Jonathan Cape.

De Costa, P., Rawal, H., and Li, W. (2018). L2 Teachers' emotions: A sociopolitical and ideological perspective. In J. de D. Martínez Agudo (Ed.), *Emotions in second language teaching: Theory, research and teacher education* (pp. 91–106). Springer.

DeCuir, J. and Dixson, A. (2004). So when it comes out, they aren't that surprised that it is there: Using critical race theory as a tool of analysis of race and racism in education. *Educational Researcher, 31*, 26–31.

Dei, G. J. S. (2010). The environment, climate change, ecological sustainability, and antiracist education. In F. Kagawa and D. Selby (Eds.), *Education and climate change* (pp. 89–105). Routledge.

Delgado, R. and Stefancic, J. (1997). *Critical White studies.* Temple University Press.

Delgado, R. and Stefancic, J. (2001). *Critical race theory: An introduction.* New York University Press.

DeMatthews, D. and Izquierdo, E. (2016). School leadership for dual language education: A social justice approach. *The Educational Forum, 80*(3), 278–293.

DeMatthews, D. and Izquierdo, E. (2017). The importance of principals supporting dual language education: A social justice leadership framework. *Journal of Latinos and Education, 17*(1), 53–70.

Denzin, N. K. (2007). The politics and ethic of performance pedagogy: Toward a pedagogy of hope. In P. McLaren and J. Kincheloe (Eds.), *Critical pedagogy: Where are we now* (pp. 127–142). Peter Lang.

DePietro, K., Ortaçtepe Hart, D., and Liu, X. (in press). Providing culturally sustaining pedagogy through mobile assisted language learning (MALL). Special Issue on Diversity and representation in the ELT classroom, *The European Journal of Applied Linguistics and TEFL.*

De Vincenti, G., Giovanangeli, A., and Ward, R. G. (2007). The queer stopover: How queer travels in the language. *Electronic Journal of Foreign Language Teaching, 4*, 58–72.

DiAngelo, R. (2018). *White fragility: Why it's so hard for white people to talk about racism.* Beacon Press.

Dixon, K. and Janks, H. (2014). Digital technologies. In H. Janks, K. Dixon, A. Ferreira, S. Granville, and D. Newfield (Eds.), *Doing critical literacy: Texts and activities for students and teachers.* Routledge.

Dixson, A. D., Anderson, C. K. R., and Donnor, J. K. (Eds.) (2017). *Critical race theory in education: All God's children got a song.* Routledge.

Dover, A. G. (2013). Teaching for social justice: From conceptual frameworks to classroom practices. *Multicultural Perspectives, 15*, 3–11.

Driskill, Q.-L. (2010). Doubleweaving Two-Spirit critiques: Building alliances between native and queer studies. *GLQ: A Journal of Lesbian and Gay Studies, 16*, 69–92.

Eberhardt, J. L. (2020). *Biased.* Penguin.

Edelsky, C. and Johnson, K. (2004). Critical whole language practice in time and place. *Critical Inquiry in Language Studies, 1*(3), 121–141.

Eisenstein, Z. (2019). *Abolitionist socialist feminism: Radicalizing the next revolution.* Monthly Review Press.

Ellsworth, E. (1989). Why doesn't this feel empowering? Working through the repressive myths of critical pedagogy. *Harvard Educational Review, 59*(3), 297–324.

Enns, C. Z. and Forrest, L. M. (2005). Toward defining and integrating multicultural and feminist pedagogies. In C. Z. Enns and A. L. Sinacore (Eds.), *Teaching and social justice: Integrating multicultural and feminist pedagogies in the classroom* (pp. 2–24). American Psychological Association.

Enns, C. Z. and Sinacore, A. L. (2005). Second-wave feminisms and their relationships to pedagogy. In C. Z. Enns and A. L. Sinacore (Eds.), *Teaching and social justice: Integrating multicultural and feminist pedagogies in the classroom* (pp. 25–40). American Psychological Association.

Enns, C. Z., Sinacore, A. L., Acevedo, V., Akçali, Ö., Ali, S. R., Ancis, J. R., Anctil, T. M., Boatwright, K. J., Boyer, M. C., Byars-Winston, A. M., Fassinger, R. E., Forrest, L. M., Hensler-McGinnis, N. F., Larson, H. A., Nepomuceno, C. A., and Tao, K. W. (2005). Integrating multicultural and feminist pedagogies: Personal perspectives on positionality, challenges, and benefits. In C. Z. Enns and A. L. Sinacore (Eds.), *Teaching and social justice: Integrating multicultural and feminist theories in the classroom* (pp. 177–196). American Psychological Association.

Ennser–Kananen, J. (2016). A pedagogy of pain: New directions for world language education. *The Modern Language Journal, 100*, 556–564.

Fairclough, N. (1992). Introduction. In N. Fairclough (Ed.), *Critical language awareness* (pp. 129). Longman.

Fairclough, N. (1993). *Discourse and social change.* Polity.

Fairclough, N. (2015). *Language and power.* Routledge.

Farahmandpur, R. (2009). A critical pedagogy of hope in times of despair. In S. Macrine (Ed.), *Critical pedagogy in uncertain times: Hopes and possibilities* (pp. 97–118). Palgrave Macmillan.

Farnsworth, V. (2010). Conceptualizing identity, learning and social justice in community-based learning. *Teaching and Teacher Education, 26*(7), 1481–1489.

Filax, G. (2006). Politicising action research through queer theory. *Educational Action Research, 14*(1), 139–145.

Fisher, L., Evans, M., Forbes, K., Gayton, A., and Liu, Y. (2020). Participative multilingual identity construction in the languages classroom: A multi-theoretical conceptualisation. *International Journal of Multilingualism, 17*(4), 448–466.

Flores, N. and Rosa, J. (2015). Undoing appropriateness: Raciolinguistic ideologies and language diversity in education. *Harvard Educational Review, 85*(2), 149–171.

Flores, N. and Rosa, J. (2019). Bringing race into second language acquisition. *The Modern Language Journal, 103*, 145–151.

Fook, J. (2014). Social justice and critical theory. In M. Reisch (Ed.), *Routledge international handbook of social justice* (pp. 160–172). Routledge.

Foster, (2012). A qualitative understanding of preservice teachers' critical examination of textbook curriculum units as political text. In H. Hickman and B. J. Porfilio (Eds.), *The new politics of the textbook: Problematizing the portrayal of marginalized groups in textbooks* (pp. 3–16). Sense Publishers.

Foucault, M. (1978). *The history of sexuality, volume 1: An introduction* (translated from the French by Robert Hurley). Pantheon Books.

Foucault, M. (1979). *Discipline and punish: The birth of the prison* (translated by A. Sheridan). Vintage.

Foucault, M. (1980). *Power/knowledge: Selected interviews and other writings.* Pantheon.

Fouch, R. (2006). Say it loud, I'm Black and I'm proud: African Americans, American artifactual culture, and Black vernacular technological creativity. *American Quarterly, 58*(3), 639–661.

Frakenberg, E., Ee. J., Ayscue, J. B., and Orfield, G. (2019). *Harming our common future: America's segregation schools 65 years after Brown.* The Civil Rights Project/Proyecto Derechos Civiles.

Fraser, N. (1995). From redistribution to recognition? Dilemmas of justice in a "post-socialist" age. *New Left Review*, *212*, 68–93.

Fraser, N. (1997). *Justice interruptus: Critical reflections on the "postsocialist" condition.* Routledge.

Fraser, N. (2008). *Unruly practices: Power, discourse, and gender in contemporary social theory.* University of Minnesota Press.

Fraser, N. (2019). *The old is dying and the new cannot be born.* Verso.

Freire, P. (1985). Reading the world and reading the word: An interview with Paulo Freire. *Language Arts*, *62*(1), 15–21.

Freire, P. (2005a). *Education for critical consciousness.* Continuum.

Freire, P. (2005b). *Pedagogy of the oppressed* (30th Anniversary Ed.). Continuum. (Original work published in 1970.)

Freire, P. and Shor, I. (1987). *A pedagogy for liberation.* Macmillan.

Fuchs, C. (2014). *Digital labour and Karl Marx.* Routledge.

Furman, G. C. and Gruenewald, D. A. (2004). Expanding the landscape of social justice: A critical ecological analysis. *Educational Administration Quarterly*, *40*(1), 47–76.

Gal, S. (1989). Language and political economy. *Annual Review of Anthropology*, *18*, 345–367.

Galloway, N. (2017). *Global Englishes and change in English language teaching: Attitudes and impact.* Routledge.

Galloway, N. (2018). ELF and ELFT teaching materials. In J. Jenkins, W. Baker, and M. Dewey (Eds.), *The Routledge handbook of English as a lingua franca* (pp. 468–480). Routledge.

Galloway, N. and Rose, H. (2014). Using listening journals to raise awareness of Global Englishes in ELT. *ELT Journal*, *68*(4), 386–396.

Galloway, N. and Rose, H. (2018). Incorporating Global Englishes into the ELT classroom. *ELT Journal*, *72*(1), 3–14.

Gao, F. (2014). Social-class identity and English learning: Studies of Chinese learners. *Journal of Language, Identity & Education*, *13*(2), 92–98.

Garber, L. (2001). *Identity poetics: Race, class, and the lesbian-feminist roots of queer theory.* Columbia University Press.

Garcia, O. and Wei, L. (2014). *Translanguaging: Language, bilingualism and education.* Palgrave Macmillan.

Garvey, J. C. (2017). Pedagogical pause: Uncovering the queerness of my classroom emotions. *The Vermont Connection*, *38*(3), 16–23.

Garza, A. (2014, October 7). A Herstory of #BlackLivesMatter. *Feminist Wire.* http://thefeministwire.com/2014/10/blacklivesmatter-2

Gay, G. (2018). *Culturally responsive teaching: Theory, research, and practice.* Teachers College Press.

Gayle, B. M., Cortez, D., and Preiss, R. W. (2013). Safe spaces, difficult dialogues, and critical thinking. *International Journal for the Scholarship of Teaching and Learning*, *7*(2), 1–8.

Gilio-Whitaker, D. (2019). *As long as grass grows: The indigenous fight for environmental justice from colonization to standing rock.* Beacon Press.

Gillborn, D. (2006). Critical race theory and education: Racism and anti-racism in educational theory and praxis. *Discourse: Studies in the Cultural Politics of Education*, *27*(1), 11–32.

Giroux, H. A. (1992). *Border crossings: Cultural workers and the politics of education.* Routledge.

Giroux, H. A. (1997). *Pedagogy and the politics of hope: Theory, culture, and schooling.* Routledge.

Giroux, H. A. (2007). Introduction: Democracy, education, and the politics of critical pedagogy. In P. McLaren and J. L. Kincheloe (Eds.), *Critical pedagogy: Where are we now* (pp. 1–5). Peter Lang.

Giroux, H. A. (2008). *Against the terror of neoliberalism.* Paradigm Publishers.

Giroux, H. A. (2009). Teacher education and democratic schooling. In A. Darder, M. P. Baltodano, and C. Torres (Eds.), *The critical pedagogy reader* (pp. 438–459). Routledge.

Giroux, H. A. (2011). *On critical pedagogy*. Continuum.

Gladkova, A., Vartanova, E., and Ragnedda, M. (2020). Digital divide and digital capital in multiethnic Russian society. *Journal of Multicultural Discourses, 15*(2), 126–147.

Glynn, C., Wesely, P., and Wassell, B. (2014). *Words and actions. Teaching languages through in the lens of social justice*. ACTFL.

Godley, A. J. and Reaser, J. (2018). *Critical language pedagogy: Interrogating language, dialects, and power in teacher education*. Peter Lang.

González, N., Moll, L. C., and Amanti, C. (Eds.) (2005). *Funds of knowledge: Theorizing practices in households, communities, and classrooms*. Routledge.

Gooding, S. F. (2016). Dear white teacher ... instructional strategies to inform pre-service teachers regarding equitable practices in the K-12 classroom. In R. Papa, D. M. Eadens, and D. W. Edens (Eds.), *Social justice instruction: Empowerment on the chalkboard* (pp. 43–55). Springer.

Gooding, S. F. and Gooding Jr., F. W. (2016). Stop! Drop. And roll ... Tackling racism. In R. Papa, D. M. Eadens, and D. W. Eadens (Eds.), *Social justice instruction: Empowerment on the chalkboard* (pp. 227–236). Springer.

Goodwin, A. L. and Darity, K. (2019). Social justice teacher educators: What kind of knowing is needed? *Journal of Education for Teaching, 45*(1), 63–81.

Gore, J. M. (1993). *The struggle for pedagogies: Critical and feminist discourses as regimes of truth*. Routledge.

Gorski, P. C. (2009). Insisting on digital equity: Reframing the dominant discourse on multicultural education and technology. *Urban Education, 44*(3), 348–364.

Gorski, P. and Clark, C. (2003). Turning the tide of the digital divide: Multicultural education and the politics of surfing. *Multicultural Perspectives, 5*(1), 29–32.

Grace, A. P., Hill, R. J., Johnson, C. W., and Lewis, J. B. (2004). In other words: Queer voices/dissident subjectivities impelling social change. *International Journal of Qualitative Studies in Education, 17*(3), 301–324.

Gramsci, A. (1971). *Selections from the prison notebooks* (translated by Q. Hoare and G. Smith). International.

Grant, C. A. and Agosto, V. (2008). Teacher capacity and social justice in teacher education. In M. Cochran-Smith, S. Feiman-Nemser, D. J. McIntyre, and K. E. Demers (Eds.), *Handbook of research on teacher education: Enduring questions in changing contexts* (pp. 175–200). Routledge.

Grant, R. A. and Wong, S. D. (2008). Critical race perspectives, Bourdieu, and language education. In A. Albright (Ed.), *Pierre Bourdieu and literacy education*. Taylor & Francis.

Gray, J. (2002). The global coursebook in English language teaching. In D. Block and D. Cameron (Eds.), *Globalization and language teaching* (pp. 151–167). Routledge.

Gray, J. (2010). The branding of English and the culture of the new capitalism: Representations of the world of work in English language textbooks. *Applied Linguistics, 31*(5), 714–733.

Gray, J. (2012). Neoliberalism, celebrity and 'aspirational content' in English language teaching textbooks for a global market. In D. Block, J. Gray, and M. Holborow (Eds.), *Neoliberalism and applied linguistics* (pp. 86–113). Routledge.

Gray, J. (Ed.) (2013a). *Critical perspectives on language teaching materials*. Palgrave Macmillan.

Gray, J. (2013b). LGBT invisibility and heteronormativity in ELT materials. In J. Gray (Ed.), *Critical perspectives on language teaching materials* (pp. 40–63). Palgrave Macmillan.

Gray, J. and Block, D. (2014). All middle class now? Evolving representations of the working class in the neoliberal era – the case of ELT textbooks. In N. Harwood (Ed.), *English language teaching textbooks: Content, consumption, production* (pp. 45–71). Palgrave Macmillan.

Griffin, P. and Ouellett, M. (2003). From silence to safety and beyond: Historical trends in addressing lesbian, gay, bisexual, transgender issues in K-12 schools. *Equity & Excellence in Education, 36,* 106–114.

Gruenewald, D. A. (2003). The best of both worlds: A critical pedagogy of place. *Educational Researcher, 32*(4), 3–12.

Gunderson, L. (2007). *English-only instruction and immigrant students in secondary school: A critical examination.* Lawrence Erlbaum and Associates.

Halberstam, J. (2018). *Trans*: A quick and quirky account of gender variability.* University of California Press.

Hall, G. (Ed.) (2016). *The Routledge handbook of ELT.* Routledge.

Hall, J., Roman, C., Jovel-Arias, C., and Young, C. (2020). Pre-service teachers examine digital equity amidst schools' COVID-19 responses. *Journal of Technology and Teacher Education, 28*(2), 435–442.

Hamad, R. (2019). *White tears/Brown scars.* Melbourne University Press.

Hamp-Lyons, L. (1997). Washback, impact and validity: Ethical concerns. *Language Testing, 14,* 295–303.

Harris, A. (2019, May 30). The Central Park Five: "We were just baby boys." *The New York Times.* https://www.nytimes.com/2019/05/30/arts/television/when-they-see-us.html

Harris, C. I. (1993). Whiteness as property. *Harvard Law Review, 106*(8), 1710–1791.

Harris, M. (2016). The politics of "being": Faculty of color teaching to social justice in the college classroom. In R. Papa, D. M. Eadens, and D. W. Eadens (Eds.), *Social justice instruction: Empowerment on the chalkboard* (pp. 15–22). Springer.

Harven, A. M. and Gordon-Biddle, K. A. (2016). Critical literacy and multicultural literature: Pedagogical strategies for the everyday classroom. In R. Papa, D. M. Eadens, and D. W. Eadens (Eds.), *Social justice instruction: Empowerment on the Chalkboard* (pp. 161–170). Springer.

Harvey, D. (2005). *A brief history of neoliberalism.* Oxford University Press.

Harvey, D. (2008). Introduction. In K. Marx and F. Engels, *The communist manifesto* (pp. 1–30). Pluto Press.

Harvey, D. (2014). *Seventeen contradictions and the end of capitalism.* Oxford University Press.

Harvey, D. (2020). *The anti-capitalist chronicles.* Pluto Press.

Hastings, C. and Jacob, L. (Eds.) (2016). *Social justice in English language teaching.* TESOL International Association.

Hauschild, S., Poltavtchenko, E., and Stoller, F. L. (2012). Going green: Merging environmental education and language instruction. *English Teaching Forum, 2.*

Hawkins, M. R. (Ed.) (2011). *Social justice language teacher education.* Multilingual Matters.

Heller, M. (2001). Gender and public space in a bilingual school. In A. Pavlenko, A. Blackledge, I. Piller, and M. Teutsch-Dwyer (Eds.), *Multilingualism, second language learning, and gender* (pp. 257–282). Mouten de Gruyter.

Heller, M. (2003). Globalization, the new economy, and the commodification of language and identity. *Journal of Linguistics, 7*(4), 473–492.

Heller, M. (2010a). Media, the state and linguistic authority. In S. Johnson and T. M. Milani (Eds.), *Language ideologies and media discourse* (pp. 277–282). Continuum.

Heller, M. (2010b). The commodification of language. *Annual Review of Anthropology, 39*(1), 101–114.

Heller, M. and Duchêne, A. (2012). Pride and profit: Changing discourses of language, capital and nation-state. In A. Duchêne and M. Heller (Eds.), *Language in late capitalism: Pride and profit* (pp. 1–21). Routledge.

Henderson, J. G. and Gornik, R. (2007). *Transformative curriculum leadership* (3rd Ed.). Merrill/Prentice Hall.

Henderson, J. G. and Kesson, K. R. (1999). *Understanding democratic curriculum leadership.* Teachers College Press.

Henry, A. (1994). There are no safe places: Pedagogy as powerful and dangerous terrain. *Action in Teacher Education, 15*(4), 1–4.

Herdt, G. (Ed.) (1993). *Third sex, third gender: Beyond sexual dimorphism in culture and history.* Zone Books.

Herrera, S. and Rodriguez Morales, A. (2009). Colorblind nonaccommodative denial: Implications for teachers' meaning perspectives toward their Mexican-American English learners. In R. Kubota and A. Lin (Eds.), *Race, culture, and identities in second language education: Exploring critically engaged practice* (pp. 197–214). Routledge.

Hickman, H. (2011). Disrupting heteronormativity through critical pedagogy and queer theory. In S. C. Malott and B. Porfilio (Eds.), *Critical pedagogy in the twenty-first century: A new generation of scholars* (pp. 69–107). Information Age Publishing.

Hickman, H. and Porfilio, B. J. (Eds.) (2012). *The new politics of the textbook: Problematizing the portrayal of marginalized groups in textbooks.* Sense Publishers.

Higginbotham, E. B. (1992). African-American women's history and the metalanguage of race. *Signs, 17*(2), 251–274.

Higgins, C. (2009). *English as a local language: Post-colonial identities and multilingual practices.* Multilingual Matters.

Holborow, M. (1999). *The politics of English: A Marxist view of language.* SAGE.

Holborow, M. (2007). Language, ideology and neoliberalism. *Journal of Language and Politics, 6*(1), 51–73.

Holborow, M. (2015). *Language and neoliberalism.* Routledge.

Holliday, A. (2005). *The struggle to teach English as an international language.* Oxford.

Holliday, A. (2015). Native-speakerism: Taking the concept forward and achieving cultural belief. In A. Swan, P. Aboshiha, and A. Holliday (Eds.), *(En)Countering native-speakerism* (pp. 11–25). Palgrave Macmillan.

Holliday, A. and Aboshiha, P. (2009). The denial of ideology in perceptions of "nonnative speaker" teachers. *TESOL Quarterly, 43*(4), 669–689.

Holly, D. (1990). The unspoken curriculum, or how language teaching carries cultural and ideological messages. In B. Harrison (Ed.), *Culture and the language classroom* (pp. 11–19). Modern English Publications and the British Council.

hooks, b. (1994). *Teaching to transgress.* Routledge.

hooks, b. (2000). *Where we stand: Class matters.* Routledge.

hooks, b. (2003). *Teaching community: A pedagogy of hope.* Routledge.

hooks, b. (2015a). *Feminist theory: From margin to center.* Routledge.

hooks, b. (2015b). *Ain't I a woman: Black women and feminism.* Routledge.

hooks, b. (2015c). *Black looks: Race and representation.* Routledge.

Houghton, S. A., Rivers, D. J., and Hashimoto, K. (Eds.) (2018). *Beyond native-speakerism: Current explorations and future visions.* Routledge.

Houser, N. O. (2007). Problem posing in teacher education: A Freirean approach. *Action in Teacher Education, 29*(3), 43–49.

Howard, T. C. and Aleman, G. R. (2008). Teacher capacity for diverse learners: What do teachers need to know? In M. Cochran Smith, S. Feiman-Nemser, D. J. McIntyre, and K. E. Demers (Eds.), *Handbook of research on teacher education: Enduring questions in changing contexts* (pp. 157–174). Routledge.

Human Rights Campaign (2020). *Violence against the transgender and gender non-conforming community in 2020.* https://www.hrc.org/resources/violence-against-the-trans-and-gender-non-conforming-community-in-2020

Human Rights Watch (2017). "I want to be like nature made me": Medically unnecessary surgeries on intersex children in the US. https://www.hrw.org/report/2017/07/25/i-want-be-nature-made-me/medically-unnecessary-surgeries-intersex-children-us

Hytten, K. and Bettez, S. C. (2011). Understanding education for social justice. *Education Foundations*, (Winter–Spring), 7–24.

Irvine, J. T. (1989). When talk isn't cheap: Language and political economy. *American Ethnologist, 16*(2), 248–267.

Ives, P. (2015). Global English and the limits of liberalism: Confronting global capitalism and challenges to the nation-state. In T. Ricento (Ed.), *Language policy and political economy* (pp. 48–71). Oxford University Press.

Jacobs, G. M. and Goatly, A. (2000). The treatment of ecological issues in ELT course-books. *ELT Journal, 54*, 256–264.

Janks, H. (2010). *Literacy and power*. Routledge.

Jean-Marie, G., Normore, A. H., and Brooks, J. S. (2009). Leadership for social justice: Preparing 21st-century school leaders for a new social order. *Journal of Research on Leadership Education, 4*, 1–31.

Jenkins, J. (2007). *English as a lingua franca: Attitude and identity*. Oxford University Press.

Jenkins, J., Baker, W., and Dewey, M. (2018). *The Routledge handbook of English as a lingua franca*. Routledge.

Jenks, C. (2017). *Race and ethnicity in English language teaching: Korea in focus*. Multilingual Matters.

Jennings, M. and Lynn, M. (2005). The house that race built: Toward a critical race analysis of critical pedagogy. *Educational Foundations, 19*, 15–32.

Johnson, J. R. (2013). Cisgender privilege, intersectionality, and the criminalization of CeCe McDonald: Why intercultural communication needs transgender studies. *Journal of International and Intercultural Communication, 6*(2), 135–144.

Kachru, B. B. (1986a). *The alchemy of English: The spread functions and models of non-native Englishes*. Pergamon.

Kachru, B. B. (1986b). The power and politics of English. *World Englishes, 5*(2/3), 121–140.

Kachru, B. (1992). *The other tongue: English across cultures*. University of Illinois Press.

Kachru, B. B. (1996) World Englishes: Agony and ecstasy. *Journal of Aesthetic Education, 30*(2), 133–155.

Kachru, B. B. (2005). *Asian Englishes: Beyond the canon*. Hong Kong University Press.

Kagawa, F. and Selby, D. (Eds.) (2010). Climate change education: A critical agenda for interesting times. In F. Kagawa and D. Selby (Eds.), *Education and climate change: Living and learning in interesting times* (pp. 241–243). Routledge.

Kanno, Y. and Norton, B. (2003). Imagined communities and educational possibilities: Introduction. *Journal of Language, Identity & Education, 2*(4), 241–249.

Kapur, K. (2016). Gender sensitization as a learning outcome. In C. Hastings and L. Jacob (Eds.), *Social justice in English language teaching* (pp. 179–188). TESOL Press.

Katz, L. and DaSilva Iddings, C. (2009). Classroom positionings and children's construction of linguistic and racial identities in English-dominant classrooms. In R. Kubota and A. Lin (Eds.), *Race, culture, and identities in second language education: Exploring critically engaged practice* (pp. 138–157). Routledge.

Kaur, B. (2012). Equity and social justice in teaching and teacher education. *Teaching and Teacher Education, 28*, 485–492.

Kautz, E. A. (2016). Exploring environmental and sustainability issues in the intermediate-level foreign language curriculum. In L. Cammarata (Ed.), *Content-based foreign language teaching: Curriculum and pedagogy for developing advanced thinking and literacy skills* (pp. 234–249). Routledge.

Keesing-Styles, L. (2003). The relationship between critical pedagogy and assessment in teacher education. *Radical Pedagogy, 5*(1).

Kendi, I. X. (2019). *How to be an antiracist*. One World.

Khan, R. (2009). Towards ecopedagogy: Weaving a broad-based pedagogy of liberation for animals, nature, and the oppressed people of the earth. In A. Darder,

M. P. Baltodano, and C. Torres (Eds.), *The critical pedagogy reader* (pp. 522–541). Routledge.

Kidder, L. H. (1992). Requirements for being "Japanese": Stories of returnees. *International Journal of Intercultural Relations, 16*, 383–393.

Killermann, S. (2012). What does the asterisk in "trans*" stand for? It's pronounced metrosexual. http://itspronouncedmetrosexual.com/2012/05/what-does-the-asterisk-in-trans-stand-for/

Killermann, S. (2017). *A guide to gender: The social justice advocate's handbook* (2nd Ed.). Impetus Books.

Kincheloe, J. L. (2007). Critical pedagogy in the twenty-first century: Evolution for survival. In P. McLaren and J. Kincheloe (Eds.), *Critical pedagogy: Where are we now* (pp. 9–42). Peter Lang.

Kincheloe, J. L. (2008a). *Critical pedagogy primer*. Peter Lang.

Kincheloe, J. L. (2008b). *Knowledge and critical pedagogy*. Springer.

Kincheloe, J. L. (2011). Meet me behind the curtain: The struggle for a critical postmodern action research. In K. Hayes, S. R. Steinberg, and K. Tobin (Eds.), *Key works in critical pedagogy* (pp. 85–100). Sense Publishers.

Kincheloe, J. L. and Steinberg, S. R. (1998). Students as researchers: Critical visions, emancipatory insights. In S. R. Steinberg and J. L. Kincheleo (Eds.), *Students as researchers: Creating classrooms that matter* (pp. 2–19). Falmer Press.

King, S. H. and Castenell, L. A. (Eds.) (2001). *Racism and racial inequality: Implications for teacher education*. American Association of Colleges for Teacher Education.

Kirkpatrick, A. (2007). *World Englishes: Implications for international communication and English language teaching*. Cambridge University Press.

Kirkpatrick, A. (Ed.) (2010). *The Routledge handbook of World Englishes*. Routledge.

Kjaran, J. I. and Sauntson, H. (2020). *Schools as queer transformative spaces: Global narratives on sexualities and genders*. Routledge.

Kleinrock, L. (2019, January). *How to teach kids to talk about taboo topics*. TED Talk. https://www.ted.com/talks/liz_kleinrock_how_to_teach_kids_to_talk_about_taboo_topics

Kocabas-Gedik, P. and Ortaçtepe Hart, D. (2020). "It's not like that at all": A poststructuralist case study on language teacher identity and emotional labor. *Journal of Language, Identity, and Education, 20*(2), 102–117.

Kolko, B. E., Nakamura, L., and Rodman, G. B. (Eds.) (2000). *Race in cyberspace*. Routledge.

Kong, S. and Hoare, P. (2011). Cognitive content engagement in content-based language teaching. *Language Teaching Research, 15*(3), 307–324.

Kress, G. and Leeuwen, T. V. (2001). *Multimodal discourse: The modes and media of contemporary communication*. Arnold.

Kubota, R. (2003). Critical teaching of Japanese culture. *Japanese Language and Literature, 37*(1), 67–87.

Kubota, R. (2004). Critical multiculturalism and second language education. In B. Norton and K. Toohey (Eds.), *Critical pedagogies and language learning* (pp. 30–52). Cambridge University Press.

Kubota, R. (2010). Critical multicultural education and second/foreign language teaching. In S. May and C. E. Sleeter (Eds.), *Critical multiculturalism: Theory and praxis* (pp. 99–112). Routledge.

Kubota, R. (2011). Questioning linguistic instrumentalism: English, neoliberalism, and language tests in Japan. *Linguistics and Education, 22*(3), 248–260.

Kubota, R. (2016). Critical content-based instruction in the foreign language classroom: Critical issues for implementation. In L. Cammarata (Ed.), *Content-based foreign language teaching: Curriculum and pedagogy for developing advanced thinking and literacy skills* (pp. 192–212). Routledge.

Kubota, R. (2021). Critical antiracist pedagogy in ELT. *ELT Journal, 75*(3), 237–246.

Kubota, R. and Lin, A. (2006). Race and TESOL: Introduction to concepts and theories. *TESOL Quarterly, 40*(3), 471–493.

Kubota, R. and Lin, A. (2009) *Race, culture, and identities in second language education: Exploring critically engaged practice.* Routledge.

Kuehn, R. R. (2014). Environmental justice. In M. Reisch (Ed.), *The Routledge international handbook of social justice* (pp. 319–338). Routledge.

Kumaravadivelu, B. (2016). The decolonial option in English teaching: Can the subaltern act? *TESOL Quarterly, 50*(1), 66–85.

Kumashiro, K. K. (2000). Toward a theory of anti-oppressive education. *Review of Educational Research, 70*(1), 25–53.

Kumashiro, K. K. (Ed.) (2001a). *Troubling intersections of race and sexuality: Queer students of color and anti-oppressive education.* Rowman & Littlefield.

Kumashiro, K. K. (2001b). Troubling intersections of race and sexuality: Queer students of color and anti-oppressive education. In K. K. Kumashiro (Ed.), *Troubling intersections of race and sexuality: Queer students of color and anti-oppressive education* (pp. 1–26). Rowman & Littlefield Publishers.

Kumashiro, K. K. (2009). *Against common sense: Teaching and learning toward social justice* (2nd Ed.). Routledge.

Kunnan, A. J. (2009). Testing for citizenship. The U.S. Naturalization test. *Language Assessment Quarterly, 6*(1), 89–97.

Kunnan, A. J. (2014). Fairness and justice in language assessment. In A. J. Kunnan (Ed.), *The companion to language assessment* (pp. 1098–1114). Wiley.

Kunnan, A. J. (2018). *Evaluating language assessments.* Routledge.

Kunnan, A. J. (2021). Revisiting language assessment for immigration and citizenship: The case of US citizenship and the Naturalization test. In G. Fulcher and L. Harding (Eds.), *The Routledge handbook of language testing* (2nd Ed.) (pp. 96–116). Routledge.

Ladegaard, H. J. and Phipps, A. (2020). Intercultural research and social activism. *Language and Intercultural Communication, 20*(2), 67–80.

Ladson-Billings, G. (1995). Toward a theory of culturally relevant pedagogy. *American Educational Research Journal, 32*(3), 465–491.

Ladson-Billings, G. (1999). Just what is critical race theory and what's it doing in a nice field like education? In L. Parker, D. Deyhle, and S. Villenas (Eds.), *Race is … Race isn't: Critical race theory and qualitative studies in education* (pp. 7–30). Westwood Press.

Ladson-Billings, G. J. (2009). *The dream keepers: Successful teachers of African American children.* Jossey-Bass Books.

Ladson-Billings, G. and Tate, W. F., IV (1995). Toward a critical race theory of education. *Teachers College Record, 97*(1), 47–68.

Ladson-Billings, G. and Tate, W. F., IV (2009). Toward a critical race theory of education. In A. Darder, M. P. Baltodano, and C. Torres (Eds.), *The critical pedagogy reader* (pp. 167–182). Routledge.

Lathan, C. (2014). Dear White teacher. *Rethinking Schools, 29*(1).

Lawrence, L. and Nagashima, Y. (2021). Exploring LGBTQ+ pedagogy in Japanese university classrooms. *ELT Journal, 75*(2), 152–161.

Leap, W. L. (2020). *Language before Stonewall: Language, sexuality, history.* Palgrave Macmillan.

Ledesma, M. C. and Calderón, D. (2015). Critical race theory in education: A review of past literature and a look to the future. *Qualitative Inquiry, 21*(3), 206–222.

Lee, E., Menkart, D., and Okazawa-Rey, M. (1998). *Beyond heroes and holidays: A practical guide to K-12 anti-racist, multicultural education and staff development.* Teaching for Change.

Lee, J. F. K. (2014). A hidden curriculum in Japanese EFL textbooks: Gender representation. *Linguistics and Education, 27*, 39–53.

Lee, I. (2009). Situated globalization and racism: An analysis of Korean high school EFL textbooks. *Language & Literacy*, *11*(1), 1–14.

Lee, I. (2011). Teaching how to discriminate: Globalization, prejudice, and textbooks. *Teacher Education Quarterly*, *38*(1), 47–63.

Lee, S. J. (2006). Additional complexities: Social class, ethnicity, generation, and gender in Asian American student experiences. *Race, Ethnicity, and Education*, *9*(1), 17–28.

Lee, S. J. (2009). *Unraveling the "model minority" stereotype: Listening to Asian American youth.* Teachers College Press.

Lee, S. J. and Kumashiro, K. K. (2005). *A report on the status of Asian Americans and Pacific Islanders in education: Beyond the 'model minority' stereotype.* National Education Association, Human and Civil Rights.

Leistyna, P. (2007). Neoliberal non-sense. In P. McLaren and J. L. Kincheloe (Eds.), *Critical pedagogy: Where are we now* (pp. 97–123). Peter Lang.

Leonardo, Z. (2002). The souls of white folk: Critical pedagogy, whiteness studies, and globalization discourse. *Race Ethnicity & Education*, *5*(1), 29–50.

Lewis Ellison, T. and Solomon, M. (2019). Counter-storytelling vs. deficit thinking around African American children and families, digital literacies, race, and the digital divide. *Research in the Teaching of English*, *53*(3), 223–244.

Liddicoat, A. J. (2009). Sexual identity as linguistic failure: Trajectories of interaction in the heteronormative language classroom. *Journal of Language, Identity, and Education*, *8*(2–3), 191–202.

Liggett, T. (2008). Frames of reference: The impact of race on teaching strategy and classroom discussion. *Urban Review*, *40*, 386–402.

Lin, A. and Luke, A. (2006). Coloniality, postcoloniality, and TESOL … Can a spider weave its way out of the web that it is being woven into just as it weaves? *Critical Inquiry in Language Studies*, *3*(2–3), 65–73.

Llurda, E. (Ed.) (2005). *Non-native language teachers: Perceptions, challenges and contributions to the profession.* Springer.

Lockhart, J. W. (2021). Paradigms of sex research and women in STEM. *Gender and Society*, *35*(3), 449–475.

Loewen, J. W. (2007). *Lies my teacher told me: Everything your American history textbook got wrong.* The New Press.

Lopez, A. and Olan, E. L. (2021). *Re-imagining transformative leadership in teacher education.* Information Age Publishing.

López-Gopar, M. E. (Ed.) (2019). *International perspectives on critical pedagogies in ELT.* Palgrave Macmillan.

López-Gopar, M. E. and Sughrua, W. (2014). Social class in English language education in Oaxaca, Mexico. *Journal of Language, Identity & Education*, *13*(2), 104–110.

Lorde, A. (1984). *Sister outsider.* Crossing Press.

Loutzenheiser, L. W. (2001). "If I teach about these issues they will burn down my house": The possibilities and tensions of queered, antiracist pedagogy. In K. K. Kumashiro (Ed.), *Troubling intersections of race and sexuality: Queer students of color and anti-oppressive education* (pp. 195–214). Rowman & Littlefield.

Love, B. J. (2004). Brown plus 50 counter-storytelling: A critical race theory analysis of the "majoritarian achievement gap" story. *Equity & Excellence in Education*, *37*, 227–246.

Love, B. J. ([2000] 2018). Developing a liberatory consciousness. In M. Adams, W. J. Blumenfeld, R. Catalano, H. W. Hackman, L. E. Hopkins, B. Love, M. L. Peters, and X. Zuniga (Eds.), *Readings for diversity and social justice* (pp. 470–474). Routledge.

Luhmann, S. (1998). Queering-querying pedagogy or pedagogy is a pretty queer thing. In W. F. Pinar (Ed.), *Queer theory in education* (pp. 141–155). Lawrence Erlbaum.

Luke, A. (2015). Documenting reproduction and inequality: Revisiting Jean Anyon's "Social class and school knowledge." *Curriculum Inquiry*, *40*(1), 167–182.

Luke, A. and Dooley, K. (2011). Critical literacy and second language. In E. Hinkel (Ed.), *Handbook of research in second language teaching and learning* (Vol. 3) (pp. 856–868). Routledge.

Lynch, B. (1997). In search of the ethical test. *Language Testing, 14*, 315–327.

Lynn, M. and Dixson, A. D. (Eds.) (2013). *Handbook of critical race theory in education.* Routledge.

McCready, L. (2001). When fitting in isn't an option, or, why Black queer males at a California high school stay away from Project 10. In K. K. Kumashiro (Ed.), *Troubling intersections of race and sexuality: Queer students of color and anti-oppressive education* (pp. 87–104). Rowman & Littlefield Publishers.

McDonald, M. and Zeichner, K. M. (2009). Social justice teacher education. In W. Ayers, T. Quinn, and D. Stovall (Eds.), *Handbook of social justice in education* (pp. 595–610). Routledge.

MacDonald, S., El-Metoui, L., Baynham, M., and Gray, J. (2014). *Exploring LGBT lives and issues in adult ESOL.* British Council – ESOL Nexus.

Macedo, D. and Bartolomé, L. I. (2014). Multiculturalism permitted in English only. *International Multilingual Research Journal, 8*(1), 24–37.

McGee Banks, C. A. and Banks, J. A. (1995). Equity pedagogy: An essential component of multicultural education. *Theory Into Practice, 34*(3), 152–158.

McIntosh, P. (1989). White privilege: Unpacking the invisible knapsack. In M. McGoldrick (Ed.), *Re-visioning family therapy: Race, culture, and gender in clinical practice* (pp. 147–152). The Guilford Press. (Reprinted from "Peace and Freedom," July/August 1989, pp. 10–12.)

McKay, S. L. (2002). *Teaching English as an international language.* Oxford University Press.

McKay, S. L. (2012). Teaching materials for English as an international language. In A. Matsuda (Ed.), *Principles and practices of teaching English as an international language.* Multilingual Matters.

McKay, S. L. (2018). English as an international language: What it is and what it means for pedagogy. *RELC Journal, 49*(1), 9–23.

McKay, S. L. and Wong, S. C. (Eds.) (2000). *New immigrants in the United States: Readings for second language educators.* Cambridge.

McKinney, C. (2017). *Language and power in post-colonial schooling: Ideologies in practice.* Routledge.

McLaren, M. (2017). *Decolonizing feminism: Transnational feminism and globalization.* Rowman & Littlefield.

McLaren, P. (2020). The future of critical pedagogy. *Educational Philosophy and Theory, 52*(12), 1243–1248.

McLaren, P. and Fischman, G. (1998). Reclaiming hope: Teacher education and social justice in the age of globalization. *Teacher Education Quarterly, 25*(4), 125–133.

McLaren, P. and Jandrić, P. (2020). *Postdigital dialogues: On critical pedagogy, liberation theology and information technology.* Bloomsbury.

McLaren, P. and Lankshear, C. (1994). Introduction. In P. McLaren and C. Lankshear (Eds.), *Politics of liberation: Paths from Freire* (pp. 1–11). Routledge.

McNamara, T. and Roever, C. (2006). *Language testing: The social dimension.* Blackwell.

McNamara, T. and Ryan, K. (2011). Fairness versus justice in language testing: The place of English literacy in the Australian citizenship test. *Language Assessment Quarterly, 8*, 161–178.

McNamara, T. and Shohamy, E. (2008). Language tests and human rights. *International Journal of Applied Linguistics, 18*(1), 89–95.

Malott, C. S. (2011). Introduction: From Toussaint L'Ouverture to Paulo Freire: Complexity and critical pedagogy in the twenty-first century: A new generation of scholars. In S. C. Malott and B. Porfilio (Eds.), *Critical pedagogy in the twenty-first century: A new generation of scholars* (pp. xxiii–lxviii). Information Age Publishing.

Mann, S. A. and Grimes, M. D. (2001). Common and contested ground: Marxism and race, gender & class analysis. *Race, Gender & Class, 8*, 3–22.

Marrun, N. A., Clark, C., and McCadney, O. (2020). Queering family difference to dispel the myth of the "normal": Creating classroom and school communities that affirm all students and their families. In C. Mayo and M. V. Blackburn (Eds.), *Queer, trans, and intersectional theory in educational practice* (pp. 99–119). Routledge.

Martel, J. (2022). *Moving beyond the grammatical syllabus: Practical strategies for content-based curriculum design.* Routledge.

Martin, I. P. (2010). Periphery ELT: The politics and practice of teaching English in the Philippines. In A. Kirkpatrick (Ed.), *The Routledge Handbook of World Englishes* (pp. 247–264). Routledge.

Martin-Beltrán, M., Montoya-Ávila, A., and Garcia, A. A. (2020). Becoming advocates: Positioning immigrant youth to share, connect, and apply their stories as tools for social change. *TESOL Journal, 11*(4), 1–20.

Marx, K. (1990). *Capital: A critique of political economy, Volume I.* Penguin Books.

Marx, K. and Engels, F. (2008). *The communist manifesto.* Pluto Press. (Originally published in 1848.)

Marx, S. (2009). "It's not them; It's not their fault": Manifestations of racism in the schooling of Latinas/os and ELLs. In R. Kubota and A. Lin (Eds.), *Race, culture, and identities in second language education: Exploring critically engaged practice* (pp. 81–99). Routledge.

Matias, C. E. and Grosland, T. J. (2016). Digital storytelling as racial justice: Digital hopes for deconstructing Whiteness in teacher education. *Journal of Teacher Education, 67*(2), 152–164.

Matsuda, A. (2002). Representation of users and uses of English in beginning Japanese EFL textbooks. *JALT Journal, 24*(2), 182–216.

Matsuda, A. and Friedrich, P. (2011). English as an international language: A curriculum blueprint. *World Englishes, 30*(3), 332–344.

May, S. (Ed.) (1999). *Critical multiculturalism: Rethinking multicultural and antiracist education.* Routledge.

May, S. and Sleeter, C. E. (Eds.) (2010). *Critical multiculturalism: Theory and praxis.* Routledge.

Mayo, C. (2016). Queer lessons: Sexual and gender minorities in multicultural education. In J. A. Banks and C. A. McGee Banks (Eds.), *Multicultural education: Issues and perspectives* (9th Ed.) (pp. 132–148). Wiley.

Meinhart, M., Vahedi, L., Carter, S. E., Poulton, C., Palaku, P. M., and Stark, L. (2021). Gender-based violence and infectious disease in humanitarian settings: lessons learned from Ebola, Zika, and COVID-19 to inform syndemic policy making. *Conflict and Health, 15*(84), 1–9.

Melchers, G. and Shaw, P. (2011). *World Englishes: An introduction.* Hodder Education.

Mendos, L. R., Botha, K., Carrano Lelis, R., de la Peña, E. L., Savelev, I., and Tan, D. (2020). *State-sponsored homophobia: Global legislation overview update.* The International Lesbian, Gay, Bisexual, Trans and Intersex Association (ILGA).

Meyer, E. J. (2007). "But I'm not gay": What straight teachers need to know about queer theory. In N. M. Rodriguez and W. F. Pinar (Eds.), *Queering straight teachers: Discourse and identity in education* (pp. 15–29). Peter Lang.

Meyer, E. J. (2010). *Gender and sexual diversity in schools: An introduction.* Springer.

Michael-Luna, S. (2009). Narratives in the wild: Unpacking critical race theory methodology for early childhood bilingual education. In R. Kubota and A. Lin (Eds.), *Race, culture, and identity in second language education: Exploring critically engaged practice* (pp. 234–251). Routledge.

Milani, T. M. (2008). Language testing and citizenship: A language ideological debate in Sweden. *Language in Society, 37*(1), 27–59.

Miles, R. (1993). *Racism after "race relations."* Routledge.

Miles, R. and Brown, M. (2003). *Racism*. Routledge.

Misa, C. M. (2001). Where have all the queer students of color gone? Negotiated identity of queer Chicana/o students. In K. K. Kumashiro (Ed.), *Troubling intersections of race and sexuality: Queer students of color and anti-oppressive education* (pp. 67–80). Rowman & Littlefield Publishers.

Mitchell, K. (2013). Race, difference, meritocracy, and English: majoritarian stories in the education of secondary multilingual learners. *Race Ethnicity and Education, 16*(3), 1–26.

Mohanty, C. T. (2003a). "Under Western eyes" revisited: Feminist solidarity through anticapitalist struggles. *Signs, 28*(2), 499–535.

Mohanty, C. T. (2003b). *Feminism without borders: Decolonizing theory, practicing solidarity*. Duke University Press.

Moll, L. C. (1992). Bilingual classroom studies and community analysis: Some recent trends. *Educational Researcher, 21*(2), 20–24.

Moll, L. C., Amanti, C., Neff, D., and Gonzalez, N. (1992). Funds of knowledge for teaching: Using a qualitative approach to connect homes and classrooms. *Theory into Practice, 31*(2), 132–141.

Montaño, T. and Quintanar-Sarellana, R. (2012). Finding my serpent tongue: Do ESL textbooks tap the linguistic and cultural capital of our long-term English language learners? In H. Hickman and B. J. Porfilio (Eds.), *The new politics of the textbook* (pp. 17–32). Sense Publishers.

Moore, A. R. (2016). Case study of an English class for LGBT learners. *TESOL Quarterly, 50*(1), 86–108.

Moore, A. R. (2020). Queer inquiry: A loving critique. *TESOL Quarterly, 54*(4), 1122–1230.

Morris, M. (1998). Unresting the curriculum: Queer projects, queer imaginings. In W. F. Pinar (Ed.), *Queer theory in education* (pp. 227–236). Lawrence Erlbaum.

Morton, M. H., Dworsky, A., and Samuels, G. M. (2017). *Missed opportunities: Youth homelessness in America*. Chapin Hall at the University of Chicago. https://voicesofyouthcount.org/wp-content/uploads/2017/11/VoYC-National-Estimates-Brief-Chapin-Hall-2017.pdf

Morton, T. (2016). Content and language integrated learning. In G. Hall (Ed.), *The Routledge handbook of English language teaching* (pp. 252–264). Routledge.

Motha, S. (2006). Racializing ESOL teacher identities in U.S. K-12 public schools. *TESOL Quarterly, 40*(3), 495–518.

Motha, S. (2014). *Race, empire, and English language teaching: Creating responsible and ethical antiracist practice*. Teachers College Press.

Moule, J. (2005). Implementing a social justice perspective in teacher education: Invisible burden for faculty of color. *Teacher Education Quarterly*, (Fall), 23–42.

Moussu, L. and Llurda, F. (2008). Non-native English-speaking English language teachers: History and research. *Language Teaching, 41*(3), 315–348.

Murphy-Oikonen, J., Chambers, L., McQueen, K., Hiebert, A., and Miller, A. (2022). Sexual assault: Indigenous women's experiences of not being believed by the police. *Violence Against Women, 28*(5), 1237–1258.

Nanda, S. (1996). Hijras: An alternative sex and gender role in India. In G. Herdt (Ed.), *Third sex, third gender: Beyond sexual dimorphism in culture and history* (pp. 373–418). Zone Books.

National Human Genome Research Institute (2003). *Human Genome Project*. https://www.genome.gov/human-genome-project

National K-12 Foreign Language Enrollment Survey Report (2017). *A comprehensive study of foreign/world language enrollments across the formal US educational system, K-12*. American Councils for International Education.

Ndura, E. (2004). ESL and cultural bias: An analysis of elementary through high school textbooks in the western United States of America. *Language, Culture & Curriculum, 17*(2), 143–153.

Nelson, C. D. (1999). Sexual identities in ESL: Queer theory and classroom inquiry. *TESOL Quarterly, 33*, 371–391.

Nelson, C. D. (2006). Queer inquiry in language education. *Journal of Language, Identity, and Education, 5*(1), 1–9.

Nelson, C. D. (2009). *Sexual identities in English language education: Classroom conversations.* Routledge.

Neto, J. N. (2018). Queer pedagogy: Approaches to inclusive teaching. *Policy Futures in Education, 16*(5), 589–604.

New London Group (1996). A pedagogy of multiliteracies: Designing social futures. *Harvard Educational Review, 66*(1), 60–92.

Newfield, D. (2011). Multimodality, social justice and becoming a "really South African" democracy: Case studies from language classrooms. In M. Hawkins (Ed.), *Social justice language teacher education* (pp. 23–48). Multilingual Matters.

Ng, C. K., Haines-Saah, R. J., Knight, R. E., Shoveller, J. A., and Johnson, J. L. (2019). "It's not my business": Exploring heteronormativity in young people's discourses about lesbian, gay, bisexual, transgender, and queer issues and their implications for youth health and wellbeing. *Health, 23*(1), 39–57.

Nguyen, H. and Yang, L. (2015). A queer learner's identity positioning in second language classroom discourse. *Classroom Discourse, 6*(3), 221–241.

Nieto, S. (2000). Placing equity front and center: Some thoughts on transforming teacher education for a new century. *Journal of Teacher Education, 51*(3), 180–187.

Nieto, S. (2009). Bringing bilingual education out of the basement and other imperatives for teacher education. In A. Darder, M. P. Baltodano, and C. Torres (Eds.), *The critical pedagogy reader* (pp. 469–482). Routledge.

Nieto, S. (2010). *Language, culture, and teaching: Critical perspectives.* Routledge.

Nieto, S. and Bode, P. (2018). *Affirming diversity: The sociopolitical context of multicultural education.* Pearson.

Noble, S. U. (2018). *Algorithms of oppression: How search engines reinforce racism.* New York University Press.

North, C. E. (2006). More than words? Delving into the substantive meaning(s) of "social justice" in education. *Review of Educational Research, 76*(4), 507–535.

Norton, B. (2000). *Identity and language learning: Gender, ethnicity, and educational change.* Longman.

Norton, B. and McKinney, C. (2011). An identity approach to second language acquisition. In D. Atkinson (Ed.), *Alternative approaches to second language acquisition* (pp. 73–94). Routledge.

Norton, B. and Pavlenko, A. (2004). *Gender and English language learners.* TESOL.

Norton, B. and Toohey, K. (2004). *Critical pedagogies and language learning.* Cambridge University Press.

Norton Peirce, B. (1995). Social identity, investment, and language learning. *TESOL Quarterly, 29*(1), 9–31.

O'Loughlin, M. (2001). Seven principles underlying socially just and ethically inclusive teacher preparation. In S. H. King and L. A. Castenell (Eds.), *Racism and racial inequality: Implications for teacher education* (pp. 59–68). American Association of Colleges for Teacher Education.

Omi, M. and Winant, H. (2015). *Racial formation in the United States.* Routledge.

Ong, P. M. (2020). *COVID-19 and the digital divide in virtual learning.* UCLA Center for Neighborhood Knowledge. https://escholarship.org/uc/item/07g5r002

O'Regan, J. P. (2021). *Global English and political economy.* Routledge.

Organisation for Economic Co-operation and Development (OECD) (2018). *Teaching and Learning International Survey (TALIS)*. https://www.oecd.org/education/talis/

Ortaçtepe, D. (2012). *The development of conceptual socialization in international students: A language socialization perspective on conceptual fluency and social identity*. Cambridge Scholars Publishing.

Ortaçtepe Hart, D. (in press). Creating anti-oppressive digital spaces for social justice language education. *TESOL Quarterly*.

Ortaçtepe Hart, D. and Martel, J. (2020). Introducing the special issue on exploring the transformative potential of language instruction for social justice. *TESOL Journal, 11*(4).

Osborn, T. A. (2006). *Teaching world language for social justice*. Lawrence Erlbaum.

Osei-Kofi, N. (2013). The art of teaching intersectionality. In P. C. Gorski, K. Zenkov, N. Osei-Kofi, and J. Sapp, (Eds.), *Cultivating social justice teachers: How teacher educators have helped students overcome cognitive bottlenecks and learn critical social justice concepts* (pp. 11–27). Stylus.

Ó'Móchain, R. (2006). Discussing gender and sexuality in a context-appropriate way: Queer narratives in an EFL college classroom in Japan. *Journal of Language, Identity, and Education, 5*, 51–66.

Paiz, J. M. (2017). Queering ESL teaching: Pedagogical and materials creation issues. *TESOL Journal, 9*(2), 348–367.

Paiz, J. (2019a). Queering practice: LGBTQ+ diversity and inclusion in English language teaching. *Journal of Language, Identity & Education, 18*(4), 266–275.

Paiz, J. (2019b). Queer ELT classroom practices: Suggestions for educators. *WATESOL Newsletter Winter, 5*.

Paiz, J. (2020). *Queering the English language classroom: A practical guide for teachers*. Equinox Publishing.

Papa, R., Eadens, D. M., and Eadens, D. W. (Eds.) (2016). *Social justice instruction: Empowerment on the chalkboard*. Springer.

Paris, D. and Alim, H. (2017). *Culturally sustaining pedagogies: Teaching and learning for justice in a changing world*. Teachers College Press.

Park, G. (2015) Situating the discourses of privilege and marginalization in the lives of two East Asian women teachers of English. *Race Ethnicity and Education, 18*(1), 108–133.

Park, J. S.-Y. (2009). The English language in South Korea. In J. S.-Y. Park (Ed.), *The local construction of a global language: Ideologies of English in South Korea*. De Gruyter.

Park, J. S.-Y. and Wee, L. (2012). *Markets of English: Linguistic capital and language policy in a globalizing world*. Routledge.

Pastor, M., Bullard, R. D., Boyce, J. K., Fothergill, A., Morello-Frosch, R., and Wright, B. (2006). *In the wake of the storm: Environment, disaster, and race after Katrina*. Russell Sage Foundation.

Pennycook, A. (1989). The concept of method, interested knowledge and the politics of language teaching. *TESOL Quarterly, 23*, 589–618.

Pennycook, A. (1998). *English and the Discourses of Colonialism*. Routledge.

Pennycook, A. (2000). English, politics, ideology: From colonial celebration to postcolonial performativity. In T. Ricento (Ed.), *Ideology, politics and language policies: Focus on English* (pp. 107–121). John Benjamins.

Pennycook, A. (2001). *Critical applied linguistics: A critical introduction*. Lawrence Erlbaum.

Pennycook, A. (2007). ELT and colonialism. In J. Cummins and C. Davison (Eds.), *International handbook of English language teaching* (pp. 13–24). Springer.

Pennycook, A. (2017). *The cultural politics of English as an international language*. Routledge.

Pennycook, A. (2022). Critical applied linguistics in the 2020s. *Critical Inquiry in Language Studies, 19*(1), 1–21.

Perkins, P. E. (2017). Canadian Indigenous female leadership and political agency on climate change. In M. Griffin Cohen (Ed.), *Climate change and gender in rich countries: Work, public policy and action* (pp. 282–296). Routledge.

Persinger, L. L. and Persinger, J. D. (2016). Gender justice in the elementary classroom. In R. Papa, D. M. Eadens, and D. W. Eadens (Eds.), *Social justice instruction: Empowerment on the chalkboard* (pp. 237–247). Springer.

Peters, M. A. (2015). Why is my curriculum white? *Educational Philosophy and Theory, 47*(7), 641–646.

Pew Research Center (2021). *The internet and the pandemic.* https://www.pewresearch.org/internet/2021/09/01/the-internet-and-the-pandemic/

Phillipson, R. (1992). *Linguistic imperialism.* Oxford University Press.

Phillipson, R. (2000). English in the new world order: Variations on a theme of linguistic imperialism and "world" English. In T. Ricento (Ed.), *Ideology, politics and language policies: Focus on English* (pp. 87–106). John Benjamins.

Phillipson, R. (2006). Language policy and linguistic imperialism. In T. Ricento (Ed.), *An introduction to language policy: Theory and method* (pp. 346–361). Blackwell Publishing.

Phillipson, R. (2008). The linguistic imperialism of neoliberal empire. *Critical Inquiry in Language Studies, 5*(1), 1–43.

Phipps, A. (2020). *Me, not you: The trouble with mainstream feminism.* Manchester University Press.

Phipps, A. (2021). Decolonising the languages curriculum: Linguistic justice for linguistic ecologies. In T. Beaven and F. Rosell-Aguilar (Eds.), *Innovative language pedagogy report* (pp. 5–10). Research-publishing.net.

Piller, I. and Cho, J. (2013). Neoliberalism as language policy. *Language in Society, 42*(1), 23–44.

Piller, I. and Cho, J. (2015). Neoliberalism as language policy. In T. Ricento (Ed.), *Language policy and political economy* (pp. 162–186). Oxford University Press.

Pollock, M. (2004). *Color mute: Race talk dilemmas in an American school.* Princeton University Press.

Preece, S. (Ed.) (2016). *The Routledge handbook of language and identity.* Routledge.

Pugach, M. C., Gomez-Najarro, J., and Matewos, A. M. (2019). A review of identity in research on social justice in teacher education: What role for intersectionality. *Journal of Teacher Education, 70*(3), 206–218.

Purkayastha, B. (2012). Intersectionality in a transnational world. *Gender and Society, 26*(1), 55–66.

Quach, L. H., Jo, J. O., and Urrieta, L. (2009). Understanding the racialized identities of Asian students in predominantly White schools. In R. Kubota and A. Lin (Eds.), *Race, culture, and identities in second language education: Exploring critically engaged practice* (pp. 118–137). Routledge.

Quinlivan, K. (2019). Hooked on a queer feeling? The paradoxes of engaging with affective silences and talk in a high school classroom. In C. Mayo and N. M. Rodriguez (Eds.), *Queer pedagogies: Theory, praxis, politics* (pp. 9–23). Springer.

Quinn, T. and Meiners, E. R. (2016). Seneca Falls, Selma, Stonewall: Moving beyond equality. In A. Butler-Wall, K. Cosier, R. Harper, J. Sapp, J. Sokolower, and M. Bollow Tempel (Eds.), *Rethinking sexism, gender, and sexuality.* Rethinking Schools.

Ragnedda, M. (2020). *Enhancing digital equity: Connecting the digital underclass.* Palgrave Macmillan.

Rahman, T. (2009). Language ideology, identity and the commodification of language in the call centers of Pakistan. *Language in Society, 38*(2), 233–258.

Ramanathan, V. and Morgan, B. (2009). Global warning? West-based TESOL, class-blindness and the challenge for critical pedagogies. In F. Sharifian (Ed.), *English as an international language: Perspectives and pedagogical issues* (pp. 153–168). Multilingual Matters.

Ramirez, A. G. and Hall, J. K. (1990). Language and culture in secondary level Spanish textbooks. *The Modern Language Journal, 74*(1), 48–65.

Rampton, B., Harris, R., Collins, J., and Blommaert, J. (2007). Language, class and education. In S. May and N. H. Hornberger (Eds.), *Encyclopedia of language and education* (pp. 71–82). Springer.

Ran, Nazım Hikmet (2008). *Bütün Şiirleri* (15. Baskı). Yapı Kredi Yayınları.

Randolph, L. J. and Johnson, S. M. (2017). Social justice in the language classroom: A call to action. *Dimension*.

Reagan, T. (2016). Language teachers in foreign territory: A call for a critical pedagogy-infused curriculum. In L. Cammarata (Ed.), *Content-based foreign language teaching: Curriculum and pedagogy for developing advanced thinking and literacy skills* (pp. 173–191). Routledge.

Reagan, T. (2019). *Linguistic legitimacy and social justice.* Palgrave Macmillan.

Reagan, T. G. and Osborn, T. A. (2002). *The foreign language educator in society: Toward a critical pedagogy.* Lawrence Erlbaum.

Reagan, T. G. and Osborn, T. A. (2020). *World language education as critical pedagogy: The promise of social justice.* Routledge.

Rhodes, C. M. (2019). A practical guide to queering the adult English language classroom. *Adult Learning, 30*(4), 160–166.

Rhodes, C. M. and Coda, J. (2017). It's not in the curriculum: Adult English language teachers and LGBQ topics. *Adult Learning, 28*(3), 99–106.

Ricento, T. (Ed.) (2000). *Ideology, politics and language policies: Focus on English.* John Benjamins.

Ricento, T. (Ed.) (2015a). *Language policy and political economy.* Oxford University Press.

Ricento, T. (2015b). Political economy and English as a "global" language. In T. Ricento (Ed.), *Language policy and political economy* (pp. 27–47). Oxford University Press.

Rich, A. (1980). Compulsory heterosexuality and lesbian existence. *Signs, 5*(4), 631–659.

Risager, K. (2018). *Representations of the world in language textbooks.* Multilingual Matters.

Risager, K. (2021). Language textbooks: Windows to the world. *Language, Culture and Curriculum, 34*(2), 119–132.

Ritchie, A. J. (2017). *Invisible no more: Police violence against Black women and women of color.* Beacon Press.

Rivage-Seul, M. and Rivage-Seul, M. (1994). Critical thought and moral imagination: Peace education in Freirean perspective. In P. McLaren and C. Lankshear, C. (Eds.), *Politics of liberation: Paths from Freire* (pp. 12–40). Routledge.

Rivers, D. J. and Ross, A. S. (2013). Idealized English teachers: The implicit influence of race in Japan. *Journal of Language, Identity & Education, 12*(5), 321–339.

Rodas, C. R. and Osborn, A. (2016). Social justice and language acquisition for English language learners. In R. Papa., D. M. Eadens, and D. W. Eadens (Eds.), *Social justice instruction: Empowerment on the chalkboard* (pp. 325–339). Springer.

Roediger, D. (1991). *The wages of Whiteness: Race and the making of the American working class.* Verso.

Roithmayr, D. (1999). Introduction to critical race theory in educational research and praxis. In L. Parker, D. Deyhle, and S. Villenas (Eds.), *Race is … Race isn't: Critical race theory and qualitative studies in education* (pp. 1–6). Westwood Press.

Rolón-Dow, R. (2011). Race(ing) stories: Digital storytelling as a tool for critical race scholarship. *Race Ethnicity and Education, 14*(2), 159–173.

Rosa, J. and Flores, N. (2021). Decolonization, language, and race in applied linguistics and social justice. *Applied Linguistics, 42*(6), 1162–1167.

Rose, H., McKinley, J., and Galloway, N. (2021). Global Englishes and language teaching: A review of pedagogical research. *Language Teaching, 54*, 157–189.

Royal, D. (2016). We are all environmental educators (whether we know it or not). In C. Hastings and L. Jacob (Eds.), *Social justice in English language teaching* (pp. 276–250). TESOL Press.

Royster, D. A. (2003). *Race and the invisible hand: How White networks exclude Black men from blue-collar jobs*. University of California Press.

Rudolph, N., Selvi, A. F., and Yazan, B. (2015). Conceptualizing and confronting inequity: Approaches within and new directions for the "NNEST Movement." *Critical Inquiry in Language Studies, 12*(1), 27–50.

Ruecker, T. (2011). Challenging the native and nonnative English speaker hierarchy in ELT: New directions from race theory. *Critical Inquiry in Language Studies, 8*(4), 400–422.

Sadker, D. and Zittleman, K. (2016). Gender bias: From colonial America to today's classrooms. In J. A. Banks and C. A. M. Banks (Eds.), *Multicultural education: Issues and perspectives* (7th Ed.) (pp. 137–158). John Wiley & Sons.

Said, E. W. (1978). *Orientalism*. Vintage.

Sánchez Bello, A. (2016). Gender studies in Spain: From theory to educational practice. In A. Darder, P. Mayo, and J. Paraskeva (Eds.), *International critical pedagogy reader* (pp. 39–45). Routledge.

Sano, J. (2009). Farmhands and factory workers, honesty and humility: The Portrayal of social class and morals in English language learner children's books. *Teachers College Record, 111*(11), 2560–2588.

Sayer, A. (2002). What are you worth?: Why class is an embarrassing subject. *Sociological Research Online, 7*(3).

Sayer, A. (2005). *The moral significance of class*. Cambridge University Press.

Schachter, E. P. and Rich, Y. (2011). Identity education: A conceptual framework for educational researchers and practitioners. *Educational Psychologist, 46*(4), 222–238.

Schmidt, S. J. (2010). Queering social studies: The role of social studies in normalizing citizens and sexuality in the common good. *Theory & Research in Social Education, 38*, 314–335.

Schneider, E. (2011). Colonization, globalization, and the sociolinguistics of World Englishes. In R. Mesthrie (Ed.), *The Cambridge handbook of sociolinguistics* (pp. 335–354). Cambridge University Press.

Schupbach, D. (2009). Testing language, testing ethnicity? Policies and practices surrounding the ethnic German Aussiedler. *Language Assessment Quarterly, 6*(1), 78–82.

Seidlhofer, B. (2011). *Understanding English as a lingua franca*. Oxford.

Seidman, S. (1995). Deconstructing queer theory or the under-theorization of the social and the ethical. In L. Nicholson and S. Seidman (Eds.), *Social postmodernism: Beyond identity politics* (pp. 116–141). Cambridge University Press.

Selwyn, N. (2004). Reconsidering political and popular understandings of the digital divide. *New Media & Society, 6*(3), 341–362.

Sensoy, O. and DiAngelo, R. (2017). *Is everyone really equal? An introduction to key concepts in social justice education* (2nd Ed.). Teachers College Press.

Shank Lauwo, M. (2019). Ubuntu translanguaging and social justice: Negotiating power and identity through multilingual education in Tanzania. In N. Avineri, L. R. Graham, E. J. Johnson, R. C. Riner, and J. Rosa (Eds.), *Language and social justice in practice* (pp. 88–96). Routledge.

Shapiro, S. (2022). *Cultivating critical language awareness in the writing classroom*. Routledge.

Shardakova, M. and Pavlenko, A. (2004). Identity options in Russian textbooks. *Journal of Language, Identity, and Education, 3*(1), 25–46.

Sharifian, F. (2009). *English as an international language: Perspectives and pedagogical issues*. Multilingual Matters.

Shin, H. (2007). English language teaching in Korea: Toward globalization or glocalization? J. Cummins and C. Davison (Eds.), *International handbook of English language teaching* (pp. 75–86). Springer.

Shin, H. (2012). From FOB to cool: Transnational migrant students in Toronto and the styling of global linguistic capital. *Journal of Sociolinguistics, 16,* 184–200.

Shin, H. (2014). Social class, habitus, and language learning: The case of Korean early study-abroad students. *Journal of Language, Identity & Education, 13*(2), 99–103.

Shin, J., Eslami, Z., and Chen, W. (2011). Presentation of local and international culture in current international English-language teaching textbooks. *Language, Culture and Curriculum, 24*(3), 253–268.

Shiraishi, J. (1996). Seito no tōhatsu to seito shidō ni kansuru ichi kōsatsu [A study on student's hair style and life guidance at school], *Hokuho Seikatsu Fukushi Kenkyū Nenpō* [Bulletin of Northern Regions Research Center for Human Service Studies], *2,* 23–29.

Shlasko, G. D. (2005). Queer (v.) pedagogy. *Equity & Excellence in Education, 38*(2), 123–134.

Shohamy, E. (1998). Critical language testing and beyond. *Studies in Educational Evaluation, 24,* 331–345.

Shohamy, E. (2001). Democratic assessment as an alternative. *Language Testing, 18*(4), 373–391.

Shohamy, E. (2006). *Language policy: Hidden agendas and new approaches.* Routledge.

Shohamy, E. (2007). The power of language tests, the power of the English language, and the role of ELT. In J. Cummins and C. Davison (Eds.), *International handbook of English language teaching* (pp. 521–522). Springer.

Shohamy, E. (2009). Language tests for immigrants: Why language? Why tests? Why citizenship? In G. Hogan-Brun, C. Mar-Molinero, and P. Stevenson (Eds.), *Discourses on language and integration* (pp. 45–59). John Benjamins.

Shohamy, E. (2017). Critical language testing. In E. Shohamy, I. G. Or, and S. May (Eds.), *Language testing and assessment* (pp. 441–454). Springer.

Shor, I. (Ed.) (1987). *Freire for the classroom: A sourcebook for liberatory teaching.* Boynton/Cook Publishers.

Shor, I. (1996). *When students have power: Negotiating authority in a critical pedagogy.* Chicago University Press.

Shor, I. and Pari, C. (1999). *Education is politics: Critical teaching across differences.* Heinemann.

Shrum, J. L. and Glisan, E. W. (2009). *Teacher's handbook: Contextualized language instruction.* Heinle.

Sierra Piedrahita, A. M. (2016). Contributions of a social justice language teacher education perspective to professional development programs in Colombia. *PROFILE Issues in Teachers' Professional Development, 18,* 203–217.

Simmonds, S. (2017). Teachers as curriculum leaders: Towards promoting gender equity as a democratic ideal. *Educational Research for Social Change, 6,* 16–28.

Skegg, B. (1997). Classifying practices: Representations, capitals and recognitions. In P. Mahony and C. Zmroczek (Eds.), *Class matters: "Working-class" women's perspectives on social class* (pp. 127–142). Taylor & Francis.

Skutnabb-Kangas, T. (1988). Multilingualism and the education of minority children. In T. Skutnabb-Kangas and J. Cummins (Eds.), *Minority education: From shame to struggle* (pp. 9–44). Multilingual Matters.

Skutnabb-Kangas, T. (2009). What can TESOL do in order not to participate in crimes against humanity. *TESOL Quarterly, 43*(2), 340–344.

Skutnabb-Kangas, T., Phillipson, R., Mohanty, A. K., and Panda, M. (2009). *Social justice through multilingual education.* Multilingual Matters.

Slater, D. (2017). *The 57 bus: A true story of two teenagers and the crime that changed their lives.* Farrar, Straus and Giroux.

Sleeter, C. E. (2001). Preparing teachers for culturally diverse schools: Research and the overwhelming presence of Whiteness. *Journal of Teacher Education, 52*(2), 94–106.

Sleeter, C. (2008). Critical family history, identity, and historical memory. *Educational Studies, 43*(2), 114–124.

Sleeter, C. (2022). Critical Family History. http://christinesleeter.org/critical-family-hi story

Sleeter, C. E. and Grant, C. A. (2008). *Making choices for multicultural education: Five approaches to race, class and gender* (6th Ed.). Wiley.

Sleeter, C. E. and Zavala, M. (2020). *Transformative ethnic studies in schools: Curriculum, pedagogy, and research.* Teachers College Press.

Smith, L. and Redington, R. (2010). Class dismissed: Making the case for the study of clas- sist microaggressions. In D. W. Sue (Ed.), *Microaggressions and marginality: Manifestations, dynamics, and impact.* Wiley.

Smyth, J. (2011). *Critical pedagogy for social justice.* Continuum.

Snapp, S. D., Burdge, H., Licona, A. C., Moody, R. L., and Russell, S. T. (2015). Students' perspectives on LGBTQ-inclusive curriculum. *Equity and Excellence in Education, 48*(2), 249–265.

Sokolik, M. E. (2007). Grammar texts and consumerist subtexts. *TESL-EJ, 11*(2).

Sokolower, J. (2016). Introduction. In A. Butler-Wall, K. Cosier, R. Harper, J. Sapp, J. Sokolower, and M. Bollow Tempel (Eds.), *Rethinking sexism, gender and sexuality* (pp. 12–15). Rethinking Schools.

Solórzano, D. G. and Yosso, T. J. (2002). Critical race methodology: Counter-storytelling as an analytical framework for educational research. *Qualitative Inquiry, 8,* 23–44.

Song, H. (2013). Deconstruction of cultural dominance in Korean EFL textbooks. *Intercultural Education, 24*(4), 382–390.

Sonntag, S. K. (2009). Linguistic globalization and the call center industry: Imperialism, hegemony or cosmopolitanism? *Language Policy, 8*(1), 5–25.

Spade, D. (2011). Some very basic tips for making higher education more accessible to trans students and rethinking how we talk about gendered bodies. *The Radical Teacher, 92,* 57–62.

Spargo, T. (1999). *Foucault and queer theory.* Icon Books.

Steger, M. B. (2017). *Globalization: A very short introduction.* Oxford University Press.

Steger, M. B. and Roy, R. K. (2010). *Neoliberalism: A very short introduction.* Oxford University Press.

Steinmetz, K. (2018, April 3). *The Oxford English Dictionary added "trans*". Here's what the label means.* Time.

Stephenson, H., Hughes, J., and Dummett, P. (2018). *Life.* National Geographic Learning.

Stibbe, A. (2004). Environmental education across cultures: Beyond the discourse of shal- low environmentalism. *Language and Intercultural Communication, 4*(4), 242–260.

Sue, D. W. (Ed.) (2010). *Microaggressions and marginality: Manifestation, dynamics, and impact.* John Wiley & Sons.

Sue, D. W. (2015). *Race talk and the conspiracy of silence: Understanding and facilitating difficult dialogues on race.* Wiley.

Sullivan, S. (2014). *Good White people.* State University of New York Press.

Sung, K. and Pederson, R. (Eds.) (2012). *Critical ELT practices in Asia.* Sense Publishers.

Tajeddin, Z. and Teimournezhad, S. (2015) Exploring the hidden agenda in the repre- sentation of culture in international and localised ELT textbooks. *The Language Learning Journal, 43*(2), 180–193.

Taki, S. (2008). International and local curricula: The question of ideology. *Language Teaching Research, 12,* 127–142.

Tamura, Y. (2007). School dress codes in post-scarcity Japan: Contradictions and changes. *Youth & Society, 38*(4), 463–489.

Tangen, D. and Fielding-Barnsley, R. (2007). Environmental education in a culturally diverse school. *Australian Journal of Environmental Education, 23,* 23–30.

Tate, W. (1993). Advocacy versus economics: A critical race analysis of the proposed national assessment in mathematics. *Thresholds in Education, XIX*, 16–22.

Tate, W. (1994). From inner city to ivory tower: Does my voice matter in the academy? *Urban Education, 29*, 245–269.

Tatum, B. D. (1992). Talking about race, learning about racism: The application of racial identity development theory in the classroom. *Harvard Educational Review, 62*(1), 1–24.

Tatum, B. D. (2017). *"Why are all the black kids sitting together in the cafeteria?": And other conversations about race.* Basic Books.

Taylor, E. (2009). The foundations of critical race theory in education: An introduction. In E. Taylor, D. Gillborn, and G. Ladson-Billings (Eds.), *Foundations of critical race theory in education* (pp. 1–12). Routledge.

Taylor, E., Gillborn, D., and Ladson-Billings, G. (Eds.) (2009). *Foundations of critical race theory in education.* Routledge.

Taylor, K.-Y. (Ed.) (2017). *How we get free: Black feminism and the Combahee River Collective.* Haymarket Books.

Taylor, L. K. and Zine, J. (Eds.) (2014). *Muslim women, transnational feminism and the ethics of pedagogy: Contested imaginaries in Post-9/11 cultural practice.* Routledge.

Taylor-Mendes, C. (2009). Construction of racial stereotypes in English as a foreign language (EFL) textbooks: Images as discourse. In R. Kubota and A. Lin (Eds.), *Race, culture, and identities in second language education* (pp. 64–80). Routledge.

TESOL Organization (2022). *Social responsibility special interest group (SRIS).* https://my.tesol.org/communities/community-home?communitykey=ca55369d-6da3-454c-a68f-68fbe03db770

Tetreault, M. K. T. (2016). Classrooms for diversity: Rethinking curriculum and pedagogy. In J. A. Banks and C. A. M. Banks (Eds.), *Multicultural education: Issues and perspectives* (9th Ed.) (pp. 98–114). Wiley.

Theoharis, G. and O'Toole, J. (2011). Leading inclusive ELL: Social justice leadership for English language learners. *Educational Administration Quarterly, 47*(4), 646–688.

Tichavakunda, A. A. and Tierney, W. G. (2018) The "wrong" side of the divide: Highlighting race for equity's sake. *The Journal of Negro Education, 87*(2), 110–124.

Tien, J. (2019). Teaching identity vs. positionality: Dilemmas in social justice education. *Curriculum Inquiry, 49*(5), 526–550.

Tollefson, J. W. (2007). Ideology, language varieties, and ELT. In J. Cummins and C. Davison (Eds.), *International handbook of English language teaching* (pp. 25–36). Springer.

Tomlinson, B. (2012). Materials development for language learning and teaching. *Language Teaching, 45*, 143–179.

Tompkins, A. (2014). Asterisk. *TSQ: Transgender Studies Quarterly, 1*(1–2), 26–27.

Torres, C. A. (2006). Schooling, power, and the exile of the soul. In L. Weis, C. McCarthy, and G. Dimitriadis (Eds.), *Ideology, curriculum, and the new sociology of education: Revisiting the work of Michael Apple* (pp. 47–65). Routledge.

Tosh, J. and Gislason, M. (2016). Commentary: Fracking is a feminist issue: An intersectional ecofeminist commentary on natural resource extraction and rape. *Psychology of Women Section Review, 18*(1), 54–59.

Ulum, Ö. G. and Köksal, D. (2019). *Ideology and hegemony of English foreign language textbooks: Globally and locally written practices.* Springer.

Unigwe, C. (2019, October 5). It's not just Greta Thunberg: Why are we ignoring the developing world's inspiring activists? *The Guardian.* https://www.theguardian.com/commentisfree/2019/oct/05/greta-thunberg-developing-world-activists

United Nations (2014). Inter-agency support agency on Indigenous people's issues (June 2014). *Elimination and responses to violence, exploitation and abuse of indigenous girls,*

adolescents and young women. https://www.un.org/en/ga/69/meetings/indigenous/pdf/
IASG%20Thematic%20Paper_%20Violence%20against%20Girls%20and%20
Women%20-%20rev1.pdf

United Nations Population Fund (UNFPA) (2020). *COVID-19: A gender lens: Protecting sexual and reproductive health and rights, and promoting gender equality.* https://www.unfpa.org/sites/default/files/resource-pdf/COVID 19_A_Gender_Lens_Guidance_Note.pdf

Urciuoli, B. (2008). Skills and selves in the new workplace. *American Ethnologist, 35,* 211–228.

van Dijk, J. (1999). *The network society: Social aspects of new media.* Sage.

Vandrick, S. (2014). The role of social class in English language education. *Journal of Language, Identity & Education, 13*(2), 85–91.

Varney, J. A. (2001). Undressing the normal: Community efforts for queer Asian and Asian American youth. In K. K. Kumashiro (Ed.), *Troubling intersections of race and sexuality: Queer students of color and anti-oppressive education* (pp. 87–104). Rowman & Littlefield Publishers.

Vavrus, M. (2009). Sexuality, schooling, and teacher identity formation: A critical pedagogy for teacher education. *Teaching and Teacher Education, 25*(3), 383–390.

Verpoorten, M. (2020). How many died in Rwanda? *Journal of Genocide Research, 22*(1), 94–103.

Vicars, M. (2016). "Queer goings-on": An autoethnographic account of the experiences and practice of performing a queer pedagogy. In A. Darder, P. Mayo, and J. Paraskeva (Eds.), *International critical pedagogy reader* (pp. 267–278). Routledge.

Villegas, A. M. and Davis, D. E. (2008). Preparing teachers of color to confront racial/ethnic disparities in educational outcomes. In M. Cochran Smith, S. Feiman-Nemser, D. J. McIntyre, and K. E. Demers (Eds.), *Handbook of research on teacher education: Enduring questions in changing contexts* (pp. 583–605). Routledge.

Vinall, K. and Shin, J. (2019). The construction of the tourist gaze in English textbooks in South Korea: Exploring the tensions between internationalisation and nationalisation. *Language, Culture and Curriculum, 32*(2), 173–190.

Walker, G. (2018). *Movie making as critical pedagogy: Conscientization through visual storytelling.* Springer.

Wallerstein, N. (1987). Problem-positing education: Freire's method for transformation. In I. Shor (Ed.), *Freire for the classroom: A sourcebook for liberatory teaching* (pp. 33–44). Boynton/Cook Publishers.

Wallerstein, N. and Auerbach, E. (2004). *Problem-posing at work: Popular educator's guide.* Grass Roots Press.

Walters, M. (2005). *Feminism: A very short introduction.* Oxford University Press.

Watson, M. (2018). Contesting standardized English. *Academe, 104*(3), 37–40.

Weber, E. L. (Ed.) (2009). *Environmental ethics: Sustainability and education.* Interdisciplinary Press.

Wei, L. (2022). Translanguaging as a political stance: Implications for English language education. *ELT Journal, 76*(2), 172–182.

Weiler, K. (1991). Freire and a feminist pedagogy of difference. *Harvard Educational Review, 61*(4), 449–474.

Weiler, K. (1994). Freire and a feminist pedagogy of difference. In P. L. McLaren and C. Lankshear (Eds.), *Politics of liberation: Paths from Freire* (pp. 12–40). Routledge.

Weis, L. (2016). Social class and education. In J. A. Banks and C. A. M. Banks (Eds.), *Multicultural education: Issues and perspectives* (9th Ed.) (pp. 42–58). Wiley.

Wesely, P. M., Glynn, C., and Wassell, B. (2016). Equity, access, and social justice: From pain to possibility. *The Modern Language Journal, 100,* 564–568.

West, G. B. (2021). "Is this a safe space?": Examining an emotionally charged eruption in critical language pedagogy. *Educational Science, 11,* 186–200.

Widodo, H. P. and Elyas, T. (2020). Introduction to gender in language education. *Sexuality & Culture*, *24*, 1019–1027.

Wiggins, G. and McTighe, J. (2011). *Understanding by design: Guide to creating high-quality units*. Association for Supervision and Curriculum Development.

Williams, D. and Evans-Winters, V. (2005). The burden of teaching teachers: Memoirs of race discourse in teacher education. *The Urban Review*, *37*(3), 201–219.

Williams, R. (1977). *Marxism and literature*. Oxford University Press.

Wilson, V. (2015). *Black unemployment is significantly higher than White unemployment regardless of educational attainment*. Economic Policy Institute. http://www.epi.org/publication/black-unemployment-educational-attainment/

Wing, A. K. (Ed.) (2000). *Global critical race feminism*. New York University Press.

Wink, J. (2011). *Critical pedagogy: Notes from the real world* (4th Ed.). Pearson.

Winograd, K. (Ed.) (2016). *Education in times of environmental crises: Teaching children to be agents of change*. Routledge.

Wodak, R. and Forchtner, B. (Eds.) (2018). *The Routledge handbook of language and politics*. Routledge.

Wong, S. and Grant, R. (2007). Academic achievement and social identity among bilingual students in the U.S. In J. Cummins and C. Davison (Eds.), *International handbook of English language teaching* (pp. 681–691). Springer.

Woodford, M. R., Kolb, C. L., Durocher-Radeka, G., and Javier, G. (2014). Lesbian, gay, bisexual, and transgender ally training programs on campus: Current variations and future directions. *Journal of College Student Development*, *55*(3), 317–322.

World Economic Forum (2020). *The global gender gap report 2020*. https://www.weforum.org/reports/gender-gap-2020-report-100-years-pay-equality/digest

Yarymowich, M. (2003). *Language tourism in Canada: Theorizing language education as a global commodity*. Master of Arts. Ontario Institute for Studies in Education of the University of Toronto.

Young, I. M. (2011). *Justice and the politics of difference*. Princeton University Press.

Young, S. L.-B. (2009). Breaking the silence: Critical literacy and social action. *The English Journal*, *98*(4), 109–115.

Zakaria, R. (2021). *Against White feminism: Notes on disruption*. W. W. Norton & Company.

Zeichner, K. (2006). Reflections of a university-based teacher educator on the future of college- and university-based teacher education. *Journal of Teacher Education*, 57(3), 326–340.

Zeichner, K. M. (2011). Teacher education for social justice. In M. R. Hawkins (Ed.), *Social justice language teacher education* (pp. 7–22). Multilingual Matters.

Zeichner, K., Bowman, M., Guillen, L., and Napolitan, K. (2016). Engaging and working in solidarity with local communities in preparing the teachers of their children. *Journal of Teacher Education*, *67*(4), 277–290.

Zembylas, M. (2003). Emotional teacher identity: A poststructural perspective. *Teachers and Teaching: Theory and Practice*, *9*(3), 213–238.

Zembylas, M. (2005). Discursive practices, genealogies, and emotional rules: A poststructuralist view on emotion and identity in teaching. *Teaching and Teacher Education*, *21*, 935–948.

Zembylas, M. (2015). "Pedagogy of discomfort" and its ethical implications: The tensions of ethical violence in social justice education. *Ethics and Education*, *10*(2), 163–174.

Zembylas, M. and Keet, A. (2019). *Critical human rights education: Advancing social-justice-oriented educational praxes*. Springer.

Zine, J. (2014). Cartographies of difference and pedagogies of peril Muslim girls and women in Western young adult fiction novels. In L. K. Taylor and J. Zine (Eds.), *Muslim women, transnational feminism and the ethics of pedagogy: Contested imaginaries in post-9/11 cultural practice* (pp. 175–197). Routledge.

Zine, J. and Taylor, L. K. (2014). Introduction: The contested imaginaries of reading Muslim women and Muslim women reading back. In L. K. Taylor and J. Zine (Eds.), *Muslim women, transnational feminism and the ethics of pedagogy: Contested imaginaries in Post-9/11 cultural practice* (pp. 1–24). Routledge.

Index

Miles, R., 94, 95–6, 97, 98, 99, 106, 112, 120
Miller, S., 30
misogyny, 127
misrecognition, 9
Mohanty, C. T., 146
Mojab, S., 158
Moll, L. C., 26
moment-to-moment interactions, tackling racism in, 117–18
Montaño, T., 59
Morris, M., 132
Motha, S,, 109
multicultural education, 47–9, 106, 149
multilingualism, 43–4, 106
multimodality, 56, 106, 119, 163

Namugerwa, Leah, 116
National Human Genome Project, 95
Native American populations, 108, 143, 148
native speakerism, 45, 81, 109–10
native-speaker status, 17, 45, 61
Ndura, E., 57–8
Nelson, C., 131–3, 135, 140
neocolonialism, 144
neoliberalism, 69–92, 111; *see also* globalization
Neto, J. N., 131, 132
'neutral accent,' 83
neutrality (presumed)
    curriculum, 8, 25
    digital technology, 170
    education, 22, 158
    English, 42, 44
    hegemonic ideologies, 6
    language learning materials, 57–8
    non-racists, 101
    teachers, 160, 164
Ng, C. K., 131
Nieto, S., xiv, 47, 48, 49, 61
Nigeria, 44, 144
No PARSNIP (politics, alcohol, religion, sex, narcotics, isms and pork), 57
non-racists, 101
nonrecognition, 9
non-standard language varieties, 41–2, 59
normalization, 131
North, C. E., 48

Obama, Barack, 12, 102
OECD (Organisation for Economic Co-operation and Development), x
offshoring, 83–4
Omi, M., 111
Ó'Móchain, R., 142–3, 151
oppression
    counter-storytelling, 106
    definition, 4, 7–9, 33
    intersectionality, 12
    language ideologies, 40
    linguistic imperialism, 43
Orientalism, 144
Ortaçtepe Hart, D., xi, xii, 53, 75, 172, 174
Osborn, T. A., xii, 45
Osei-Kofi, N., 11, 12, 13
Othering
    colonialism, 144
    counter-storytelling, 105
    digital technology, 171
    'empathy,' 162
    foreign language education, 45–6
    native speakerism, 109–10
    social class, 111
    unlearning 'normal,' 30

pain, acknowledging, 160–2
Paiz, J., 60, 132, 136, 139
parental engagement, 159
Park, J. S.-Y., 81
Parkland school shooting, xiii
paternalistic attitudes, 28, 163
patriarchy, 28, 33, 124, 125, 127, 147; *see also* heteropatriarchy
Pavlenko, A., 60
Pavo's story, 177–80
pedagogy of discomfort, 166
pedagogy of hope, 161–2
pedagogy of pain, 161
Pederson, R., 34
Peltier, Autumn (Anishinaabe), 116
Pennycook, A., xvii, 42, 44, 52, 80, 85
Persinger, L. L., 139
personal is political, 167
Peters, M. A., 108
Philippines, 84
Phillipson, R., 42–3, 44, 58, 64, 82, 110
Phipps, A., 46, 55, 144, 147, 148, 149
plurilingualism, 110